Best Wishes

It's Tougher At The Bottom

For every book sold the Author and
Publisher will both make a donation to:

RACEAID
BACKING THE FIGHT AGAINST CANCER

I hold The Ayr Gold Cup after So Careful's victory. I had dreamt about winning this race for some thirty-five years; 'Albert' made my dreams come true on the greatest racecourse in the British Isles on 16th September 1988.

It's Tougher At The Bottom

Jack Berry

Foreword by Peter O'Sullevan, O.B.E.

LAMBOURN

LAMBOURN PUBLICATIONS LTD
12–14 High Road, London, N2 9JP.
9 Queen Street, Melbourne 3000, Victoria, Australia

First published 1991
© Text – Jack Berry
© Foreword – Peter O'Sullevan, O.B.E.
A limited edition of 100 signed and specially bound copies is published
by
The Marlborough Bookshop and Sporting Gallery
6 Kingsbury Street, Marlborough, Wiltshire

Editor: Sir Rupert Mackeson, Bart. (as Rupert Collens)
Assistant Editor: Peter Fitzmaurice
Production: Jeannine Alexander
Indexing: Michael Mullins
Jacket Design: Ann Doolan
Typesetting and Origination: Footnote Graphics (Warminster)

Photographs Courtesy of: Kenneth Bright (including front cover),
Kris Photography (including back cover),
Barncroft Photography, E. L. Gibbs Equine and Livestock Photography,
Provincial Press Agency and Jack Berry's family, friends and associates.

ISBN Limited Edition 1–872708–09–9
Trade Edition   1–872708–08–0

Printed in Great Britain by
Billing & Sons Ltd, Worcester

FOREWORD

by Peter O'Sullevan, O.B.E.

I have known and admired Jack Berry since the relaunch of his unpromising career on the Turf in 1960 after his National Service. 137 rides in his next two seasons as a jump jockey yielded a total of 3 winners and visits of varying duration to just about every hospital within range of a National Hunt circuit. Kamikaze Jack's reckless eagerness to travel anywhere, anyhow, to share the hazards of steeplechasing with untutored partners as well as those of proven deficiency in the jumping department ensured that he broke more bones than records.

His ultimate 47 winners – at a cost of 46 fractures – reflected the unquenchable spirit which inspired Jack and his wife Jo to set about building a dream with their bare hands. To outsiders the Lancashire farmland site – remote from traditional equine centres – appeared an improbable setting for the realisation of a viable training stable.

For years the going was tough at the bottom but resilience is an essential ingredient for anyone involved in the race game. Jack has more than his quota and, amazingly, at the end of the 1990 Flat season the 127 winners "Trained Jack Berry" constituted a record for a northern trainer. No man has worked harder for his achievement. He still wears the same size in hats (and obligatory red shirt) and when anyone professionally involved in racing says, as I do now, "Good luck Jack", they mean it.

Author's Acknowledgements

Without the help of certain people it would have been very difficult indeed to have put this little lot together. Many of them have put themselves out by foregoing some of life's normal pleasures, such as going out in the evening, watching TV, or even just sitting down to meals, in order to give me the information I required in getting part of a story together.

I should like to take this opportunity to thank all these people for the invaluable help and tolerance they have shown me over this past year. Jo, my wife, for helping me out with research. Also for putting up with me diving out of bed and disturbing her sleep in the early hours in order to get something down on paper which I had on my mind, or returning to bed at unearthly hours from working late on the book.

Jack Allen, a long-time friend, who kept records of all our wins over the years and very kindly lent me his book to note our winners. Chris Pitt, a proper Leslie Welsh on racing statistical records. Chris is very much like myself, he doesn't take very kindly to wasting too much of his life in bed. Many times I have phoned Chris, who lives in Birmingham, well past midnight for confirmation of racing facts. Our office staff who have made and answered phone calls, written letters and helped initially in deciphering my scribble for putting onto a computer. Tricia and Claire Harrison for allowing their home to be turned into a hive of industry. Apart from housing the computer and printer, my thanks to Claire for her typing services, amending, updating and producing the numerous copies of my typescript. I shouldn't forget either the computer expertise of Les Pickstock. Les has given up his leisure time to sort out computer problems in order that my publisher's deadlines could be met. Even when Les came out of hospital he readily volunteered his services over a very busy period leading up to Christmas.

Miles Baird-Murray, Brian Durkin, Paddy and Mary Farrell, Tony Potts, Sally Hall, Charles Fry, Michael White, Colin Dukes, my brothers and sisters, Mr. Wildblood, James Kearsley, Ian Bolland and Anne Charlton for listening to my requirements, going over the past and for the chaos I must have caused in their homes getting them to rummage for old photos to reprint. At times they must have thought I was a real pain!

Colin and Jean Bradford-Nutter for lending us their beautiful home for a few days as a retreat from the everyday hassle and disturbances like the "ever loving telephone", in order to concentrate on working on the book.

It would not be fitting not to mention James Threadgold for lending me the photo of Osbourne Lad with Colin Dukes, Ben Robinson and himself on. When it arrived recorded delivery and wrapped as if it was the Crown Jewels, within two hours of it being in my care, yer man, Jimmy phones up ... "Has the photo been delivered yet?"

In the South, a particularly warm vote of thanks to my old friend Peter O'Sullevan, O.B.E. for taking so much trouble to write a smashing foreword. Tim Cox was wonderfully quick in checking facts and figures, and of course I must not forget the gang at Lambourn, Jeannine, Rupert, Peter, Mr. Mullins and Eddie who made this all happen along the lines I wanted and not always as they wanted.

Last, but definitely not least, Pat Knight. This past year Pat has gone racing at weekends and during her holidays with me. She has taken dictation whilst I have been driving, made countless phone calls and helped me in my dealings with the publishers. Pat has worked with me for numerous hours with an abundance of effort and energy on the project. In addition to all that, she introduced me to Tricia, Claire and Les and organised the computer work for them. Pat is only small, but as we say in racing "she's a little good'un".

Thank you Pat. Thank you all.

Jack Berry

PREFACE

by Jack Berry

Most of this book was written while on holiday in Tenerife, January 1990. On a few occasions I have worked right through the night, going over my past and getting it down on paper, and I have enjoyed doing it. Mind you, even in Tenerife one can get disturbed. Once, when I had been up all night writing, I went out for a break around 8.00a.m. the following morning. Sitting by the pool, I was distracted by a man splashing about in the water. Looking up and glancing towards this fellow I thought he didn't seem very happy.

"Jo, that man's in difficulties!" I said to Jo, my wife. As laid back as Jo is, she did manage to drag her head out of the book she was reading and replied, "No . . . he's alright."

Shortly after, he disappeared under the water; I thought I'd better get in and dig him out, never mind about Jo. That man was glad to see me I can tell you!

In the 1989 season, the white Mercedes that kept tearing up and down all the roads leading to race meetings throughout the country travelled 54,000 miles with me in it – the one motorway police seem to delight in stopping, as Jo Berry, Alan Berry, John Carroll, my friend James Kearsley and yours truly have all had our licences endorsed whilst driving it. On one occasion, John Carroll drove twenty-one miles on the hard shoulder of the motorway to get us from a day meeting at Haydock Park to a night meeting at Pontefract. When we got there, our horse was the only one walking around the paddock without any tack on, because I was to do the saddling-up, and John was riding. When the Clerk of the Scales, Jim Isherwood, asked us where we'd been, John and I both looked at each other and cracked up laughing!

To cut out more hassle like that in future I would love a helicopter or a 'plane. If ever I get straight, that is a definite on my agenda. I hate hassle: once, I named a horse "No Hassle"!

Also in 1989, we trained the winners of ninety-two Flat races and three jump races.* In doing so, we sent runners to every Flat racecourse in the country. Most of the winners were 2-year-olds, and speaking of 2-year-olds, I'd better get back to them; so, sit back, and enjoy the book.

* Editor's Note. In 1990, Jack trained an incredible 127 Flat winners, more than any other trainer in the British Isles.

LIST OF ILLUSTRATIONS

CONTENTS

I dedicate this book to a lovely girl who lives in our village,

my mate Andrea Campion.

1

EARLY DAYS

BORN: 7th October, 1937, at 57 Glensdale Grove, East End Park, Leeds 9, Yorkshire.

There were eight of us kids in the family: in order of arrival Betty, Elsie, Harry, myself, Frank, Joan, Goff and Susan, who died as a baby. My mother was called Nancy, she was a slave in the house tending to us lot.

My father was called Harry, as was his father. He was very strict with us – in fact, much too strict at times. He was a Regimental Sergeant-Major in The Royal Army Veterinary Corps, and after the War, I sometimes wondered if he realised he had been demobbed! Dad was always well-dressed, well-mannered, and sharp; he couldn't be doing with idiots, time wasters, wind-ups, or small talk; he didn't flap, and was always in total command. From listening to the Doncaster, Nottingham, and Leicester racecourse farrier, Jock Murray (who was a close friend of father's in the army), father was apparently very easy going. However, countless tales of stunts my father pulled during and shortly after the Second World War have been told to me by the likes of the late Tommy Sheddon (the trainer), Major Daddy Briden (the vet who practised at Boston Spa, Yorkshire), and Jock.

As a kid I was small and thin, but hyperactive. I was running around within months of being born, which was far too early and consequently I damaged my knees. I had to wear leg irons on both legs. I was sent to a childrens' orthopaedic wing attached to Harrogate General Hospital, which was then wooden huts which have since been demolished. My grandad used to come and visit me there, bringing sweets with him for me and all the other kids. When he was coming up the road, us kids could see him through the iron railings of the hospital grounds where we used to play (most of us were not bed cases), and we would all shout "Grandad! Grandad!" as he approached. By the time I reached him, being a bit one-paced with my irons on, I was lucky to get even one sweet! Everyone loved my grandad.

Grandad walked with a stick, and used to swing it as he walked. He always wore a black bowler and walked with a lot of presence, as if he had a purpose in life. Whenever he passed ladies in the street whom he knew, he would always take his bowler off to them and pass the time of day. He had the credentials of a gentleman, which he was. A chemist by profession, he later became a pork butcher, and also a pig dealer. He was a very fit man. He had been known to go to Wetherby Market on the bus to buy pigs for his clients, then walk the fourteen miles back home. He never did own a car, and I never saw him on anything other than a bus or tram. Except for the short time when he lost his memory, to the best of my knowledge he was never ill until he died.

Grandad never bought anything unless he could afford to pay for it there and then, and never owed a penny to anyone. "Pay and be paid", he always said. It's a good job he isn't around now to hear me talking to my bank manager, telling him how important it is to expand. "We need another all-weather gallop . . . We need more boxes up . . . We need a new horse-box . . . We need more land draining," etc. etc.

At Cockerham, in the main yard, we have a clock-tower with a lovely weather-vane with horses on it. Underneath, it says 'Moss Side Racing Stables'. We once had a treat – a visit from the bank manager – and under 'Moss Side Racing Stables', especially for the occasion, I got one of the lads (who fancied himself as a bit of an artist) to paint 'and Midland Bank'! My grandad would have got an even bigger shock if he could have watched me performing at The St. Leger Yearling Sales every September at Doncaster, with no owners lined up to pay for the majority of my purchases!

After my legs had got strong enough to hold me without the irons, I was still very thin and weak. I was definitely the runt of the family. It's a good job I wasn't born into a litter of pigs – I might have had a knock on the head!

From the age of about four or five, I suffered from swollen glands and had to have three operations for them. I was regularly attending Leeds Infirmary with my poor old mum. She was a lovely woman, and was just like a hen with chicks when it came to her children.

Attending the Infirmary as an out-patient one day, the doctor mumbled, "Leave him (or it – I wasn't quite sure which) and we'll put it on the operating list tomorrow to have the tonsils out." I cut up a bit about this at the time, especially as they had dropped it on me at such short notice and because I couldn't see what tonsils had to do with swollen glands. Alas, it was to no avail. Mum took me upstairs to the wards. I can still see her now, crying as she waved and left the ward. Mind you, I think I might have been crying as well!

The following day, I was taken down on a trolley to a side room of the operating theatre by a nurse and left there for ages. The nurse who had taken me down then came back and told me that she was sorry for the delay, but they had had an emergency – a young woman had a broken sewing needle stuck in her finger – so my operation had to be delayed. I was absolutely crapping myself! My fear was not of the operation to take the tonsils out, but the thought of being put to sleep with that damned ether. This was going to be my fourth time, and I hated it, really hated it. In the operating theatre, on trolleys and hanging around the walls were frightening looking gadgets and apparatus, also lots of people flying around in white uniforms, presumably doctors and nurses. They would hold me down on the operating table, then someone would put cotton wool or gauze over my mouth while another poured the awful smelling ether over it. Some berk would say "Count to one hundred", but I was much too busy fighting the system to be bothered about counting! I also had the problem of having nightmares, not dreams, whilst under the anaesthetic. On one occasion, hundreds of horses were galloping over me!

When I was returned to the ward and my senses finally came back, I could hear a lady talking to another, "That's young Jacky Berry back, poor little sod. He suffers with swollen glands," she was saying. "He regularly comes in here for operations." She must have thought I also suffered with my ears! No offence though – she meant well. The elders in the ward could not have been nicer towards me. When visiting time was over, they often came to my bed with goodies that they had had brought in by their relatives or friends, or they would send things down to me via the nurses.

On this occasion, I felt really rotten. The smell of ether was still there, and lingered on for two or three days. Thank God there's a more civilised method nowadays of putting people to sleep by a simple injection! Looking out of the window, I remember a very big bill-board on the wall of the building opposite. It had two posters on it – one advertising Andrew's Liver Salts, and the other saying 'Arthritis Can Kill'!

Our house must have been about ten minutes walk from Victoria School, and as a toddler I would go to see my brother Harry, and sisters Betty and Elsie, at play-times. I remember they wouldn't always talk to me through the iron railings of the playground once I had spotted them – they must have thought I was a bit of an embarrassment. One particular day when they wouldn't have anything to do with me, I saw our Betty, my eldest sister. "Bett, I've got your knickers and shoes on!" I shouted, to draw her attention. What with living in such a large family, and being drawn fourth of the remaining seven runners, my draw was the worst, so that remark could have been the truth!

My first day at school soon arrived. Our Betty took me to the infants' class of Victoria School, York Road. I didn't like it. The feeling I had has never left me. I was crying, and the lady teacher gave me her handkerchief to wipe my eyes with. My first school scolding followed as I blew my nose with it!

As a youngster, I didn't fear much. I was always lively, always on the go, and always in trouble. There was a bully-boy at school who got a lot of pleasure out of hitting our Harry (who was a softy, mind you). This particular day, he was giving Harry a hard time in the garden. In our garden was an iron clog (weighing about 1 st.) which was to put in front of a wheel of our horse-and-cart whenever my father called home and parked it outside the house. When I saw the bully getting at Harry, I picked up this clog and told "matey-boy" to leave him alone or I would drop the iron clog on his foot. He came tearing at me like a lion, and so, with all my force, I dropped the clog on his foot. He didn't half yelp! Needless to say, it broke his foot. He should have thanked me – he changed from being a bully to being a really nice boy. He was heading towards becoming a gangster as he was!

Life always seemed hectic at home. Father, thankfully, wasn't in much. The rest of us were always messing about and getting on my poor old mum's nerves. Mind you, my two elder sisters were the worst. They were always squabbling about who had whose clothes on, and the like. "Who's pinched a piece out of one of the apple pies I've made for tea?" my mother would demand as she went into the pantry. "You won't get another bite to eat until the greedy so-and-so owns up!" Even if Sherlock Holmes and Doctor Watson had been called in, she would still not have got a result. It's a good job she was only threatening us, or we would have starved to death!

Whenever we were naughty, mother would send us to bed. Imagine me, with all my energy, cooped up in bed during daytime. I'm bad enough as it is, now, at getting to sleep in the dark. I was also a bit claustrophobic (for which I blame the nurses who held me down for that terrible ether), so that didn't help. There was a dust-pan and brush upstairs in a cupboard, and I used to tidy and sweep up all the bedrooms, the bathroom, and the stairs. I also collected the rubbish up, and there was always plenty of that in my sisters' room. When I had collected all the rubbish and put it in the bath-room basket, I needed to go downstairs to empty it. At the bottom of the stairs, the door leading into our front room would be locked to stop me getting out. So, I would knock on it to get my mother's attention. On my first couple of attempts, she didn't let on that she had heard me. When she finally weakened, I'd reel off all the things that I had done, finishing with, "I have the rubbish here, in the bathroom basket. Will you let me out so I can empty it, please?" In time she would soften up and open the door. I had been known to climb out of the bathroom window and scale down the drainpipe for my freedom. After a confrontation with my dad on my return home I decided that course of action was not a good idea!

One of my daytime bedroom visits was for ordering some coal. The coalman was delivering in the street, and I asked him the price of a bag of coal. After he'd told me, I said, "My mum could do with a ton of it." "Is that your house, Son?" he asked, pointing. "Yes," I replied. He put one ton of coal down our coal-hatch. When he knocked on the door for the money, my poor old mother didn't have anything like that kind of money. She ended up having to pay for the coal at so much a week!

Whenever I got the chance, I nipped round to grandad's house. (This used to be at least once a day). He lived in between our house and Victoria School in 19 Raincliffe Street, and it's still standing to this day. If it was around tea-time when I went, grandad would ask me, "Have you had your tea, yet?" I'd say I hadn't, and have tea with him there instead of at home. Afterwards, we would wash up and tidy up the table. Then I would get the cards out of their drawer and we would play. Grandad had a tin of half-pennies which we used. We always put them all back in the tin at the end of our card session. As it got towards night-time, I dreaded grandad saying, "Isn't it time you were going home, Jack?" When he did, I would say, "Let's just play for a few more minutes." We always played a card game called Fish. Eventually, he would say, "All right, then, that's enough. In the bath." I would have a bath while he went round to tell mother that I was spending the night at his house. He needn't really have bothered – with all us kids, she surely wouldn't have missed one! We only had a four-bedroomed council house, and I can't remember how many slept in one bed, but I can remember waking up many times with a foot in my face! When he got back from our house, we would have some supper and then he would send me to bed. I've never known more pleasure than I used to get from those evenings. I think he liked me going round there, too, as the only other company he had was his canary, Joey.

"When I grow up, I'm going to save like mad and buy a nice house like this," I would think whilst lying in bed. It was only a two-bedroomed terrace house, but grandad kept it like a palace. In his living-room, he had a grandfather clock which struck once every quarter-hour, twice every half-hour, and then the relevant amount of strikes for the hour on the hour. I felt just like a king in my grandad's spotlessly clean house. I even had eggs and bacon for breakfast before I departed the next morning.

Granny had died before I was born. I don't know what of – grandad never told me, and I never asked him. I could tell that he loved her from the way he talked about her, and he never married again. He used to tell me all sorts of wonderful stories about things that happened before my time. God, I loved him.

Long before I was born grandad had owned two lovely hackneys, called Archer and Dolly. He'd had their portraits painted and hung them up in his house, one on each side of the chimney-breast in the alcoves. They were his pride and joy, hung up there on the wall, both standing to attention with their tails docked. They were a lovely sight, for sure. I often caught him admiring them. When grandad died, the portraits were passed down to me, of course. I treasured them for years. When my sister Betty's daughter, Julie, got married, I had the paintings cleaned, put into nicer frames, and gave them to her as a wedding present. Needless to say, she already knew the importance they held for our family. Julie got married to an accountant. She's a good girl, and cherishes them. I thought it was best to pass them on to a younger member of the family, as my job as a free-lance jump-jockey

15

wasn't exactly as safe as playing marbles! At the time, our sons, Alan and Sam, weren't old enough to take on the responsibility of them.

Grandad also owned a horse-flesh shop. I wasn't keen on this side of his business, which, incidentally, father was in charge of. It was in Accommodation Road, which has all been pulled down and rebuilt now. Grandad rented a stable yard on York Road which was behind Hemmingway's Brewery. It had about twelve stalls (or 'standings', as they were called) and a couple of loose boxes. He also rented a field towards Seacroft, which is all houses now. There would be more than thirty horses in it at any given time, and most of the poor beggars usually ended up in the shop. Father was a great man to drive horses. He could even drive a six-in-hand, and was rated one of the best around. When he collected horses out of the field, he went up with a horse-and-cart and put halters on the ones he wanted, tying them to the back of the cart. Many times he would bring three or four horses down at a time in this way. He was also a good dealer – if any horses he bought were good for other jobs, he would sell them on, no doubt for a profit.

My first recollection of riding is when I was only four or five – around the swollen glands period. Dad would take the horses he had bought to grandad's house to show him how his money was being spent (or rather, what he had to pay for!). Often, I would pick up a bit of courage and ask dad for a ride, but he always said "No". He probably thought, from looking at me, that I wouldn't be able to hold my own water, let alone hold a pony up and down the street! I then realised I was going about things in the wrong way, and decided to work on grandad instead, as he was much more civilised. This plan worked well, and the next time dad brought something along which looked reasonable, I asked grandad if I could have a ride. "Harry! Let young Jack, here, have a ride on that one," he said, having heard all the bullshit dad gave him to try and justify its price.

"He doesn't want to be riding in his condition," replied my dad.

"Just let the lad have a ride," said grandad, adding "And take him steady."

With that, dad loaded me up and walked me down the cobbled street. It didn't take as much courage to ride the pony as it would have done to ask my sire for the ride! We turned round, and dad jogged me back, going much too fast for someone who was supposed to be looking after me. However, I wasn't for coming off. It had been too big a struggle getting the ride in the first place, also I was loving it!

After that, I started to ride most of the horses and ponies which dad brought up, and in return he would give me instruction – if that's what you call it. Him shouting, bawling, swelling-up in the neck and going bright red! I thought then, should I ever have children, I would work out a different way of teaching them to ride!

2

YOUNG GRAFTERS

By the time my brother Harry and I were about eight and ten years old, we had to earn our keep. The old boy would have us out by 6.00a.m. every morning. We often saw the knocker-up woman, whose job was to go around the streets with a long pole giving early morning calls by banging on the bedroom windows of the occupants who needed a knock to wake them up. My father got up so early that he could have given her a call! He walked with us down to the yard before school (or rather we had to run to keep up with him!). Once there, the first thing we did was feed all the horses that we had in, which could amount to as many as a dozen. Then Harry and I would start mucking out and haying up, etc.

While we mucked out, father would be putting the harness on the horse he was driving that day. The horse would be eating his/her breakfast as fast as he/she could, knowing full well it wouldn't be long before Mr. Berry had him/her walking down the passage, complete with blinders, collar, aims and traces, breechings with crupper attached (which the lesser members of the Berry household would be cleaning that weekend). The horse would be yolked up in the flat cart with the two carriage lamps that dad had lit along with his cigarette as soon as he arrived at the yard. As the horse jogged out of the cobbled yard into the darkness, heading for York Road to get to the abattoir for the day's meat for the shop, dad would be shouting, "Do this, do that, do this and that", until out of earshot. At this point it would have been a good time for Harry and I to have a skive, but we couldn't because we had so much to do. Betty, who worked full-time in the shop since leaving school, would have to start making her way at about 7.00a.m. to open the shop and let in Mr. Kitchiman, the full-time butcher, in order to be ready for dad and Mr. Kitchiman to make up the joints ready for Betty to serve. When things got going dad would leave and get on with any other business he had to do.

School, a good 1½ miles from the yard, started at 9.00a.m. There was always an assembly during which the pupils sang a couple of hymns and said a prayer together. It finished at 9.30a.m. Harry and I legged it like hell to get there on time, and we would be as hungry as church-mice because we wouldn't have eaten all morning. The first chance we had of getting something into our stomachs would be at 11.00a.m. (play-time) when we got a half-pint of free milk. I absolutely hated milk, and still do. With luck I would be able to trade mine for a sweet or something edible. If no-one had anything to swap it for, I gave the milk away, and needless to say there were always plenty of takers!

If we managed to get to school before the morning assembly finished, we had to stay in the cloakroom where the duty teacher took our names, gave us our regular bollocking, and reported us to the Head (but at least we could get a wash and a drink of water in there!). If we got to school after assembly, when the duty teacher had gone from the cloakroom, we were really up the creek. We had to go through a side door, off the huge assembly hall, to get to where our class would have started lessons. I would end up standing in front of the class, getting my usual dressing down, stinking like a polecat from mucking out, blowing like a train from running, and not exactly dressed as if I was going to Sunday school! The only good thing was that none of the lads took the piss because I was late, like they did when most other things happened in class. This was probably due to the fact that there was only one kid in the class who I couldn't beat in a fight, which created a certain amount of respect. They sometimes called me 'blackberry' or 'gooseberry', but that was harmless ribbing. Imagine what Richard Head, the ex-trainer, or P. Ennis, the ex-jump-jockey, might have been called at school!

On days like those, it was bad enough handling the hassle and abuse from the teacher. If we were late twice in one week (and I can't remember when we weren't!) we got caned by the Head, Mr. Hunter personally. As this occurred last thing on a Friday before we broke up for the weekend, I used to look forward to that day with mixed feelings!

Whatever happened at school, though, was preferable to facing my ex-R.S.M. father for not doing the jobs at the yard properly. Mind you, dad worked very hard himself, and he was as strong as an ox. I would have thought he weighed around 12 to 13 st. He could lift a whole side of beef which, apparently, takes a very strong man to do. To achieve it, he had to get the half-body swaying on its hook, then take it forward very fast. Next, someone had to quickly unhook it and free it so that he could walk off, in rhythm, with the side on his shoulder. Otherwise, the side of beef would have flattened whoever was under it! One day, things didn't turn out quite right, and my darling father ended up in Leeds Infirmary. He had to have several stitches in his shoulder because the hook had stuck into him. They didn't keep him in, though (or rather, he wouldn't stay in), and some time later he asked my mother to remove his stitches. She said she wouldn't, and told him to go to the doctors or back to the hospital. So, I immediately volunteered for the job – and got it! His shoulder was all wet and pussy – a real mess. He had still been working with the stitches in, and they should really have come out sooner. Household scissors were not the most delicate of tools to be performing this minor operation with, especially without the aid of tweezers, but they were all I could find! I tugged on the catgut a few times before I even attempted to cut the loops of the stitches, just to see if this hard-nut had any feelings. He didn't even bat an eyelid! He just said, "Thank you, Son" when I'd finished, and put his shirt back on. He didn't even give me a chance to clean up the wound. (He nearly always called the lads in the family "Son", very seldom using our christian names. This was probably because he had so many names to remember! He only started using them later in life).

School lunch-times, we ran home for something to eat. As we were all in different classes, we didn't wait for each other. It was always a race to get home first. We didn't have school meals, father wasn't always consistent at coughing up the money to my mother. Eating at home was safer – it saved the embarrassment of going to school without dinner money. It was bad enough having to take one shilling on Mondays to The Yorkshire Penny-Savings Bank at school (collected by the teacher), and then having to find the gall to draw it out again every four or five weeks for mother because she said she badly needed it. My money never earned a penny interest.

School-banking was a real pain. If anyone wanted to (or could afford to) put money in the Yorkshire Penny Bank, they could have taken it to the branch at the top of my grandad's street (this was the first property in Raincliffe Street). It would have saved the embarrassment in class that us kids from big families had. Some of the little darlings in the class would say, "I'm putting two and sixpence in the bank, today." The teacher collecting the cash must have been on commission. When he had collected and booked in all the deposits, the prat would say, "Any withdrawals?" I would stroll up to the front of the class, often on my own, and draw out my savings. Sometimes, I stayed at my desk and didn't go up, to save the embarrassment. In the end, the teacher and I made a pact that I didn't have to bother banking any more.

We were never late back to school after lunch. In fact, we had enough time to play football and cricket in the school playground, even allowing for the time I spent galloping off to the Thrift Store where we had an account (or rather, we were allowed credit). We'd be downing our soup or eating sandwiches at home, when mother would say she wanted one of us to go to the shop for her. It usually fell on deaf ears, and in the end it was always either Betty or I who went. As I ran out to the shop on York Road, I'd tell them, "You lot need Dad's foot up your backside!" On the way, I would be saying to myself, "Two loaves of bread, three pints of milk, ¼lb. of tea, and a packet of Oxos," over and over again. I often got it wrong, and probably brought back three loaves of bread, two pints of milk, and ½lb. of tea – completely forgetting the Oxos!

Our woodwork teacher was called Mr. Clegg, and if ever there was a head-banger, it was him. He knocked us about just for the fun of it, and we were frightened to death of him. We had to climb up three flights of exterior metal stairs to get to the woodwork room, and if he heard one sound as we were coming up, he would make us all go back down again until we could do it in complete silence. I remember once, when we had run out of wood, he had us all kneeling down, asking God to ask Illingworth and Ingham (a Leeds haulage firm) to deliver our wood. What a plonker – as Del Boy in Only Fools And Horses would say!

On most days, come 4.00p.m. home-time, father would be waiting at home to take Harry and myself back to the yard to get the horses done up. He never took my next youngest (by two years) brother, Frank, with him, as he did not consider him to be a horseman. My brother was therefore useless, and was a weekend harness cleaner.

After school in summer-time, on most nights, we went with father on the horse-and-cart to mow a load of grass for the horses to eat, probably Round-hay Park or some big verge near Harehills Lane. In those days, there were lots of big grass verges around Leeds – the town wasn't contaminated by fumes from cars as much as it is now. Sometimes father might have bought a horse or a pony which would end up being tied to the back of the cart. He wouldn't have to say anything; I knew I had to ride the horse or pony behind the cart, with no saddle, sometimes no bridle just a halter, and nearly always trotting (my father could not drive at a walking-pace for long; he was always in too big a hurry). Searching for grass to mow, we would drive for miles, depending on the condition of the horse or pony and how my backside stood up to the ordeal!

When we got to the mowing place, my father mowed the grass in lovely straight lines. Harry and I raked it up afterwards, and forked it onto the cart. Sometimes, while the old boy was mowing away, singing his hymns, I would have a crafty feel to see if I was bleeding! Periodically he'd stop to say, "Keep those corners square!" As anyone who has ever loaded grass onto a flat cart before will know, it's important to have good square corners or else the load won't hold.

On our way back home, I had to ride the horse which was still tied behind the cart. Dad made me do this, as it was his way of breaking or "getting them going", as he said. Sometimes, if I was hidden by a high enough load of grass on the cart, I would bob off the horse to give my backside a rest. From time to time the old soldier gave the reins to Harry and, as quick as a flash, jumped off the cart. If I was running alongside the horse or pony, Harry drove as fast as he dared to give me a chance, but the old boy was as cunning as a fox – he would know if Harry had increased the pace. One day, I had only just got off the pony's back to take a breather; there he was, ready to give me a crack. So, I ran the other way. Dad ran after me for a short while, but couldn't catch me as I was very sharp when I was on the retreat from him. Harry kept the horse-and-cart going while this happened. We were a long way from the stable yard, dad had to catch the tram back home. As I was in no rush to confront him again, I took the remainder of evening stables off, thinking that I may as well swing for a sheep as a lamb. I don't know what dad said to Harry when he finally caught up with him, but no doubt it wasn't complimentary! If I was still on the poor horse's back when dad jumped off, he would say, "Sit up! Keep your hands down!" I never managed to get it just right, or if I did, he never let on!

To be fair to dad he wasn't a drunkard or anything, but one summer night, after we had cut a load of grass, it was still quite early. He must have fancied a pint. We stopped at a pub and put the horse-and-cart on some wasteland opposite. He told us he wouldn't be long.

We undid the reins at the bit of the horse in the cart and extended the halter rope of my steed behind the cart, so they could eat while father was taking refreshments. Harry and I were fooling about wrestling in the rough grass. Somehow I rolled over onto the bottom of a broken bottle. It cut just below the right knee very badly, for which I still have the scar. When dad came out of the pub I told him, "I can't ride the pony back because of my leg!"

He gave us a right ticking off about couldn't be left out of his sight for a few minutes and were in trouble. To be fair to us also, it was more like an hour. He could hardly have expected us to sit waiting for him like a pair of choirboys. He drove to Leeds Infirmary, gave me some money for my tram fare home and left me there to get my leg stitched up and a damned injection – I suppose for tetanus.

Those days in Leeds, a horse-and-cart or pony-and-trap was common-place. If I was mounted behind the cart I knew when one was in sight on our side of the road because the pace would quicken. The old man always had a good steed in the shafts, and they were always for sale. Being the showman that he was, he'd give the driving whip one good crack, which could nearly be heard in the next county (he called this "stroking it up"), and the horse would jump straight into the bridle. As we passed the other horse-and-cart, Dad just gave a little nod. I bet those drivers loved him!

The railways, rag-and-bone men, breweries, the Co-op, and lots of coal merchants had horse-drawn vehicles. I can even remember seeing a horse-drawn hearse. Wouldn't that be a sight, today! The highlight of some people's week came on Sundays when they would get out their immaculately pre-sented pony-and-traps and go for a drive in the country. Sometimes the horses were plaited-up and tied with ribbons; the harness was nicely polished and the brasses shone like new shillings; every kid was in Sunday best, and invariably spent the whole day in the traps, probably with a packed lunch.

21

No-one told father that Sundays were for pleasure, though. He could always find something to do, and even something for the rest of his family also.

I don't think dad knew a single song, and yet throughout the day, no matter where he was, he would be singing hymns. Isn't that amazing? I'm sure he knew every hymn in the book. He had been a choirboy in his youth, as had grandad. Some nights, we sat around the fire, either at home or at grandad's, and dad had us all singing hymns. When someone either lowered their voice or dropped out, he would say, "Sing up! Sing up!"

Once, father bought four donkeys from a dealer, and one Sunday, when he wasn't about, Harry and I fitted the donkeys out as best we could with bridles of their size (and some others made to fit by adding a few knots here and there), but no saddles. We set off to take them to an area where there were plenty of kids, and, being in Leeds, that wasn't too difficult. We thought we could earn ourselves a crust by selling donkey rides. We did a grand job drumming up trade, but unbeknown to us the little donkeys hadn't been broken, and they were dumping the budding Lester Piggotts as fast as we were putting them up. We had to move out pretty sharpish with our long-eared friends when the jockeys' parents started whingeing and threatening to call the law.

Dicky Yates, the grocer on Temple View near our house, gave a penny in exchange for every empty one-pound jam-jar. He would fill the jars up again with treacle, which had either been bought in bulk or had fallen off the back of a lorry. Whichever it was, he was definitely a crook who would have made Al Capone look like The Milky-Bar Kid!

I collected dozens of jars in my spare-time (which I didn't get a lot of) from knocking on people's doors, having asked them to save them for me. When the supply was in Dicky's favour, the cunning old fox would only pay half a penny. I used to collect these jam-jars up in a rickety, home-made barrow, and store them at the yard for weeks on end until Dicky put his price back to a penny. On one occasion, my dad sold them all. He swore blind that he hadn't, saying he had given them to some needy soul. All I know is that I saw a roughneck with a spotted muffler round it, coming out of our yard with my jars rattling on his horse-and-cart. When I questioned him about where he was going with my jam-jars, he said, "They're not yours!" and kept going.

Another time, down at the yard, father was selling a young pony to some old boy. We had only had the pony for a few days, and were just pulling him about, getting him broken. Dad put me quietly on his back with just a snaffle bridle on, as we had not got as far as putting a saddle on him yet. Anyway, the little chap was doing great until this silly old bugger tapped the pony on the backside with his walking stick and said, "Trot him on, lad, and let's see it move."

Move he did! – straight out of the yard, down the street, and on to York Road (one of the busiest roads in Leeds). The poor, little fellow ran straight into the side of a moving tram, and later had to be put down. I got concussion.

On another occasion, we were up in the field catching horses. Some of them were big and strong – real handfuls. We only put halters on them when they were caught. If ever they messed about, dad would shout, "Hold tight! Hold tight!" Whenever we let one go, he would go bananas. Well, on this particular day, one took off with me. "Hold tight! – Hang on!" the old man shouted to me, as I ran almost as fast as Brendan Foster, trying not to let go of the end of the halter. Still hanging on, I hit ground that was like Market Rasen in August. My face and legs got cut and grazed really badly – they looked like raw meat! Worst of all, though, when the horse finally stopped I had no trousers on – they had worn completely off! I just stood there, still holding the horse. How degrading!

On Saturdays, Harry and I used to go to the market with dad. He and Harry would go to the abattoir which was next door. I had been to the abattoir with them on a few occasions, but it wasn't my scene. I have always liked to see animals alive. Those slaughtermen are a breed apart. Twice I've seen a Rabbi cut a beast's throat as it was turned upside-down in a box which the poor mite couldn't get out of. I don't want to get involved in the religious do's and don'ts, but that is really cruel. The first time I saw a horse being shot was in our field. It had a twisted gut, and this man who had a wagon with a winch on it shot the horse, cut its throat, towed the poor horse onto his wagon, then drove away. I was violently sick.

The Leeds market was, by far, the best market I have ever seen. The small animal part: I loved it – really loved it. This is why some crackpot reporter stated that I began life as a street salesman, which simply isn't true because I hadn't even left school. If a ten-year-old lad gets 5s per week for cleaning the house windows, one would hardly say that he had set off in life as window-cleaner. What I did, in fact, was rent one of the market's permanent cages for sixpence a day which could be divided into sections. I'd walk around to barter with the owners of other cages, which had various small animals in. For example, if one of the cages contained a litter of nice looking pups, and the man in charge wanted 5s for each of them, I would buy them all for 3s 6d each and agree to pay him when I had sold them. I would deal like this all day, with pups, rabbits, chicks, bantams, mice, guinea-pigs, and all sorts of small animals. At the end of the day I would go home on the tram with two or three pounds to the good, or if I hadn't quite sold-up, possibly with a pup and a couple of rabbits in a box, or two or three mice in my pocket. I would try to sell them to the kids at school during the week or swop them for something. Failing this, I took them back to the market the following week to sell on. Invariably, most of the money I earned I would give to mum when I got home because she needed the money more than me in order to feed us all. Even at my early age I could appreciate it was a struggle for my mum. I mainly did it for the crack.

Nowadays, I still have to back my judgement – as I did all those years ago – at Yearling Sales, the only difference today being the size of animal. The main object for the vendor is to get as much money as possible for an animal. The people selling their yearlings often say, "This is the best one I have ever bred," and so on, and I have to riddle a lot of chaff away from the corn before I get committed. After I have bought their yearling, and if they still own the mare, no matter how many phone calls the ex-owners make to me to see how he/she is getting on, I know their main interest is whether or not the yearling I have will win as a 2-year-old because if it did, future offspring of a mare are more valuable.

On Wednesday and Friday nights, from about 7.00p.m. till 9.00p.m., I used to go to a boxing club at Harehills. I enjoyed going there, especially working out, sparring, skipping, shadow-boxing, and of course, the real thing – boxing. The smell of lubrication and liniment around the place was something I really liked. It created a great atmosphere the same way the buzz of excitement and crack, combined with the smell of tack does in weighing rooms at race meetings. I could not afford to get hooked on it though, as I always wanted to be a jump-jockey. However, I did have a few fights for the club, and was not disgraced. It certainly built me up and made me stronger. When I was letting off steam to get more weight into the punches, I would often imagine that the punch-bag was my dad, Mr. Hunter or that crackpot Mr. Clegg!

Once, as I was going to the boxing-club, I found a National Dried Milk tin. I picked it up and had a struggle to get the lid off. Inside was full of water, and six little kittens – dead. At the time, thinking who could be so rotten and cruel to these poor little mites, I could have understood anyone drowning the kittens because they didn't want them. But at least they should have had the decency to bury them afterwards or even to have put them in the dustbin, rather than have someone nosey like me discover them. I took the tin to the nearby police station. The bobby took the tin off me and said he would make some enquiries.

After finishing stable duties one evening, Harry and I were passing The Princess Picture house in Pontefract Lane. Outside was a board saying 'Free Meeting – Everyone Welcome'. There were lots of people going inside. "Come on, we'll have a bit of this," Harry said.

It was actually a Labour Party meeting. We found ourselves nice seats up front, and then some guy started speaking a lot like the Reverend Ian Paisley. He was thumping hard on the table and shouting, "Is it a sin to wear glasses? Is it a sin to wear false teeth? Is it a sin to wear a wig? Or walk with a limp and need a stick? Isn't it bad enough for these unfortunate people that they need to? Why, why, why should they be penalised further by having to pay for them? Wouldn't it be fairer if the people who don't require such things are made to pay for these unwanted extras rather than the people who do?"

Harry and I were laughing so much at this, that the Reverend Paisley lookalike stopped the show and had us thrown out!

24

3

WORK AND PLAY

When Wetherby Races were on, adverts were posted on bus shelters and other places in Leeds. I made a mental note of the date, and then took the whole day off school. Borrowing my pal Eddie Foster's bike, and despite all the chores I had to do at the yard, which included doing some of Harry's jobs so he wouldn't be late for school, getting to Wetherby before the first race never posed a problem. There was a level-crossing near Wetherby where I rode Eddie's bike to and parked by. After climbing the racecourse fence, with my secretly home-made sandwiches safe in my pocket, I headed for the open ditch in the straight with my *Sporting Life* or *Sporting Chronicle* which had been bought in Leeds at the start of my journey.

In between races and going to watch the jockeys at the starts I would read my paper. I never went to the start right up by the Grandstand because I thought my clothes weren't smart enough to be seen in near the paddock. Having got to know lots of the lovely jump-people since, I don't think they would have given a monkey's what I looked like! I was there – that was the important thing.

Back at the ditch, I knew the names of most of the jockeys who were riding over it. I desperately wanted to be out there with them some day, and I often went to the jockeys who fell at my fence. They seemed pleased to have someone to talk to, and were always down to earth. It made me feel really good talking to the likes of M. Prendergast, T. Molony, and A.P. Thompson. These men were idols to me. It was brilliant! If they were hurt after their falls, the unsung heroes of the St. John's Ambulance Brigade soon saw to them, and they would sometimes give me a cup of coffee from their flasks. I hoped that I'd make it as a jockey as I wouldn't have liked to have been a first-aid man all my life!

I loved every minute of the races, whether it was cold, raining, or whatever. As a kid I was always cold in winter, but I could stand any type of weather at Wetherby Races. On the way back home on Eddie's bike, I would

25

be jumping imaginary fences wherever there was a line or a shadow on the road; trying to see my stride and sitting back like the jockeys did; pushing and kicking the bike to a winning post I had sorted out further up the road.

When I finally did get home, a low profile was kept because dad would give me a good wallop or two when he found out where I'd been. He always seemed to know, and gave me loads of useless verbal about how I could get killed on the roads going all that way on a rickety, old bike like Eddie's. It was safer than riding some of the horses he had tied to the back of the cart! If he had put his hand on his heart for the truth, he was more concerned about absenteeism from work at the stable yard.

Other than wanting to be a jump-jockey, I also had an urge for a time to be a bull-fighter and had read many books about matadors and bull-fights. I am not a cruel person, in fact I absolutely love my animals (and I own plenty!), but there is a lot more to bull-fighting than just killing the bulls. Lots of people don't approve. I didn't approve of the way the Rabbi killed the cattle in the Leeds slaughter-house. When I've been fox-hunting, however, there have been people protesting about hunting, carrying boards and banners condemning it. I have never seen one protest about the method some animals are slaughtered by, be it outside Leeds abattoir or any other.

I would have dearly loved to have ridden jumpers during the winter, then fought bulls in Spain during the summer. However, it couldn't be – I would have had to serve an apprenticeship in both fields – I chose racing.

To get a breather away from us lot, Mum would do her best to get us all out of the house at the same time, instead of us using it like a warren. Knowing that I was less of a house bug than the others, she told me to take Joan, my younger sister, for a walk or something. There was a good chance that I would be gone for longer than just a few minutes, because I loved the open air. Joan was all right, but a bit of a gawp. If she saw any kids playing football, or whatever, and we either stopped to watch or joined in at some stage, her mouth dropped open and she dozed off into a trance. Seizing my opportunity, I would back off, and by the time she awoke I'd be gone, fully aware she would tell Mother later on that I had left her.

On one of my compulsory outings with Joan I took her to York Road swimming baths. There she got lost in one of her stupid gazes, so I pushed her in. Unluckily, she caught her ankle on the side of the pool as she fell, and broke it. Eddie and I took her to hospital to have a pot put on. Returning home, I bribed her with all my possessions – all the money I had, my jockey cigarette cards, my marbles, conkers, everything – just so she wouldn't tell mum what really happened. She agreed not to tell, but as soon as we got home, although I had even carried her (by way of a piggy-back) all the way from the tram, she blabbed. The whole story gushed out, and it wasn't the fictitious one that we had told her to say. I was soon back upstairs again, cleaning out the bedrooms!

Pushing Joan in the water didn't do her any permanent harm, for she

Watercolours of grandad's hackneys, pictures which have now been treasured in the Berry family for around 100 years.

Left: My only picture of my mum.
Below: My grandad.

grew up to become a top-class swimmer. She won lots of prizes for York-shire, and on one occasion beat Anita Londsborough. She later suffered polio and had to have a few operations. Now she has to wear a caliper on one leg. She has since married, lives in Australia, and has three children, two boys and a girl.

Often Eddie, my brother Harry and myself would go to Leeds City Varieties, the theatre where they employed a Master of Ceremonies to intro-duce the acts. For a bit of devilment we would go on the balcony armed with oranges. When everyone was settled down and enjoying the show, I'd lean over the balcony to pick out a bald-headed person in the audience directly beneath us. I would get him lined up before squeezing the juice out of my orange onto his head. By the time the man looked above him I had moved to the left or the right of the balcony to see his reactions. One day a solo act was performing on stage and he saw me doing this. He could hardly continue doing his turn for laughing. It wasn't long before some misery whinged to the management and they employed an usherette to prowl the balcony.

Some nights, Eddie, myself, and others went to The Princess Cinema. We had whip-rounds to get together enough money so that one of us could pay to get in. When the picture started, at a time when loud music was playing, (so no-one could hear the back door bar drop), the one that paid to get in went to the toilet and let the others in through the back door. Very often, this was my job. Unless it was a really good picture, there were always plenty of empty seats for us.

In those days, a doorman sat on the first seat of the front row. He tore the tickets in two, then kept one half and gave the other half back. At The Princess Cinema, this man was called Ernie. He was a very big, rough bugger with a grumpy, frightening voice. Sometimes, he would realise that more people had come out of the toilets than had gone in. Having noted where we had gone to sit, he would come over to our seats, shining his torch in our faces. "Where're yer tickets?" he'd grunt.

We would search in all our pockets for the lost ticket we never had, then Ernie would grab us by the scruff of our necks and throw us out. He made such a fuss for so long that people lost interest in the film and began watching us. It was like Dick Barton – Special Agent! Would Ernie kill them or let them live?? Will Jack and Eddie survive?? Tune in next week for the next thrilling instalment of 'Ernie And The Intruders!'

Bob Tate was the owner of a small pig-and-poultry farm in Boston Spa. He had a cattle-wagon and used to bring horses back to Leeds for us when dad had bought them from places far afield. Bob also owned two really nice show ponies which I sometimes rode in shows for him. I stayed at his place for the summer holiday of 1950, when I was twelve years old. He had recently left his wife and moved into a smaller house in the village with his mistress, Peggy, and so I stayed there.

I rode the ponies, mucked out the pigs, and collected and graded the eggs before packing them into wooden cases. These eggs would be sent off to the packing station every week. There was one employee of Bob's who used to pinch the eggs. I saw him nick some and put them in a pocket of his overcoat, which he kept hung up in the boiler room. When he was out of sight, I went over to the coat and squashed all the eggs still in the pocket! He needn't have pinched them – if he'd have asked, Bob would have given him some for nothing, as Bob was a very kind man. He had some cracking sayings, such as:

"If a man's poorly, he's not well."

"If things don't alter, they stop as they are."

"You'll make a man before your mother," and lots more.

I really liked it at Bob's – there was so much open countryside, not like Leeds. I went all over the place in the cattle-truck with him. On market days at Wetherby, I used to see my grandad. We would go and have a cup of tea and a sandwich in the place where all the farmers went for their meals and a banter. It was really good. The only thing missing to make my world complete, was my own piebald pony, Gamecock.

Originally, my grandad had bought Gamecock from Bill Walmsley of the show jumping family, and I had liked him so much that my grandad gave him to me. He was one of the best gymkhana ponies in the business, and often we would win the musical chairs, the potato race, the sack race, or whatever, without even coming out of the ring. It was brilliant going round the local shows. Most towns and villages held a show in those days, and they were such fun. Recently I met John Walmsley, Bill's son, at Thirsk Races and he remembered the pony all these years afterwards. He also told me that Gamecock had hunted all season as a 2-year-old! What a tough little fellow he was. When you think of all the horses and ponies this family have had through their hands he must have been out of the top drawer for John to remember him.

When I went to Bob's, I took my bull-terrier with me. His name was "Pal", but sometimes he wasn't much of a pal to me! He landed me in all kinds of trouble. He killed four dogs and countless cats, although he had only done so when they had come down the lane where the farm was. This didn't cut a lot of ice with the policeman who kept calling in on us with people's complaints about Pal! Anyway, to keep the peace, I got the vet to put Pal down, then I buried him. This was tough, and really upset me, as I loved the old boy. At the time it was very difficult for me to survive without the added aggro from Pal.

I had also brought my yellow ferret with me from Leeds, who was brilliant at bolting rabbits. There were lots of rabbits at Boston Spa, where we worked the banks. By netting the holes up, we could catch up to a dozen at one session, and afterwards I would sell them to the local butcher (in those days, rabbits didn't have myxomatosis!). There was always a good market for them.

When the summer holidays were over, I didn't like the idea of going back to Leeds. Bob had said that if it was all right with the authorities, and my parents, I could stay with him, because I wasn't just a bum – I could, and would, work. I was still there a few weeks after the school holidays had finished, as I wouldn't go home! Word had it that a posse from Leeds was coming to take me back there. On the day in question I hid on the roof of the large pig barn so they couldn't find me, staying up there for hours until they left. I had felt it was the best way to handle things, rather than to try and reason logically. Soon afterwards, I was told that if I went to school in Boston Spa, it would be all right. So, I agreed, and that's what I did. Alternatively, I would have been sent to a remand home for playing truant.

I am about to make a confession, now, which I have never mentioned to anyone before. While I was at Bob's, my swollen glands started to play up again. The bottom scar from a previous operation on my neck was very red and swollen, even when it was warm I wore a polo-neck sweater to hide it. The swelling continued until it grew to a size of a golf ball, and whenever I got the chance I would strip to the waist and bathe it praying it would be all right and I wouldn't have to go back into hospital with it. The glands had been trouble free for a few years, and now it was such a worry to me. Eventually, the swelling got so big and raw looking that one night it burst, splitting where the old scar was. Whenever possible I bathed it and applied a dressing of lint with zinc and castor oil ointment. I kept the ointment and the lint in my pocket all day so that no-one would find it and ask me what it was for. I had bought the ointment from the chemists. When I had asked the chemist what the best thing would be to put on an open wound, I was fearful he might want to look at it – it looked so nasty that he might have called an ambulance for me! Thankfully, he didn't, and it settled. Thank God – yes, thank God – it has never bothered me since. I can appreciate how people feel when they find out they have something radically wrong with them!

David Sheddon, the trainer's son, went to my new school at Boston Spa. I went down to Mr. Sheddon's yard with David at lunch-time on a few occasions. On the first, he asked me if I was any relation to Harry Berry from Leeds. "Yes, he is my father," I said. He then told me a few yarns about their army days. After he had finished reminiscing, I told him that racing was for me when I left school. He then said that when I did leave, he would give me a job if I wanted one.

At certain times of the year, when potatoes were being harvested, farmers would ask schools for volunteers to pick them. These volunteers got a week off school to perform the task and were paid something like 5s per day. I jumped at the chance, and went to work at a farm at Thorpe Arch, the next village. It was just a family farm with only one field of potatoes to pick. It took us exactly a week to complete the job, and, at the end of it, the farmer asked me if I could come back on the following Saturday morning to help him pick up the harrowings. He told me he wasn't getting any younger, and that if I wanted a job when I left school, he would give me one. So that really chuffed me. I'd been offered another job, and was at least sure of employment when I left school.

Out of the blue, Bob Tate announced he was selling up and looking for a smaller place. He had worked hard all his life, driven mile upon mile in his cattle-wagon over the years, and I think he wanted an easier time. He would be about age fifty, then. Bob sold everything except his cattle-wagon, his pigeons and their loft. We all moved to the village pub in Ryther, a village about thirty miles away from Boston Spa. The pub was called The New Inn, and was tenanted by a pal of Bob's called Ron Ward, who also had a cattle-wagon. The two of them would transport horses, cattle and sheep to and from shows, cattle markets, etc., which is how they originally met (no doubt in the market canteen!). They probably had been discussing business, of some sort. Ron may have asked Bob to stay at his place, until he found somewhere permanent.

So, there we were. Straight away I was sent to Ryther village school so that we wouldn't get any more trouble from the authorities. There were only about twenty of us in the entire school. We were divided into two classes and I was by far the eldest there. The teacher had taken me on, saying it only looked like being temporary and that there was nowhere else within a reasonable distance for me to go.

A few weeks later, Bob brought home some good news. He had put in a successful offer for a shop in none other than the village of Towton, the very same village where jump-trainer Charlie Hall trained. This was great news, and the shop itself was actually next door to Ben Robinson, Mr. Hall's headman. Although Ben was shortly to move and become 'mine host' at the village pub, The Rockingham Arms, it didn't take me too long to knock on his door and ask if I could help in the yard.

The next morning, I arrived at the yard at 7.00a.m. Ben gave me a horse to muck out, and then at 7.30a.m. we rode out. To be honest, I can't remember which horse it was, but everything went well. I loved it. Without a shadow of a doubt, this was the life for me. "I'll have a chat with you, when I get a minute, to see how we can arrange things for you," Ben said. "You seem keen and willing."

It was now 1951 and I was thirteen years old. Bob and Peggy didn't need me to help them as much because they didn't have the livestock – only a couple of dogs and his racing pigeons. This was good for me, it meant I could spend more time at the stables as Ben had said I could ride out and help in the yard. However I still had to do my bit by stacking shelves and helping out in the shop.

By now, I had saved up a few pounds (£8 or thereabouts) from the various hand-outs that Bob had given me, and I was a little better dressed than I was at Leeds. Bob said he was taking me to Wetherby because he had a surprise for me. He took me to the cycle shop of Horton and Hollinders and showed me a beautiful Phillips 3-speed bike. He bought it for my fourteenth birthday. It cost him around £14, and I offered to put my £8 towards it, but he wouldn't hear of it. What a smashing man Bob was. He was going to tie the bike down in the boot of his car, only I told him I wanted to ride it home. Besides, I thought I would go on a spending spree with my £8 while I was in town. I went to Foxes, the saddler, and bought myself a pair of cavalry-twill jodhpurs, a pair of jodhpur boots, and a flat-cap. I blew my £8, and enjoyed doing it. It should all have cost more than I had, but my Leeds market days spent bartering had stood me in good stead. I was now starting to get some collateral together by way of clothes and my bike. From then on I was determined to save really hard and try to make something of my life.

4

GOOD YEARS

I didn't say anything to the teacher about moving to Towton. Rather than change schools again and go the four miles on the bus to Tadcaster, I cycled on my newly acquired bike the seven miles from Towton to Ryther every day. I mucked out and rode out with the first lot, then set off on my bike for school. School finished at 3.30p.m. and I biked straight back to the yard for evening stables to do the horse which Ben had given me. The horse was called Three Two's, and he was a fine little fellow. He was really quiet to ride and didn't pull at all. To be fair to the others, though, ability-wise Three Two's was not one of the best in the yard. I ended up getting 10s a week for something I loved doing. If I'd have had the money, I would have willingly paid to do the work. It was great.

When on roadwork, sometimes, we would ride towards Ullerskelfe, near to where Uncle Walter trained (that's Walter Easterby – Mick and Peter's uncle). Ann and Sally Hall, The Guv'nor's two nieces, always referred to him as Uncle Walter. One day, while riding round the roads, a horse slipped up and got loose. I jumped off my mount to catch it, and while I was holding the two horses together, waiting for whoever had fallen off to come and remount, one of them squealed and reared up. While the horse played up, I got struck on my head with a front foot, and I was only wearing my flat-cap. Those days, no-one wore crash-helmets when riding out. Jump-jockeys' crash-helmets were only made of cork, and Flat jockeys only wore the cap of the colours of the owner without any helmet at all. It's a pity John McCririck hadn't been around then, as he was the one who advocated that even trainers should wear crash-helmets! I got a nasty cut on the top of my head. Having it seen to (bathed, etc.) made me late for school, so I decided not to go at all and rode the next lot out instead, which I considered to be a fair exchange.

Going to school at Ryther didn't have the same aggravation for me as at Leeds. If ever I was late, I would just say, "Sorry I'm late, ma'am." She would fill me in on what I'd missed, then we all got on with our work – that was the end of it. The lady teacher never once gave me (or anyone else) the stick, or even grumbled. I learned as much at that village school as I ever did at Victoria School. I was enjoying it there, too, because we worked as more of a team. She was far more civilised than the teachers at Leeds. With her living at Barkston Ash, a couple of miles south of Towton, I soon blew my cover regarding my new home, because the teacher saw me riding out. She used to drive past us on her way to school in the mornings. The first time she saw me she had a chat with me about it when I got to school. I told her I now lived at Towton and I was prepared and happy to cycle the mileage involved. After our chat whenever she saw me riding out she went out of her way to give me a wave. Often when I arrived at school she would say, "That was a nice horse you were riding today, Jack. What was his name?" I couldn't imagine those teachers at Leeds reacting in such a nice, friendly manner. She was a lovely and understanding woman.

The owner of the village shop at Ullerskelfe was called Mr. Mottram. He played the fiddle in the Ullerskelfe Village Hall Dance Band every Saturday night. It started at 7.30p.m., and The Guv'nor made us young ones go along. Mainly for the older people there would be a whist-drive before the dance, and The Guv'nor roped us into attending this as well. He had a live interest in Ullerskelfe village affairs because he was courting Maurice Camacho's (the present trainer) mum, and she lived there at the time. He wanted us mainly to make up the numbers and to clear the chairs away after the whist to get ready for the knees-up. Sometimes we had to partner the old folks in a game of whist. For devilment, if our partner played an ace, we would put a king on it, or better still, trump it if we didn't have a card of the same suit. They would go mad! Winning a game of cards meant so much to them. They even went as far as to tell our boss what we had done.

After the whist, we did our job of clearing away the tables and chairs, have a buffet-supper in a side room and then carry on with the Gay Gordons, Veleta's, old-time waltzes, barn dances, and the like. Accompanying Mr. Mottram would be Mrs. Mottram on the piano and an old boy on drums. Some of the lads moaned, but I loved it. They whinged because they had an urge between their legs, and most of the old biddies who attended the Ullerskelfe village-hop were a bit past it! They would rather have been at The Riley Smith Hall dance at Tadcaster which had been held on Friday, the night before, and where a bit of young skirt attended.

One of our lads, Jimmy Threadgold, was taken short at the Ullerskelfe dance. He had an upset tummy, as I think he had been drinking too much. He dashed to the toilet, which was an old-fashioned, outside one without a light or a lock on the door. Straight down with his pants, he sat on the knee of a woman who was already sitting on the toilet! He frightened the life out of the poor dear! During the rest of the evening, she was pointing Jimmy out to people, "That's him! That's him! The blond one!"

35

Mr. Mottram loved a punt on the horses. One particular morning when we saw him as we were riding round the roads, he asked us, "Have you anything for me to bet on today?" Although our yard was a really good one, with plenty of winners, most of the lads couldn't tip muck out of a barrow, let alone tip a winner. The only account the bookie ever closed on our lads was for not paying their bill, not for winning too much! Tommy Lynch, one of the lads, said, "Mr. Mottram, today I'm going to do you the biggest favour you have ever had. Go to Westmoorlands and put your maximum on Osborne Lad at Doncaster."

Westmoorlands was the local bookmakers. It was owned by two brothers, Ray and Jeff. It was an unofficial betting shop because off-course betting wasn't allowed in those days. Periodically, shops got raided by the police, and the bookie would have to pay the fines of all the people who were in at the time. Usually, however, the shop about to be raided would be given a tip-off, so the bookie only let a few punters stay, therefore limiting the amount he had to pay by way of fines. He always made sure our lads got out, as The Guv'nor wouldn't have liked them being in there.

Osborne Lad (Ozzy) was a lovely little horse, but he was not gifted with much speed. He was even slower at home than Glorious Days, which Mrs. Camacho used to come to the yard to ride out. We told Tommy he was a rotten prat for telling the old boy to back Ozzy, but he didn't give a damn. At Doncaster that day, on 15th February 1951 in the Butterscotch Selling Hurdle on heavy going, Ozzy, ridden by Colin Dukes, trotted up at 20/1. On the following Saturday, at the village dance, Mr. Mottram brought cigarettes and bags of sweets for us all, and gave a nice bung to Tommy, who was blowing to Mr. Mottram about how he had thought Ozzy would win as he had been going so well at home. (At home, one could cry faster than he galloped!)

Tommy was a good lad. All he ever wanted was a quiet life and a bit of fun. Later on when we were all living at The Manor, The Guv'nor's house, whenever we got ready to go out anywhere, Tommy would be the first in after work, and was always the best-dressed because he would put anyone's gear on. He once passed The Guv'nor going through the big kitchen. "Isn't that one of my collars and my tie, Tom?" The Guv'nor asked, head down, looking over the glasses resting on the end of his nose (in those days, collars were often separate from shirts).

"Now Guv'nor, would I wear your things?" he replied. "My mother sent me these in a parcel from Ireland only last week." (I can't remember Tom ever getting a letter, never mind a parcel).

"That's funny," The Guv'nor said, walking away nodding, head on one side. "They look like mine. Funny . . . funny!"

We had a colt, called Sashcord, who was a really randy sod. Once, as we walked the horses down to the gallops to work, Sashcord spotted a little mare, called Marenka (ridden by Tommy), half-way up the string. Sashcord took off with his lad and jumped straight onto Marenka's back. He tried to give her one while Tommy was still on her back. You could tell that Tommy had no ambitions to become a jump-jockey by the screaming and yelling he was doing under Sashcord's belly! Tommy was really frightened, and as white as a ghost. "Now you know what it feels like to get stuffed!" one of the lads shouted.

There was a girl who lived in Saxon village, whose parents were quite well off. She had a lovely car. She couldn't keep a permanent boyfriend, as she was a bit plain. Tommy, Colin 'Shadow' Dukes, and the old lads would cut cards to see which one had to take her to The Riley Smith Hall dance and stay with her all night, so they could get a lift home in her car. To make matters worse, she didn't even do a turn – the nearest they ever got was occasionally getting a finger in the neck-strap!

I rode out, then cycled to school, every day until I left on 7th October 1952. It was my fifteenth birthday, and I had decided that I had had enough schooling. I should have stayed on until Christmas, but no-one seemed too bothered. I thought I'd done my bit, so I started full-time in the yard. I left the shop and moved into the big house with the rest of the lads.

There was another young lad working in the yard called Harry Crudace, from Spennymoor, Co. Durham. Harry was a nice kid, but he was small and didn't have the bottle for racing. He was just getting over a fall from Culworth. The old horse had run off with him up the lane near The Rocking-ham Arms. Harry had bailed out and broken his leg in doing so. With him being so small, he got away with murder, as he was very cheeky! I remember him best for his saying – which I had never heard before nor have ever heard since – "Jesus to me, man!"

On 4th January 1954, my apprenticeship agreement arrived from Bromet & Sons, solicitors of Tadcaster. I signed and so did my father; my father's signature was witnessed by H. Parnaby, who served his own apprenticeship with George Formby in Malton. I doubt if the terms of my indentures had changed since the days of Fred Archer, nearly a hundred years before. I can't imagine staff signing such an antiquated agreement today, and stick-ing to it. However, I am sure we would all be better off though if we still served apprenticeships.

On one of Tommy Lynch's walkabouts, he once brought back a black Labrador pup. He called him Fagin and he grew into a super dog. Everyone loved Fagin. He was the best ratter I have ever seen. We took him round the stables, late at night, and let him loose in the boxes. One of us went inside the box, with a fork, and pulled the straw down from the sides, then another turned the light on. Fagin would catch the rats as they scampered away in panic – we caught lots of them in this way.

As we mucked out our horses, we put the muck into a great big fold-yard which was full of bullocks. Periodically, our farmers would clean it out with tractors and muck spreaders, then spread the manure on the land. Many times we rode the bullocks, ending up taking some nasty falls off them. Often bruised and sore, we never reported our injuries. It didn't help to get the bullocks fat, but they were certainly fit!

Jim Aldridge, the farm foreman, occasionally came back at nights to check on the cattle and sheep, especially at lambing times. We were always on the look out for him. He would creep round as quietly as possible, trying to catch us riding the cattle when he came into the fold-yard. We would turn a light on and off quickly then Jim would head for the switch and trip over things we had put in his way. One of us then made a noise at the end of the yard. If Jim got near anyone, someone else would say (in an altered voice), "You're getting warmer, Jim!" Then, to his rear, "You're going cold, Jim!" He would find the main light switch to the fold-yard and turn it on. He wouldn't see us, though, because we would be hidden behind the tumbrels they fed the cattle out of, which were strategically placed so that all the beasts could feed without any particular animal getting bullied. We wore sweaters or jackets over our heads so that he couldn't recognise us! One of us would then nip around the back of Jim and turn the lights off again. He got into such a state, shouting, swearing, and going berserk like a wild animal! "You little b*****ds!" he would shout at us. "If I ever catch you I'll break your bloody necks!" Jim always walked around with a thick stick, a bit like a brush-handle. A crack from that could have killed us! He'd go back into the house and tell The Guv'nor about us. When The Guv'nor, or whoever, went to the attic to check, we would all be in bed, asleep!

We had an old, grey cart mare turned out in a paddock adjacent to the gallops (except during severe weather, when Jim would put her in a box). The only work the old mare did was raking-up at hay-time, which often used to be my job. She was fairly old; The Guv'nor didn't want to sell her, as he liked her – we all liked her.

Some nights, we took her out of her paddock and onto the gallops, where four or five of us would get on her back without any tack on. We were like a giant caterpillar, with all our little legs kicking like mad. She would take off with us, and gallop under the two trees (which had low branches) on the left-hand side of the gallop to get us dragged off her back, just for the fun of it. It could take us up to two hours to catch her, put her back in the paddock, and tread the footings in. If Ben had seen her hoof-prints, especially on the woodside gallop, he would have gone bananas! But honestly, I do believe that the old mare enjoyed it.

In the stack-yard, we kept straw for the horses' bedding. It was all in loggings or batons, and was always nice, long, clean wheat straw. It was a pleasure to set a box fair with that kind of straw, which was nothing like the short stuff we get now after a combine-harvester has mashed it up. Some nights, after work, we would take a logging of straw right to the top of the stack, then sit astride it and ride it all the way down the stack. "Look at this – Becher's Brook!" we said, sitting back and calling cabs.

Sally Hall lived at Towton, in those days, as did her sister, Ann, who rode Stormhead out at the front of the string. I rode upsides Ann with either Ozzy or Three Two's, who were both quiet. We walked and jogged the horses right round Saxon village, past Barkston Ash, along the main road, and then cantered them. (For a change we might take the Ullerskelfe route.) Stormhead was a really strong, thick-set 'chaser – he didn't like traffic at all! He wouldn't settle if he was dropped in. In fact, he hardly ever settled up front: he would jig-jog every inch of the way. Jack Hanson (the later-to-be Wetherby trainer) had, as well as a racehorse transport business, a fleet of wagons carting coal and coke past the Saxon route every day. Stormhead used to hate these, but the drivers would be good and stop for us. They got to know Stormhead's antics.

Ann paid the wages every week on Friday tea-times when we had finished evening stables. We had to get up from the great, big table (which we all used to eat off in the kitchen), then, one at a time, walk to the office and receive our wages from her. Now that I was living-in and a signed-up apprentice learning my trade, I got 5s a week and had my board and clothes paid for. The other paid lads got £3 10s. They were fed, but had to buy their own clothes. It's no wonder Tommy borrowed The Guv'nor's collars and ties! If I wanted any clothes, I had to ask Ann for them. She would always put up such a defence as to why I didn't need any new ones, saying, "It wasn't so long ago you had such-and-such."

The classic thing she always bought were grey trousers from the Co-op in Tadcaster. They were something else! Drainpipes with white lines down them, and made us look as though we came from a naughty-boys' home!

Ann once told all of us to get changed and cleaned up from the waist upwards, as we were going to Wetherby to have our photographs taken. We were told that we would need them for some passports, as the racing authorities were starting a new security system which meant that stable employees would now need a passport to get into any racetrack's stabling-area. Jim Aldridge took us all on the farm's flat wagon. Ben and old Bill Hodgson (the odd-job man at the yard) were in the cab with Jim.

Except for the old mare, I don't think Jim liked horses. I do know he didn't like stable-lads – he gave us some ride on that wagon! Although the machine was several years old, this was the day that Jim thought he would try it out – flying round the bends, never missing a bump! It wasn't possible to stand up, as the sides were low and there was nothing to grip onto. He must have had evil thoughts on his mind, driving like that; probably thinking "I'll pay those so-and-so's back for riding the cattle and giving me a hard time in the fold-yard". We bounced up and down like balls. When we arrived at Wetherby, bruised, battered, and bedraggled every one of us could have qualified for the role of Compo in the Last Of The Summer Wine series!

In June 1954, Ann married a farmer called Teddy Charlton who had been courting her for quite some time. She left Towton amd moved into their

39

newly bought farm in Tockwith, not far from Wetherby. One afternoon, Ann asked me if I would help Teddy on their farm. He was spreading some fertiliser on a field, and he wanted me to drive the tractor for him while he tilled the land, by way of shovelling it out of the attached trailer. I have never been very mechanically minded, so my lines were not very straight as I was driving. At times, I drove over places that Teddy had already tilled (or got very close to them!). Teddy was a little annoyed, but he could hardly give me a proper bollocking because I was only doing it for him as a favour. Having only just bought the farm, Ann and Teddy hadn't got any workers or up-to-date machinery yet. They would have been struggling, no doubt, for cash too!

The lads who lived outside the yard, like Tad Joe (Michael Hanegan was his real name), got a bus and food allowance in their wages. Mind you, he and everyone else cadged lifts from the yard. Our yard was on a main road, and most people knew that we were from the stables and gave us lifts to and from Tadcaster. Once, as I was hitch-hiking, my long-time friend, Gerry Blum (the Newmarket trainer), gave me a lift in his car. That was the day he left Harry Wraggs' Newmarket yard to take up his post as travelling head-man for Captain Charles Elsey.

Every day, we used to see Joe Sime (one of the best Flat jockeys around, at that time) as he drove through our village on his way to ride out for Rufus Beasley, the Malton trainer. Joe was a super chap and an absolute gentleman – he always found time to have a word with everyone.

Bill Hodgson lived in the house with us. He looked after the only brood-mare we had, until she was sold at Newmarket Sales. He saw to the chickens, cleaned The Guv'nor's boots (and a good job he made, too!), got the coal and wood in for the house, peeled the potatoes, and did a few other jobs besides. Anyone who came to the yard knew old Bill, and they used to drop him a few bob. With all the tips he got, he must have been the best paid worker on the place!

Whenever The Rockingham Arms opened for lunch, Bill was always the first customer and he never came out until it closed. It was the same at nights, too. He got drunk every single night, but always managed to find his way back home. At night he rambled on before he went to sleep, and sometimes used to curse and swear. "Those f*****g lads must be pinching the bloody eggs! . . . Last week I was getting eight-a-day!" he would say. "I wouldn't let George Slack ride *my* bloody bike!" (which was strange of him to say because George was our stable-jockey, and on the rare occasions when he turned up at the yard, Bill was always hovering around him. He must have been on Bill's bung-list, too). ". . . That Mary! I wouldn't piss on her if she was on fire! . . ." (she was later to become The Guv'nor's wife!). ". . . What a useless bitch that Jenny is!.." (she was our housekeeper). ". . . That son of hers is a bloody mongrel, I tell you! No good will come of that lad!" he would say. ". . . That Lynchy's a lying sod! I wouldn't trust the bugger. Take the head-collar off a nightmare, he would.." and on and on he went.

If ever we shouted at him to try and shut him up, he would turn on us and tell us what useless f****rs we were. It was best just to let him ramble on (sometimes we would talk to him and egg him on). In all fairness, though, he never once slagged off The Guv'nor or Ann. He would say Sally ought to have been a lad, and that she was wasted being a lass. "Should have had a spout on!" he would say. "She smokes and drinks like a bloody man: she should definitely have been one!"

Mrs. Wariner was the village nosey parker, and made a point of knowing everything. When we rode past her house, we often saw her staring at us through the curtains. "Do you fancy that Mrs. Wariner, Bill?" we would say. "Do you call in to see her on the way to the pub? Would you give her one?" (It was common knowledge that she didn't approve of William Hodgson spending so much time in The Rockingham Arms – you can imagine the things he said about her!). He would go on non-stop until he finally went to sleep, which could have been one or two o'clock in the morning.

Old Bill's bedroom was one floor below the attic. It was a very big room and in there were five or six single beds. At some stage through the night, still chuntering Bill always got out of bed and used the potty which he kept underneath. He must have waited until he was almost bursting as no sooner had he picked the potty up than we could hear his liquid bouncing off the bottom.

On top of his wardrobe Bill kept a black bowler. He said it was for wearing when he went to funerals. The last time he wore it was when he buried his dad. One night we swopped it for his potty. He must have staled for a full minute before he realised that he was pissing into his bowler. He went berserk and chased us all out of the house. We spent the rest of the night playing cards around the AGA in the kitchen.

The attic (or 'Arctic' as we called it, because it was freezing in winter) stooped to its lowest level around the right-hand side. The whole length of it was boarded-off, about three feet or so from the existing wall. There was a little door in the middle of the boards to allow access to the electric cables behind them. The area was riddled with mice. We held competitions from 7.00p.m. to 9.00p.m. to see who could catch the most mice (during these 'mousing sessions', we would also be playing cards). We each had our own individually marked mousetraps, and the winner would take the kitty which we had each put 2s into. The rules were as follows:

1) Once the traps had been put behind the door, no-one could look at them until one went off. When one did, we all had to put our cards on the table, face down, to avoid cheating.

2) The door had to be left open until the trap which had gone off had been re-set and put back in its position.

3) If it was a tie at 9.00p.m., we would continue until a result was gained.

The record catch stood at eleven. We would throw the dead mice out of the attic window for the cats. If ever we caught a big one that looked as though it was carrying young ones, one of the lads, Robin Rhodes (who came from Church Fenton, near where the aerodrome is), would fumble for his pen-knife and say, "Let's open it up!" We would never let him. Rob was a nice enough lad, but he did have a morbid approach to things. Rob and I used to go fishing together in the evenings or on our Sunday afternoons off. We would go on our bikes to a big pond at Scarthingwell, near Barkston Ash. There were some lovely tench in there. Whenever Rob caught one, he took it off his line and killed it by crushing its head between his teeth. I would go mad at him for doing it, but he wouldn't stop. He used to hold maggots in his mouth, too – he said it was to "keep them warm"!

One afternoon, though, we were watching Major Briden, the vet at the farm, perform a Caesarean section on a sheep that couldn't lamb and, lo and behold, Rob passed out! After that, I ribbed him many times for being a "soft boy"!

5

FUN AND GAMES

Ben Robinson was one of the best head-men in the business. He was an absolutely brilliant feeder, and all credit must go to him for anything I know about feeding horses. He was also a great man with horses' leg problems. Ben's day started by knocking me, 'the apprentice', out of bed at 6.20a.m., when we used to feed the horses. The other lads started work at 7.00a.m., except for Tad Joe, whose bus didn't get in from Tadcaster until about 7.15a.m.

Wednesdays and Saturdays were 'mash' days. On the nights before, we would put the linseed in water to soak, and lay the fire for a quick start (so that all we had to do the next morning was put a match to it). We would then go to the house for a cup of tea, and Ben would have a smoke. Often, I would have liked one too, but dared not because of Ben being there. He would not have approved of me smoking at so young an age.

Ben suffered badly some days because of asthma. Sometimes he could only manage to give me a shout from the bottom of the stairs in the morning and tell me to get some of the others up to feed with me. When he did, I would always go for the youngest, as the bigger and older ones would tell me to go away (only in stronger language than that!). Ben would have recovered by 7.00a.m. when the rest of the lads started work. After he'd drunk his cup of tea, a couple of squirts with the inhaler which he kept in his pocket, then a fag, and he was away.

After mucking out the first lot and tacking up, we would go back to the house (except Tad Joe) for breakfast, cooked for us by the housekeeper. Our horses pulled out at 7.30a.m. looking really good, and I mean *good*. We always rode our own horses out. In those days we did two each, and it was very rare that we had to do a third. At 7.26a.m. Ben, with his hands behind his back, under his jacket and tucked in his belt, would shout, "C'um, me lads!" Whether we had finished breakfast, saved it for later, ate it whilst riding out, given it the dogs, or whatever, every single rider would be riding

43

around that yard for 7.30a.m. with tack on properly, their horse wiped over and the feet picked out.

One day, Ben wasn't in the position where he shouted from at 7.25a.m. So, I put my hands behind my back and shouted, "C'um, me lads," just as Ben came round the corner from the house. He kicked my backside so hard that it hurt all day!

After the roadwork we would come back to walk round a big ring at the top end of the gallops (made by constant wear from the horses walking), where any pilot changes were done. We waited there for The Guv'nor to come and work the horses, which could be ten or fifteen minutes of walking round, as our Guv'nor liked his bed! We sometimes saw him with just a night-shirt on, yawning and scratching his private parts as he looked out of his bedroom window!

When the horses carted us young lads, or went a bit free, Ben would say to us, "Ask a boy to do a man's job! Instead of asking Ann to get you some new boots on Friday, ask her to get you a pair of boxing gloves!"

One tack-cleaning day, we were going through the spare tack and tidying up, when someone came across a whacking great, big stirrup-iron. The lad was amazed at the size of it. "It looks big enough to fit that saddle that hangs outside The Chase Hotel at York!" he said. "Who the hell ever rode with this?"

"A bloody jockey rode with it years before you were born, son," said Ben from the bottom of the steps which led from the feedhouse up to the tack-room.

"He must have been a big sod. Who was it? Goliath?" asked the lad.

"It was me, you cheeky little bugger!" Ben snapped back, flying up the stairs, coughing and spluttering, to give the lad a crack.

Whenever Ben was talking about his past, he often said, with his hands behind his back and in his belt, "When I worked for Ossie Bell and Bert Cleminson . . ." Or, if we didn't come up to scratch with something we had done, he would say, "If Ossie Bell saw that he would go f*****g mad! The poor sod would turn in his grave!.." Captain Ossie Bell came over here from Australia (where he was born) and trained the 1928 Derby winner, Felstead, and also the One Thousand Guineas and Oaks winner, Rockfel. Bert Cleminson was one of the best judges of a horse who ever walked in a pair of shoes.

Afternoon stables started at 4.00p.m. We used to go to the kitchen for a cup of tea at about 3.40p.m. and we had to dig all the lads out of their pits. If they hadn't been to the bookies at Tadcaster, then that's where they'd still be. Ben walked into the kitchen and I'd pour him a cup of tea (me being the apprentice). He would light up a cigarette, go straight to the grandfather clock standing against the wall and open the door of its brass face. With one hand in his belt behind his back, fag still in mouth, he pulled out his pocket-watch, then put the clock on five minutes with the hand from behind his back. In unison, all the lads would look at their watches, but there were never any arguments – Ben's watch was right. We once put the clock on five minutes before he came in, but it made no difference, he still moved it on. Ben made mistakes, but he was never wrong! During stables, though, he must have gone back into the house and put the clock right again, because when we finished stables for the evening the clock was no longer five minutes fast.

The Guv'nor and Ben walked round to see the horses every night. You couldn't have worked for a nicer man than Mr. W.A. Hall. He was an absolute gentleman whom everyone respected. He never once swore, and very seldom shouted: he was a first-class trainer. His two brothers, Sam and Tom, also trained. They are all dead now. Tom Hall had three daughters – Jean, Ann, and Sally. Jean married trainer Ryan Jarvis (father of William Jarvis, the Newmarket trainer).

A lad started work in the yard, and he was always going on about how he wanted to be a jockey. He never let up, but he had absolutely no ability. One day we got our amateur jockey, Miles Baird-Murray, to tell him that a *Sporting Life* photographer was coming at 4.15p.m. to take his photo. He told the lad that *The Sporting Life* had heard all about him, and wanted to take a photo of him in racing colours and do an article on him for their paper. We got all his gear together: Miles' racing breeches (Miles struggled to do 11st. 7lb., and this self-opinionated up and coming Lester Piggott weighed about 8st., if that, so you can imagine how the breeches fitted!), and a pair of lady's black wellies (which we all wore in those days). We put on him a set of The Guv'nor's famous red, white and blue colours, and told him to go downstairs to sit in the kitchen and wait for *The Sporting Life* man to come. "Whatever you do," we said, "you must be down by 4.15p.m. and no later." We told him that particular time because it was when Ben came back into the house to wait for The Guv'nor to start his rounds, or maybe even to put the clock right. We knew that when Ben saw the lad dressed like that, he would go berserk.

As soon as the lad went downstairs, we heard Ben shouting and raving. "You stupid looking bugger! (upon which he rived off The Guv'nor's racing colours and kicked the kid's arse out of the house with every stride he took, never missing him once). Get your bloody horses done, you barmy b*****d! What a f*****g idiot!!"

Ben was brilliant at getting his tongue round those kind of words. I don't think he was much of a church-goer. I can't remember him ever going to church, anyway! How he would have put up with the authorities and staff of today, I shudder to think!

Sometimes we worked our horses on Uncle Walter's rotavated gallop, especially when our grass gallops got a bit firm. It was situated on the bottom side of Grimston Park, and we got to it by heading towards Ullerskelfe, then cutting over somewhere near Mr. Easterby's stud. It was a bit hairy there if ever there was anyone being carted. The gateways were quite narrow, and we also had to pull up only a short distance off the main Tadcaster to Sherburn-in-Elmet road. It was always best to let the horses do a bit early than late. It's a good job that Dr. Allen, of The Jockey Club (who found twelve stones on the all-weather course at Lingfield Park), didn't see this gallop! On some afternoons, Ben took us young lads up there with a tractor and trailer to pick stones off this almost straight, 7-furlong track. We would collect half a trailer load without breaking sweat!

In the autumn of 1953, my mother was poorly. She had an abscess on her leg which was giving her a lot of pain. Someday through the week, I would catch the bus to Leeds and go and see both her and grandad. Although my mum wasn't the type to complain and could handle most things, her leg was really getting her down. Whenever I went to see her, she would often be upstairs in bed, resting her leg. Now believe it or not, as a kid I wasn't a bad singer. After we had been talking for a while, mum would ask me to sing the Harvest Hymn I had learnt at Boston Spa School. It was called 'Fair Wave The Golden Corn'.

1) Fair wave the golden corn
   In Canaan's pleasant land,
   When full of joy,some shining morn
   Went forth, the reaper band.

2) To God so good and great
   Their cheerful thanks they pour,
   Then carry to this temple-gate
   The choicest of their store.
   . . . and so on.

It's a lovely hymn. I have asked Jo, when she plants or cremates me, whatever the season – Harvest, Christmas, or Lent – to be sure to have this beautiful hymn sung for me. She has promised me she will. If any of you reading this book have the chance to attend on the day, sing up when you hear 'Fair Wave The Golden Corn'. If it's at all possible, wherever we go when we pass on, I will be joining in with you.

6

MY FIRST PUBLIC RIDE

Paddy Farrell, a young, Irish jockey, came over to ride for our stable. He had been riding in Ireland for the well-known trainer Paddy Sleator from Grange Con, Co. Wicklow. When his taxi came, I was working in the yard. He walked in and asked where he should go. "I'll show you where to go, Mr. Farrell," I said, eagerly, "I'm Jack." We shook hands. (Paddy and I are still very close pals to this day!). I offered to carry his case inside for him, but when I tried to, I couldn't even budge it. "God," I thought, "I know the Irish are superstitious but this one's brought the bloody Blarney Stone with him!" He laughed at me struggling with his case, and swapped it for his other, lighter one. He wrestled with the big fellow and managed to get it off the ground. I took him, cases and all, into the house. Later that day, at tea-time, he sat opposite me at the table. We kept those same two places throughout the time we worked there together.

"I like this fellow," I thought. "He must be a really good jockey – he's ridden quite a few winners in Ireland, and he doesn't claim. I'll watch every move he makes." Unbeknown to him, I was hoping he would teach me a lot about riding. The first winner Paddy ever rode was called Port Lunar, and he later named his house after that horse. Also, he went on to win The Galway Plate on a horse called Amber Point. One of the first horses he rode for us was Average, owned by Mr. Clifford Nicholson.

Unfortunately, there was a brilliant novice around at the same time called Chatham, trained at Royston by my old friend, Willie Stephenson. On 13th March 1954 after the horses had been let go to canter down to the start of the Lucifer Novices Chase at Manchester, Chatham's lad, Manch, and I got talking. "Today, Average will make Chatham pull out all the stops, as he has never been better," I said. Manch agreed with me because the horse looked so well. As we were walking to the stands to watch the race, we had to pass the winner's enclosure. This saucy devil put his paddock (clothes and sweat) sheet in there, and sauntered up to the stand to watch Chatham

47

easily beat Average by 4 lengths. After the race, the cheeky beggar just gave me a wink.

Later Chatham went on the win the Victory Chase at Manchester in 1955 and 1956.

All of a sudden, Jenny, the housekeeper, left. She had seen an advert in a paper asking for a housekeeper for a farmer in Kirkby Moorside, and had decided to take that job instead. I have since passed through Kirkby Moorside and thought of Jenny. She was a nice lady, regardless of what old Bill said about her. Her son would have been aged eight or nine at the time. She probably wanted something easier and with a bit more security. She did a good job, and I think she was the longest serving housekeeper that The Guv'nor had ever had – certainly in my time.

Another housekeeper came, called Miss Haig. She was about sixty years old. It must have been the 'Miss' part that impressed Ann. It was obvious that she had been employed over the phone after answering an advert in a newspaper. Looking at her when she arrived, you could tell there was more life in a tramp's vest! For the first three days, she didn't once come out of her room. Ann ended up doing all the cooking and cleaning, with the help of Bill (when they could find him) and Evelyn, our daily. Bearing in mind that Ann was also the secretary, she had enough to do, and Sally was still at school. Mind you, I don't know what for – she had about as much interest in that as I had in becoming Prime Minister!

Sally was a fine little rider – she had good hands and was very strong. It was very seldom Sally got carted, and she had lots of bottle. Saturdays, or in the afternoons Sally and I, for a bit of fun, would jump over our schooling fences. She had a point-to-pointer called Finnlass Road and I had Gamecock there at the time. Often we would ride these two cross-country. There were a couple of big ditches down at the bottom of our land, and Sally and I used to sail over these flat out. The things we asked our horses to jump, it's a wonder we weren't killed. If girls then had had the opportunities of riding that they have now, Sally would have ridden lots of winners. She represented England, once, in a race in Italy.

Ann began to show signs of not being pleased with our new housekeeper. She elected Tommy Lynch to go and have a word with the woman. We all seconded this, because Tommy was best person around where women were concerned! If Miss Haig had been younger (or anything half-decent!) he wouldn't have needed any persuading to go up there and dig her out. If there was a human stud farm, Thomas Lynch would have been another Northern Dancer!

When Tommy knocked on her door, Miss Haig squeaked out that she hadn't been very well lately, but was feeling a bit better now and was contemplating getting up soon. She came down, but it couldn't have been at a worse time for her. It was lunch-time, and we were all sat round the table eating. Bear in mind that this was the first time most of the lads had seen her. When this frail, ashen-faced, ghost-like creature, with her hair like sore fingers and a fag lit in her mouth, entered the room, we all burst out laughing. Tears were running down all our cheeks. We couldn't have laughed more, even if we'd been listening to Bernard Manning in a night club! She went straight to the sink and started washing-up as if she'd been there all day.

The next day, Miss Haig got up early and made all our breakfasts. She stank of gin and perfume (the scent was probably intended as a camouflage for the gin!). She still had a fag wedged between her lips. The ash would get really long – I've never known anyone who could keep ash on the end of a cigarette for as long as Miss Haig could. I must look in *The Guiness Book of Records* to see if she holds the record! Her breakfasts were by far the biggest meal of our day, and were also the only meal we didn't have time to dwell on. Anyway, thankfully she left very soon afterwards. Our next housekeeper was Mary Furlong from Baltinglass, Co. Wicklow, in Ireland. This young lady was none other than Paddy Farrell's long-standing girlfriend. When she arrived, she soon put the ship back on course. She was a lovely woman, and still is, but she was no push-over. She would clean the house until you could eat off the floor, and she even hired Rentokil to get rid of our mice. We now had to take our boots off before entering the place, and there was never one bit of straw to be seen anywhere. "Go outside and shake those filthy sweaters!" she would say.

She was really bossy towards us, and was the same with Paddy. I have never known a man get as many haircuts as he did. It's a shame, really, considering people like Duncan Goodhew and Elton John can't grow any! She would always go on at me to get a haircut, and still does. Despite her faults, though (if that's what you can call them), I liked Mary.

By now, The Guv'nor must have thought I was safe enough to give a ride to, as one day Ben said, "The Guv'nor told me to tell you that you can ride Sussex Way in the apprentice race at Pontefract next Saturday."

Sussex Way was our best Flat horse. The Pontefract trip was a mile, although it was a stiff mile, it wasn't going to bother him. That night I went home to tell my mum and my grandad. Mum was still suffering with her leg at the time and said she wouldn't be able to make it, but grandad said he'd be there – even if he had to walk it. I was really excited about having a ride: I rode the race over and over in my mind many times.

The Guv'nor only had four or five Flat horses in the yard, and I knew they weren't brilliant. If they had been any good, they would have been up at his brother Sam's. By the same rule, if Sam had any good potential jumpers they would be sent down to us. Towser Gosden sent his good Flat horses for a few days to break their journey on the way to the Western Meeting at Ayr, because it was such a long haul to travel from Lewes in one go. With me being so light, I rode them out with one of Mr. Gosden's lads. They were proper Flat horses, and after riding our big, hairy jumpers, they were something else!

Mr. Gosden invariably had a horse entered in The Ayr Gold Cup, and won it with Orthopaedic in 1954, ridden by Jimmy Lindley, and Precious Heather in 1956, ridden by Edward Hide and owned by the gambler who was an artiste on time – Alec Bird.

Mr. Gosden also trained a horse called Tintinnabulum, and Norman Marshall, one of our lads, couldn't pronounce the name – he always called the horse Tintinnablumblum. Even that far back, I can remember thinking that, if ever I was lucky enough to become a racehorse trainer, I would dearly love to have my name on The Ayr Gold Cup.

On 22nd May 1954, the day of my ride on Sussex Way, I went to Ponte-fract in the horse-box. Our horses were transported by Bill Pearce from Flaxton Moor, near Malton, whose driver was called Tom. Ben got in the front with Tom (as he always did whenever we had a runner) and I got in the back with Percy Hinchcliffe, a jump-jockey who still claimed. In those days, a jump-jockey had to have ridden fourteen winners before he lost his 7lb. allowance and started to ride as a fully-fledged jockey. Percy always had one winner to go before he lost his allowance. He rode two or three more winners over the years while I was at Towton, but afterwards he was still claiming his 7lb. allowance with one to go!

Tom told us to keep our eyes open for the cops, but there wasn't much use saying it to Percy, for as soon as we got out of the yard the lazy bugger fell asleep!

In the paddock at Pontefract, it was great to be dressed in my jockey's outfit. Chris Cunningham was my valet, and he only retired at the end of the '89 season. How old he must be! He's weathered well, and you can tell he's only been getting jockeys ready for races and not riding the horses – there aren't many jockeys riding at his age. He gave me lots of good advice before the race, like "Look after my breeches and boots and don't lose any of my tack", etc, because he owned most of the gear! My biggest concern was that I didn't cock it up. Percy was always game to make a deal, especially when the balls were in his court like they were today. He knew I would be messing myself, with it being my first ride and all. At one point of the journey, not far from the course, Percy woke up and said, "Mr. Bowler (the owner) is a very generous man, you know, Jack". This I already knew because, if he hadn't been, Percy would not have been doing Sussex Way! Percy didn't always look after horses for the love of them! He looked after a horse called Starwings, a 2-mile 'chaser owned by Mr. L. Hyman. This horse had a real kink in that he wouldn't go down to the gallops. On the occasions he went, he didn't always jump off. Often he stayed down there for ages, just rearing up. Imagine the kind of owner Mr. Hyman must have been for Percy to have put up with Starwings' antics!

Normally, in those days, the jockey of a winner gave the lad who did the horse £1, and if it was a decent race, £2, but Percy reckoned that since he'd been doing Sussex Way all season, I could forget about paying him any money as a jockey. He said he would risk it if I was prepared to share with him whatever Mr. Bowler gave me as a present, if I did win. I agreed to this, because I valued riding a winner more than the money I might get afterwards.

Walking round the paddock, Sussex Way looked a bomb. He was a lovely, big chestnut, and had nice dapples on him, like one sees on a Tamworth pig. He was beautifully plaited-up. Percy had really worked hard to justify his hopeful-half of Mr. Bowler's present to me. Then it was time to mount up, and The Guv'nor gave me my instructions. He didn't spend long over it. "Be handy, and don't hit him," he said. "If it was that easy," I thought to myself, "I might as well have gone to sleep in the 'box, like Percy, and risked Tom getting caught by the police!"

As we walked across the paddock, The Guv'nor questioned Percy.

"Did you show him the course, Perce (The Guv'nor always called him Perce instead of Percy), and where to start from?" "Yes, Guv'nor, I did," Percy replied. To be fair he had done, but I think The Guv'nor had intended him to walk round with me! Percy pointed to the mile-gate from the stands. "That's where you start from," he said. "Don't forget your draw number. The starter will give you a real bollocking if you go from the wrong position, so get it right." There were no stalls in those days, just a starting gate.

I was really keen to ride a winner so I walked the course by myself, and on the walk back, I visualised myself being 6 lengths clear of the pack on Sussex Way, coming round the bend in the short straight and hearing the crowd shouting for Sussex Way.

Sussex Way normally pulled a bit, and so he usually ran in a cross-noseband. On this day, though, he didn't have it on. "Ben forgot to pack it," said Percy. "You big, soft bugger!" Ben told Percy. "You do the horse – you know f*****g well he runs in a cross-noseband!" So who do you believe? Ben's dead, Percy's alive. Make up your own mind. I'd put my money on Percy!

Cantering down to the start, I had my full-nelson on Sussex Way so he didn't cart me. Thankfully, he lobbed very sweetly down the course as when Willie Nevett had ridden him last time at Pontefract, the horse had gone down very free. Percy, in fact, said that the horse pissed off with him, but that may have been Percy's way of giving me a bit of confidence!

At the start we walked round for a few minutes. It was a lovely day. I hadn't seen my grandad in the paddock, but I told myself not to think of such things at a time like this. I tried to keep my mind on the race, but the main thought I had was; "With all these people – Mr. Bowler, The Guv'nor, Ben, Percy, Tom, and me – here for the one runner, think of the expense for the entire lot!" As Harry Crudace would have said, "Jesus to me, man!"

The starter climbed onto his rostrum. He had already called out our names to see if we were all there, and if the other budding jockeys all felt the same way as I did, then it's no wonder he wanted to check!

"Go on!" the starter shouted, and the gate went up.

It was a fairly level break for an apprentice race, and by about half-way we were fourth. Sussex Way wasn't trying to run away, though. In fact, he was off the bridle. Although it was my first race, I did have all my faculties with me throughout, and managed to stay on to finish fifth of the ten runners. The second horse got disqualified for crossing, so I was moved up to fourth. Everyone seemed pleased enough. Mind you, the phone didn't trouble me with too many calls afterwards, so I can't have made too big an impression on the other owners and trainers. It was quite some time before I got another ride, so I must not have made all that much of an impression on The Guv'nor, either!

7

A DOUBLE LOSS

By now, I was riding plenty of schooling – and I loved it! I would ride out, canter, gallop, and school horses all day if I could: a real saddle-tramp. I was still quite light, too, at around 7st. 10lb. Paddy had taught me a fair bit, as he was a good horseman as well as a good jockey. He rode with such a long rein and a good length of leg, he switched the horses off and they ran for him when he shook them up. He was also riding winners and getting plenty of outside rides, too. On the Northern Circuit, the number board with P.A. Farrell on was getting to be a familiar sight.

Sometimes Paddy and Mary, after work, would come to Leeds with me to my grandad's where we played cards. During the course of the evening I popped round to see my mother. She still managed to get up and down, although her leg hadn't healed very well and she was in a lot of pain. I very seldom saw my dad on these visits. Mind you, I had heard on the grape-vine that he was keeping another bird.

I would get back to my grandad's house in time for the three of us to catch the bus back to Tadcaster. That bus connected up with the 10.15p.m. to Sherburn-in-Elmet, which went through Towton, and we would be home for about 10.40p.m. On one of my visits, I mentioned to my grandad how I hadn't seen him at Pontefract. He told me that he was there, but he hadn't come into the paddock because he didn't want to put me off.

Mr. Hall trained for established owners like Clifford Nicholson, Mr. Cullington and the like, and this, along with the fact that the majority of our horses were big strapping 'chasers, led to the owners usually putting good jockeys on their horses. It was through Mr. Nicholson that Paddy was imported from Ireland. George Slack was our stable-jockey before Paddy came. He was a very good jockey, and a gentleman too, but once Paddy had started to ride Mr. Nicholson's horses, he was soon riding all the others as well. We didn't train enough horses to merit two retained stable-jockeys, so George had to go.

Paddy and Mary said that in the summer, when I got my week's holiday, I could go to Ireland with them. This really excited me because Ireland was where lots of good jump-jockeys and horses came from. When Paddy arrived at Towton, he had brought with him the nicest pair of jodhpurs you ever did see. There are lots like them nowadays, but they were a rare thing, then: most of the jodhpurs were like the breeches Biggles wore. Paddy's were beautiful – fawn cavalry-twill, with one long piece of buckskin going down the whole inside leg, and a two-inch band going right round the bottoms. They had a zip on the outside at the bottom of the legs, and were hand-stitched. Having asked Paddy about them, he told me a tailor, who traded by the name of 'The Heron', made them in Newbridge, Co. Kildare. "If ever I get to Ireland, and have a few quid in my pocket, I'll pay 'The Heron' a visit," I thought. From then on, I started to save so that I would have enough money to go with Paddy and Mary.

My wages had now risen to 12s 6d, which was 2s 6d more than The Guv'nor needed to pay me. I had a few pigeons, some bantams, and a ferret dragging on the rations, so I decided to get rid of them. I was finding it difficult to find the time to look after the birds properly. There's a bit more to looking after pigeons than giving them the occasional bowl of beans or peas!

I kept them in a hut which I had made, down at the bottom of the stack yard. Tending and feeding them twice a day took up a lot of time in my busy schedule. Pigeon races were started from Newark, Grantham or Peter-borough. When training them, it was important that they flew back in the same direction. When the horse-box was going south to a race meeting, as part of their training I would put a few in a basket and ask the lads to release them at a certain part of the journey where there were no telephone wires or overhead cables so they wouldn't get hurt flying into them. Needless to say, if I was travelling in the 'box I would release them myself.

I had joined 'The Pigeon Club' at Tadcaster, and attended the meetings with Bob. I used to share his clock, for which I got a time allowance. I had got one of my birds, a pied hen, as a squeaker from Mr. Cropper, a Southport potato merchant. He was a friend of The Guv'nor's, and an even bigger pal of old Bill's. I thought a lot of this bird – her mother was bred by Sir Gordon Richards, the twenty-six times champion jockey.

After lunch one day, when the 'box had taken my birds for a ride, I went to the loft and found my pied hen was in. I was so excited! She was so early I thought the little girl could win the Penzance race on this form. I immediately went up to the shop to tell Bob. I was really chuffed about her. Bob said it was impossible. After the customary interrogation of the lads when the 'box came back from the races (Did they circle? Did they fly in a straight line? . . . etc.), the lads started laughing. It turned out that one of the prats had let the hen out early to give me a thrill and get me wound-up, as the bugger knew that I thought a lot about this particular pigeon.

To enable me to swell my funds to go to Ireland, I did a few odd-jobs. In the afternoons, I would help Jim Aldridge on the farm by striking weeds from potatoes, turnips, or mangels. He paid me 2s an hour. I helped Mary as well by sweeping and mopping the kitchen floor after tea, and I would get the table ready for morning breakfast too. For this I got 10s per week. In haytime, we worked afternoons from 1.30p.m. to 3.30p.m. in the fields. By the time we all returned to the yard (as some of the other lads also did overtime) and had a cup of tea, it was 4.00p.m. and stable time. Then, after stables at night, I worked in the fields, if there was any work going. Harvest followed haytime, and that lasted for a few weeks because ours was a big farm. Whenever the farm workers did overtime, I would be there with them.

At Christmas, The Guv'nor gave either a turkey, a chicken, or a duck to owners and friends. He paid the lads and a woman to dress these birds. We received 1s 6d for dressing them, and the same for gutting, which was my job. Doing the gutting and setting them up was messy, but it was easy! I singed them and cleaned them out, then set them out nicely, ready for the oven. When they were finished, I would lay them all out on big stone slabs in the pantry. They would then be given to the relevant people.

As Arthur Daley might say, I had a few little earners going on. Kent Road, a filly I looked after, went to Stockton Sales but didn't fetch her reserve. A few days later, ridden by Paddy, she won at Doncaster, beating one of Willie Stephenson's horses called Captain Hornblower, ridden by Tim Molony. A nice white fiver appeared in my wages the following Friday, as was practice for doing a winner.

While at the races, there were always plenty of spare lead-ups going. Every lead-up I could manage, I did. The going rate those days was ten bob – nearly a week's pay! One particular day, as Tom came to take us to Manchester, the trainer, Peter Easterby, was in the 'box with his runner, but with no lad to lead up. I led and did that horse up as if it were my own. I plaited him up, washed him off after the race, the lot. At the time, Peter wasn't in anything like as big a way as he is now, and when we stopped for a cup of tea and a sandwich on the way to Manchester, Peter paid for it. "What a super chap this is," I thought, "but he can't be doing so well if he has to travel in the 'box with the horse and no lad." I couldn't see The Guv'nor doing this. I took Peter's 10s though.

One day when I went to see grandad he was ill in bed. My sister Betty, who lived directly opposite in the same street, used to look in on him every day and had been taking care of him.

The very next day after my visit, he went into a nursing home. He was in there for a week or so, then he wanted to come home (I think he knew he was going). While he was in the home, Joey, his canary, pined and died. Grandad died shortly afterwards, at home, on 17th March 1956, aged eighty. We buried him at Harehills Cemetery, Leeds. It was a very sad day – there were lots of people mourning him. Mother couldn't go as she wasn't well enough. It was a bitterly cold day, and I didn't have a coat with me. Dad told me to put on my grandad's, which I did. I have still got that coat, and it's still as good as ever. It's a standing joke at the yard in winter – me going around in my grandad's coat. On a cold day, our Alan and most of the lads say to me, "You should have your grandad's coat on, Boss!"

I started riding out on Sundays for Cliff Boothman. Every Sunday morning, I used to cook the lads' breakfast before I went to Cliff's. I would cook the bacon and sausages first, then put them in a big dish in the bottom oven of the AGA to keep warm. I cooked the beans and tomatoes, then left them in their pans on the hotplate. I also made their toast, which I left on a plate on the top of the AGA. I left out some eggs next to the frying-pan for the lads to just drop into it when they came in. Before I went, I made sure that the lads were going to wash all the pots afterwards, as I was paid to wash up as well as cook. Then, I would get on my bike and burn up the road to Cliff's. That was *every* Sunday.

In return for cooking breakfast, the lads did my horses, mucked them out, and did them at evening stables as well, because I would never manage to get back on time. On Sundays that's about all we did – muck out, hay and water, and finally sweep the yards up. We might ride out any horses which were down to run up to the following Wednesday (Ben would tell us which ones they were; if I had a runner, I would ride mine out early, before I started to cook the breakfast), but we still finished for 9.30a.m. A couple of the lads would come back and feed with Ben at lunch-time, then again at evening stables. Sunday was a nice, easy day, and we only worked every other Sunday afternoon. We didn't get whole weekends off like they do in racing, today.

Cliff trained in a fairly modest way at a village called Biggin, near South Milford. He only had a small set up – just himself and a couple of girls doing the horses. Cliff and Mrs. Boothman were a lovely homely couple. When we had finished riding the horses Cliff and I used to go in the house for a cup of tea and a chat about the horses, (we mainly covered the same ground as we had done in the previous week, but I was a good listener and I was keen). Cliff kept his wellingtons in the bottom oven of their kitchen stove. This particular day he opened the oven door to put his wellies in and a ginger moggie jumped out. I couldn't stop laughing. I got the giggles. Cliff kept saying, "What's the matter? What are you laughing at?"

He looked after his horses thoroughly and they were always well fed, well bedded down, and had plenty of rugs on to keep them warm. Cliff and I used to work the horses, and he made Sunday his workday. We had an arrangement whereby he didn't give me anything for riding work, or schooling, but he would give me a ride whenever possible. He rode the horses in races himself, so he would have had to have two horses in one race, runners at two meetings in a day, or have got broke up, before he could give me a ride. Such a situation was unlikely, however, as he only had six or seven horses! I was so keen that grabbing at such straws seemed worth it – it was very difficult to get rides from Towton. In addition to Paddy Farrell, Leo McMorrow rode Colonel and Miss Judy Thompson's horses, Derek Leslie. rode for Tom Corrie, Colin Dukes was coming back from National Service, George Slack still had the occasional ride, Rodney Mansfield from Ashby-de-la-Zouch owned and rode Magic Thread, there was our own amateur, Miles Baird-Murray, and of course there was Percy Hinchcliffe, claiming 7lb. with one to go. Plus the fact that our owners wanted good jockeys to ride their horses, not kids like me just trying to get going.

On occasions, when we could work it, Robin Rhodes cycled down to Cliff's with me. The journey was about twelve miles down country roads, so we used to put our heads down and just pedal like stink. One day Rob and I were riding our bikes upsides and our front wheels touched. The pair of us went a right purler! Rob's front wheel was buckled and, unlike Reg Harris, we didn't have a back-up team following us with spares!

This all happened about half-way to Cliff's, so we hid the bike behind a hedge (with the intention of picking it up on the way back) and I gave Rob a ride on the crossbar for the rest of the journey. When we finally got there, Cliff made a point of telling us the horses had been saddled up for an hour or more. We rode the horses as usual. Then on our way home we couldn't find the right hedge where the bike was hidden (or some thieving so-and-so had nicked it!). Rob, on the crossbar, did nothing but moan telling me that I must be stupid to cycle all that way every Sunday for nothing.

"That berk looks like he's never going to give you a ride. In fact, you haven't even got a f*****g licence yet. I've busted up my bike and some bugger's pinched it – are you going to buy me another? . . ."

By now, I had a few quid in the Post Office Savings Bank, but that had been earned to go towards my trip to Ireland and some new clothes (I didn't fancy going to Ireland in Tadcaster Co-operative Society trousers!) and I was desperate to acquire a pair of the Heron's jodhpurs. In saving every penny I could, the lads were already calling me a tight b*****d, and I had to be very careful not to say anything daft that I might later regret, such as, "I'll give you a fiver towards another bike!" or the like.

A few weeks after this, still persevering with my Sunday outings to Cliff's, something must have been pricking at his conscience as he told me he had put Dombleue in a Selling Hurdle at Hexham on Monday, 30th April 1956, and that I could ride her. This really chuffed me – I galloped my bike back to Towton to ask The Guv'nor if he would send off for my jump-licence. He gave me nearly as hard a time as Rob did when he lost his bike! At this stage it seemed such a struggle to get going that nothing seemed to be slotting into place. I wondered if I'd have been better off working for the farmer at Thorpe Arch, as Mr. W.A. Hall didn't seem to be going out of his way to make a Tim Molony or an A.P. Thompson out of me! Considering that I had disturbed The Guv'nor during his evening spare-time in order to ask the all-important question, I realised that it was not the most appropriate of times. I tackled him again, however, on Monday. All he said was, "You'll kill your damned self."

Having made arrangements to ring Cliff Boothman on Monday afternoon to let him know the score about what The Guv'nor had said, Cliff asked if he should give him a ring and ask him if he would send off for my licence. "No, no! Don't do that. I'll catch him again when he comes round to evening stables," I replied.

When he did come round (with Ben, as usual) I noticed Ben's stern face and square jaw, so I bottled out. That night, though, I plucked up enough courage to knock on The Guv'nor's living-room door, heart in my mouth. He told me that he had already sent for my licence, so I rang Cliff to tell him the news.

"Good," he said, "Can you pop round through the week and have another sit on her before she runs at Hexham? We don't want to be doing too much with her on Sunday."

"I'd love to," I told him, "but it will be impossible."

"You can ride some of the others out on Sunday, then," he replied. "Will you be coming on your own?" he asked.

"I think so," I told him.

Within the next day or so, the licence duly came. It wasn't automatic – I kept reading it to believe it. The authorities were starting to tighten-up on who they issued jockey-licences to, as in the past a 16 st. bookmaker could have applied for one!

On the day of the Hexham meet, we didn't have any runners there, and Paddy didn't have any rides, so I organised a lift with Jack Boddy, W. Easterby's jockey. Jack nearly always came to work on a motor-bike and sometimes rode it to race-meetings, but on this particular occasion we went in his car. The horse ran well and finished in the middle of the pack. Cliff was pleased, and thankfully was to give me three or four more rides in races shortly afterwards.

After the Hexham meeting, I was supposed to see Jack in the car-park. Well, I couldn't find his car amongst the others for love nor money, so I went back to the stable-yard. Luckily, I managed to get a lift back to Towton Bar, just a couple of miles from home, in Walter Easterby's 'box. The next day, Jack came down to the yard on his bike and gave me such a bollocking! He was telling me what a "dozy bugger" I was, and in front of everyone, too! "It's a wonder you managed to find your way around the 2-mile hurdle course yesterday, you thick prat!" he yelled. Jack and I later became the best of pals, and both of us served on The Jockeys' Council at the same time.

We had a lad in the yard called Mick Thornton, who had served his time with Avril Vasey at Middleham and had ridden a couple of winners on the Flat. We called him 'Mad Mick', not because he was a nutter, but because he was always playing foolish pranks on people, like the day when I had taken the droppings from my horse at evening stables and gone to get some hay. I had left my horse tied up and beautifully set fair, but when I got back the horse was stood still and between his hind legs there was a heap of droppings nearly up to his hocks. This fool, Mick, had got everyone from the bottom yard to put all their droppings in his mucksack and he had put them there while I was getting my hay!

One of my horses was in the passage-boxes in the main yard and, unfortunately, was next to one of Mad Mick's. He would ask which horse I was doing first so he could do his at the same time, just to have a bit of a crack. This lad was a bad influence on me as I wanted to set a good example and get on in life. All this dickhead seemed to do was undo it all!

Rock 'n' Roll had just started, and Elvis Presley had just brought out a song called 'You Ain't Nothin' But A Hound Dog'. At the bottom of the passage, Mad Mick used to stack up hay and straw for the stables there, and once, as we were doing evening stables, this nutter suggested that we should take turns in singing "You ain't nothin' but a rabbit . . ." whilst the other jumped out from behind the bales, arms in the air, singing "And you ain't no friend o' mine!" His timing was brilliant!

After he had sung "You ain't nothin' but a rabbit . . .", I thought he had rushed it a bit, but I still jumped out from behind the bales, arms waving in the air, singing "And you ain't no friend o' mine!" as loudly as I could, just as the old man and Ben were coming through the passage entrance to see the horses. Mick was in his 'box, grooming away as if he knew nothing about it! "Good evening, Guv'nor," he said. Ben was behind The Guv'nor, staring at me with eyes like knives. There was I with a face as red as a beetroot, feeling a right twit! I could have crawled down a mouse-hole!

Mr. Clifford Nicholson was a very smart and well-to-do man who farmed land by the mile in Lincolnshire. All the gates on his land were painted scarlet and grey, as was the woodwork of his cottages and farm buildings. He always wore a fresh, red carnation in his coat, and a bowler hat. All his horses ran in a white breastgirth. Just after the War, he had a second favourite running in The Grand National, a horse called Limestone Edward. The horse was up with the leaders with an excellent chance, but a slipping saddle in the last mile meant he finished 6th so all future horses ran with a breastgirth. Mr. Nicholson's two main ambitions were to farm 10,000 acres of land and to own a Grand National winner. He farmed 10,000 acres of land. The best chance he had of winning The Grand National from our yard was with Witty in 1956, but he fell when going well. Although Witty had won races, he never got his act together on the big occasion. Mr. Nicholson had some of the best 'chasers around, but he couldn't win The National despite all his money. Stormhead was a really good horse of his who loved Aintree, and he won a few times around there over shorter distances than The National: The Molyneaux in 1956 and '57, and The Topham Trophy in 1955. He also won The Emblem 'Chase at Manchester twice, on one occasion beating Halloween, but he couldn't stay the National trip.

Mr. Nicholson won lots of big races with the likes of Ace Of Trumps, Average, and Doorknocker. One year I remember well; it was a severe winter, and we took all our best Cheltenham horses to Filey so they could work on the beach, as all the gallops and fields were frozen up. Ingoe was one of the favourites for The Champion Hurdle. We had Doorknocker in for the race as well, although not at as short a price as Ingoe in the ante-post market. Doorknocker didn't stay over to work at Filey as he was a poor doer, and worried a lot.

Paddy wanted to ride Ingoe at Cheltenham in The Champion instead of Doorknocker. I argued with Paddy that Doorknocker was the horse he should stick with, even though he was only a novice. Doorknocker never did anything quickly, and used to get behind in races. He had already won three Novice Hurdles on the trot, the last being at Wetherby carrying 12st. 10lb., where he was nearly last turning into the straight. Previously he had been trained in Ireland by Paddy Sleator. He had awful, bad legs. He must have broken down in Ireland before he came to Towton as he had been fired.

Harry Sprague, one of the best hurdle-jockeys around then, stepped in for the ride on Doorknocker in the 1956 Champion Hurdle at Cheltenham. While I was leading Harry out, I told him all about Doorknocker.

"Paddy and company fancy Ingoe, but don't think that this fellow is out of it," I told him. "Don't be too worried if he gets left out at the back early on – when he gets himself organised, he can really turn the tap on. Just sit still on him and he'll get going after half-way. The fast pace of The Champion will suit him."

From two out, the writing was on the wall. There was only going to be one winner – Doorknocker. Ingoe finished 7th. You wouldn't believe that in Doorknocker's next race, The Coronation, a Novice Hurdle at Liverpool, he was beaten at big odds-on. Luckily for Paddy, Harry Sprague had come in for the ride, again. Otherwise, we might have been getting George Slack back at Towton!

A phone message came to the yard that my mother was very ill. She was taken to St. James's Hospital, Leeds. Having arranged to meet my dad in Leeds, we went to see her but she was so ill she couldn't recognise us. It was to be her birthday the following day and all her birthday cards were already on display on her bedside table. The next day, her birthday, she died – it was 25th September 1956, just six months after grandad had died. Mum was only forty-nine. What a shame, and how she suffered. Life is cruel to some at times.

There wasn't much point in me going to Leeds any more, now that grandad and mum weren't there. However, my father got in touch with me, asking if I'd meet him in Leeds. So, I did. He brought the bird I had heard about with him! We went to a pub and had a couple of lagers. She wasn't a bad woman, but he needn't have involved me in his love affair. Shortly after, the pair of them fell out. At least I didn't have to attend a wedding! Dad had done a bit of spending, living it up since grandad's death and I felt his job wasn't exactly booming because I rang up, one day, and the number was unobtainable.

After a while, dad got a new job working for Mr. Wildblood of Barwick-in-Elmet. Previously, my brother, Harry, had worked for him. My sister Joan trained with Mr. Wildblood's daughter, Susan, at York Road swimming baths. Susan was a very good swimmer and was a member of the schools' Olympic Squad. She later married Maurice Camacho, the Malton trainer and step-son of Charlie Hall.

Dad was teaching Mr. Wildblood to drive a four-in-hand: he was very keen to learn. The horses they put together were greys. Dad later teamed up four Dutch horses which got spooked while Mr. Wildblood was driving them in London and they bolted. Mr. Wildblood ended up in East Essex Hospital with a broken hip!

There was a pub near Aberford which used to be a coaching-house, and someone once said to dad that there wouldn't be room to drive a four-in-hand through the entrance. "If it used to be a coaching-house, there'll be plenty of room," my dad said. Not satisfied, the man got out his money. Father, never known to run away from a challenge, asked the man which pub it was, then told him to make sure the entrance was clear and that there were no cars in the yard at a given time the next day.

At the time stated the old man trotted straight through the entrance, with just inches to spare at either side. He turned round in the yard, still trotting, then on the way out took his bowler off to the people who were there to witness the event.

Later father found work in Mr. Horner's piggery at Potterton, a village near Barwick-in-Elmet. I suppose it gave him time to take stock. Anyway, he was showing definite signs of mellowing. I would visit him occasionally, and we would go to his local pub, called The Fox And Grapes, which was just up the road from the village. The landlord there, Gerry Oddy, was a very good friend of Tony Doyle, the Wetherby trainer. He had a lovely photo on the pub wall of Tony Doyle coming over a fence at Aintree when he was a jockey. My dad would introduce me to everyone there. "Hey, so-and-so! Meet my son, Jack, the jockey," he would say. That really annoyed and embarrassed me, and I told him so. Blood being thicker than water, though, I suppose it was just his way of showing people he was proud of me. I don't know what of, though – I hadn't exactly pulled any trees up!

During this period, I was doing a little, grey horse named Sarsta Gri. Paddy had schooled him over hurdles, and the horse had a lot of ability, but, given the chance, he was prone to run out. One schooling day when I was on Sarsta Gri, Mad Mick was riding Repeat Performance, a seasoned 'chaser who jumped for fun and was as safe as houses, and Pat Gulwell was riding another horse. The Guv'nor's instructions to us were, "Jump off together, keep Jack in the middle so his horse can't run out. Jump the three flights of hurdles at a nice even pace."

I thought, hacking down to the start, that had it been a dance I would have chosen a better partner than this wally Mick! He never gave any indication of what he was going to do next. Jumping off, we ran to the first flight of hurdles and this pillock took a pull on Repeat Performance. Sarsta Gri ran straight through the wing and I took an awful fall, bruising my kidneys, which put me in bed for a few days. Also a nail from the wing of the hurdle went through my right ear-lobe. Mad Mick thought it was a huge joke, and came to take the mickey out of me while I was in bed, bringing with him a bunch of buttercups and daisies that he had picked out of a field. "How's yer ear?" he asked. "Can you piss all right?"

A few weeks later, Sarsta Gri more then compensated for burying me. On Easter Monday, 22nd April 1957, I rode him in the Bilton Hurdle at Wetherby. We won the race at 10/1 beating Larry Wigham on King James by a neck and Barney Cross was third on Blue Hussar a length further back. It was my first winner. Paddy finished 4th on the 5/2 second favourite, Depreciation, also trained by The Guv'nor.

What a brilliant feeling that was. To ride my first winner at Wetherby, our local course, on a Bank Holiday. Sarsta Gri's owner, Mr. Kingston, gave me £20: four white fivers! With me also looking after the horse at home I didn't have to do any deals with Percy either. It was all mine!

In the first race that same day, I rode a mare of Mr. Clifford Nicholson's. Getting changed for the race, I felt so honoured to be wearing those famous scarlet and grey colours that I had led up such good jockeys in on countless occasions. Later Paddy got hurt and I stepped in for some good rides of his the following day. In the first I rode Turbid trained by Mr. Nicholson and in the next race, The Montagu Hurdle, I rode the Irish import, Casamba, which was also owned by Mr. Nicholson and was now trained by The Guv'nor. Casamba was absolutely hacking. He stood way off at one hurdle, caught the top, and turned over. I broke a collar-bone. Mr. Nicholson came to the ambulance room to see me. He was very good about it, and didn't blame me, or anything. In fact, he told me I had a bright future, and that if a broken collar-bone was the worst injury I would ever get, then I wouldn't be doing too badly.

8

IT WAS ALL HAPPENING

When we went to the pictures, it was mainly The Regal at Tadcaster. For a change, we would go to The Rodney at Wetherby. It was a small, cosy picture-house, nearly always showing a good cowboy film, the type where the cowboys had abandoned their horses and had to cross miles of desert with very little water. As they staggered about in the blazing heat with burnt faces, vultures hovered overhead.

While the picture was in progress the heating would be turned up so much that the punters peeled off their coats and sweaters and undid their shirt collars. Standing in the aisle at the interval would be the usherette selling ice creams and cartons of pop. The queues would be miles long and the manager dashed about bringing in reinforcements. We would completely forget about the weather outside being freezing cold.

At a race-meeting, I had met one of Walter Wharton's girls and arranged to take her to The Rodney pictures. Sitting on the front seat on the top deck of the bus, I spotted this girl standing at the bus stop where I was to meet her. She was wearing a skirt and a pair of jodhpur-boots which didn't even have elasticated sides – just straps. Seeing her dressed like that, I stayed on the bus and went to Harrogate pictures on my own! I could imagine the lads at Wetherby taking the juice out of me for going out with a girl dressed like she was.

There would be lots of stable staff around at that time as Wetherby was quite a large training area – with Donald Oates, Billy Newton, Percy Vasey, Walter Wharton, Tony Doyle and just a few miles away Tommy Sheddon. Someone I knew was bound to have seen me. When I mentioned this girl's dress sense to Johnny East, who was Walter Wharton's stable-jockey, he said that I was lucky because none of them had even seen her legs – they were always in slacks! Today, one can get away with things like that, but not then.

The Guv'nor announced that he had got married. We hadn't been invited to the wedding. Instead, he had left some money for us with Ben so we could all have a drink at The Rockingham Arms. Big changes were taking place at Towton. The biggest of all was that Mrs. Hall moved in. The first thing she did was to turf us all out of the house with a style that Margaret Thatcher would have been proud of.

"Lads," she said, "I want you to take all your things out of the house today, and move into the cottage that's empty in the village next to Jim Aldridge's. What you don't take, just leave and I'll get rid of it."

When we went in for lunch, she started up again.

"Don't forget, lads, you're moving out today, with all your belongings, into the cottage. Take it all up there when you've finished eating."

"How are we going to move all our stuff?" Paddy asked.

"That's your concern!" she replied.

Paddy must have thought that she was going to hire Pickfords or some other removal firm, because he got a bit upset at this. He invited me to go with him to The Lonsborough Hotel in Tadcaster for lunch, which I did. After lunch, mind, things were no different than before. So, we were moving beds, wardrobes, etc., full of our gear, all afternoon with a lad at either end, up and down the village. We must have looked like Steptoe and Sons!

The attic, where we had been, was divided in two. In the half we didn't live in, hams were hung. They were awful – nearly all fat! Only old Bill and The Guv'nor seemed to like the stuff. Hung on a beam was the skin of Carton Duke Of Connaught, a hackney of The Guv'nor's (or his parents'). There were sacks of harness and all sorts of things which held happy memories for The Guv'nor. Mrs. Hall called it rubbish. She opened the sash window which looked onto the yard below, and threw the whole lot out.

"You can't throw that away! . . . or that!" the ex-boss of his home shouted. "Mary! . . . Not that! . . . Stop it, woman!" Anyway, it all arrived down in the yard at great speed. "You should have wives on a trial basis before you go wading in and marrying them!" The Guv'nor was muttering. From that day on, we only went into the house for meals.

Culworth, one of our best horses, a great old campaigner who had won lots of races (including The Becher's 'Chase around Aintree), had a heart attack and died in a race at Wetherby. It came as a shock to everyone, especially The Guv'nor. He loved him. The old horse had been a marvellous servant to Towton. He was owned by Mr. G. Cullington, who named all his horses Cul-something. Culworth was the only horse I ever saw The Guv'nor ride. He was a very superstitious man. He would never get his hair cut on a Friday or even allow us to clip the horses on that day. It was bad luck if he saw a single magpie, and if the level-crossing gates at Newton Kyme were closed on the way to Wetherby Races, we would be hard-pressed to have a winner. The day old Cully died, the gates had been closed.

Once every year the Bramham Moor Foxhounds met on our gallops. One year in particular the ground was quite soft. Near the wood we kept a strip of land which we only galloped on occasionally as it was our best gallop. Ben was on tenterhooks in case the hunt-riders strayed over there and cut it up. The Guv'nor, who was a member of the hunt-committee, was chatting away to the followers as they drank his sherry. Ben was anxiously strutting up and down. One of the whips and some of the followers edged towards our best gallop. Ben couldn't bear it any longer, and said, "Hey lads, don't take those dogs over there on that best going!"

Once, at a Wetherby meeting, we won the Selling Hurdle and a man bid for and bought our winner. He asked Ben if we could take the horse back to our yard until he had sorted transport out to take the horse to his new home. A couple of days later, this chap came with a car and trailer to pick up the horse. No apologies for being two days late, however.

"Have you got some straw for the trailer-floor?" he asked. We gave him some straw.

"Are you going to leave that rug on him?" he then asked.

"No," said Ben. "You'll have to buy your own."

"Oh," said the man. "Well, can I have a bit of hay to see him on his travels?" So, we filled up a net and gave him that. He never gave anyone a drink, or anything. As he was pulling out of the yard, Ben walked over to the man's car. The man rolled down the car-window, then Ben said to him (as Ben could often be a dry wit), "Would you like a bag of f*****g oats for him as well?!"

Whenever we had a runner, before we set off for the races, we would muck out, ride and canter the horses that we looked after which weren't running. Sometimes we would see foxes at the bottom loop of our figure-eight gallop, and it was such a smashing sight. Some days, it was dark when we rode the horses. On one occasion, when we had three or four horses out early, whoever was leading misjudged the gallops and we had a pile-up in the wood. Fortunately, no-one got hurt, but it wasn't easy catching loose horses in the dark!

The Guv'nor bought a new car, a Rover 105. For the first few months of its life, he had us lads washing and polishing it at least once a week. Not to be outdone, Paddy followed suit. By now, P.A. Farrell was the North's leading jockey, and he announced that he was getting married. Mary handed in her notice, then she and Paddy left on a trip to Ireland to return as man and wife. They rented a house in Scarthingwell Estate which had a very large pond where Rob Rhodes and I fished. The Estate was owned by the Catholic Church, and their church was on the grounds. They had a boat tethered on the side of the pond, and on one of our fishing trips Rob and I decided to borrow the boat and fish in the middle of the pond for a change. Rob and I were having a really good run – the tench were biting like mad, and we had caught three or four beauties – when the priest came to the pond-edge and started shouting to us. Not only were we in the wrong for using the boat, but we were also trespassing.

"You boys! Come here with that boat!" he was saying.

"Rob, whatever you do, don't look up," I said.

"Hey! You boys!" continued the priest, in a fairly polite manner. His voice gradually got louder and louder. He even began to shout threats about calling the police. Quietly I said to Rob, "We'll make for the path that leads to Paddy's house as soon as he's gone!" The priest wasn't in a hurry for going – but we didn't care as the fish were biting and we were having a ball. "Don't you dare bite their heads off while he's here," I whispered to Rob.

Thankfully, he didn't: any we caught while the priest was there, we put straight back into the water. Eventually the priest went away (no doubt to call the police), so we paddled his boat to Paddy's path on the opposite side of the pond to where the good father had stood. We hurriedly packed up our gear, tied a piece of string around the 2 to 3lb. tench that we had already caught, then made a quick retreat. We hung the fish on the doorknob of Paddy and Mary's house to prove a point, as Paddy would never believe us when we said we had caught big fish in the pond. We decided to let the dust settle for a few days before we went back to fish there again!

On one of the many occasions Paddy and Mary invited me round for Sunday lunch, I noticed that there were baby clothes hanging on the washing line. My immediate reaction was that someone with a baby must be staying with them. I went bouncing in, "Well, Mary, where's the baby, then?" "I haven't had it yet," she said. "I'm just getting ready." It shows how naive I was. I didn't even notice that she was in foal! They stayed on there for quite a while, then they bought a lovely house near the 9-furlong pole of York Racecourse.

One Manchester race meeting, I travelled there with Paddy in his car. The yard didn't have any runners, we were just going because we had some spare rides. Percy came with us; he had now left Towton and was working at John Smith's Brewery. He came for the beer, so to speak. It was foggy on that Barnsley/Manchester road. Suddenly, a car passing us ran straight into an oncoming car. The overtaking vehicle was pushed into our path, we couldn't avoid hitting it. The impact caused Paddy to hit the steering wheel and break his nose. Percy hurt his knees and the woman passenger in the oncoming car, who had a baby with her, was carted off to hospital with a broken ankle. Neither of us rode at the races that day, as it took time to clear all this up. Paddy's car wasn't injured too badly, it had just hurt a wing. He still drove it, and on the way home he got his nose fixed at Barnsley Hospital.

One day, I was riding at Wetherby and took a spare ride in the Novice 'Chase on a horse trained by J. Wetherall. The ride had been going round the weighing room and no-one was falling over themselves for it because it's form wasn't brilliant – O F U (The 'O' had been in a hurdle race when the horse was tailed off). The horse jumped all right, but he was very slow. I pulled him up after the second last as he had got out of touch with the rest of the field. The thing I remember most about that horse was his width. He was so wide that it was like sitting astride a small table! I enjoyed it though, and he gave me a taste for fences, as this had been my first ride in a 'Chase. Mr. Wetherall came to meet us as we came off the racecourse into the paddock. "Look at him," he said. "He's hardly even sweating. He's not blowing much, either." "No, he's not," I replied. "The horse is fit, he just isn't fast enough. He would make a good hunter, though."

Because the horse was slow and had very little ability, Mr. Wetherall was trying to pass the buck to me by making out that I hadn't given the horse much of a ride. He couldn't doubt me on that score, though, as I had pushed and kicked the poor thing from start to pulling him up. Besides, at that stage of my career I would have ridden the horse's grandmother round, I was that keen! The horse had never jumped so many fences in a day at the races, before. Mr. Wetherall was out of order. In the next schooling session we had at Towton, a couple of days after Wetherby we gave a novice his first pop over fences. "You ride that one, Jack," The Guv'nor said. "You seem to be going out of your way to get yourself killed!"

Anyway, back to the racecourse at Wetherby. After riding the Wetherall slow-coach, I was called to the weighing-room door and hoped it was a trainer to offer me another spare but it was Mr. Chapman, father of David, the trainer. "That pony you've got turned out – he keeps getting loose." he said. "He's been in my field for the past two weeks."

Gamecock went back to Leeds because my dad said he knew someone with a field who had some youngsters that would look after the pony. Mr. Chapman asked me how much I would take for him, saying he would buy Gamecock for his grandchildren. I didn't want to sell him; we'd had lots of fun and ridden miles and miles together – we were such pals. I said, "Keep him where he is. Provided you don't sell him, you can have him for as long as the kids want him."

That was the end of my association with Gamecock. I was sent £20 through the post which I gave to my younger brother, Goff, as I hated the thought that I had sold a pony of Gamecock's calibre for that kind of money. I saw Mr. Chapman many times afterwards (I even rode for him), and always wished I knew of my pony's whereabouts. I never asked, though – I was afraid he might have sold him.

9

A HOLIDAY OF A LIFETIME

Paddy was recovering from a broken collar-bone at the time of my trip to Ireland with him and Mary. Ann said I could have two weeks holiday instead of one, seeing as I was going so far away. For this kind gesture, I was grateful.

The Irish boat sailed from Holyhead to Dun Laoghaire. To get there we had to catch a bus to Leeds, a train to Manchester and a further train to Holyhead. That was the first time I had ever been on a proper boat. It was certainly bigger than the one Rob and I fished from at Scarthingwell! Mind you, I hadn't actually seen the sea until I went to Bob Tate's. Tommy Tutty, Paddy's brother-in-law, met us as we got off the boat. He drove us to Paddy's home in Grange Con, Co. Wicklow. Paddy's mum was a lovely, homely woman, and I also met Kitty, Paddy's sister. What a really nice family they were, they made me feel very welcome.

Later we moved on to Mary's parents' home on the outskirts of Balting-lass. Her mum and dad were just the same as Paddy's – lovely, warm, friendly people. Mary had some brothers and sisters, one of whom was an absolutely brilliant singer, called Anne. She could have earned a living from singing if she had wanted to. She had a beautiful voice. We would all get together round their peat fire and talk and sing away. We had a great night.

Next day, Paddy took me down to the yard of Paddy Sleator (the ex-home of lots of our best horses). Paddy introduced me to Mr. Sleator – who all the lads affectionately called "Bossman". He was wearing a beautifully-cut, cream pair of cavalry-twill slacks, and in his mouth was a cigarette in a cigarette holder – in his yard!! My mind drifted to over the water. What would Ben have said if he saw someone was smoking, like this chap, going in and out of the stables? He would have blown a fuse! As Paddy and I were talking with The Bossman, he said if I wanted to ride out the next day, I would be welcome. Also, he added, if he had known I was coming I could have ridden out that day.

"We're pulling out in ten minutes, though," he said.

"If you've a horse for me to ride, I'll be back before then!" I replied.

"Yes, we've got a horse." He shouted to one of the lads, "Paddy, put some tack on that hoss for this young fellow."

I went off like a shot to change into my jodhpurs, and got back before any of the lads had pulled out. There are sixty seconds in an English minute; this isn't always the way in Ireland. When eventually we did pull out, only two or three of the lads were wearing jodhpurs. They mainly had slacks and wellies on. Ben should have gone there for his holidays – it would have done him good. Nobody was rushing around, and the horses looked super. No two were tacked-up alike, but they looked really good. Even though I had just arrived at the yard, the staff made me feel very welcome. Everyone was saying "Hi, Jack!" as though they had known me for years. By, I liked this place!

The Bossman led the horses out (one couldn't call it a string, as the horses were all over the road!), still with his cigarette and holder in his mouth. I remember thinking at the time, "Is this man really Paddy Sleator, or Fred O'Carno?" Whoever it was of the two, I liked his style. It was such a different sight to 7.30a.m at Towton!

After we had been on the road for ten minutes, the stragglers on their horses trotted to catch us up. No-one seemed to give a monkey's, and the crack from the lads was great. "How yer today, Jack?" they'd say, riding two or three abreast. "You'll be going to Naas, today, will yer now? . . . seeing as yer on yer holiday? . . . will yer?" and all that. (At home, it was an effort for anyone to ask how you were the day after taking a bad fall!)

When we got to the gallops, The Bossman told some of us to canter quietly around this big field for what seemed like ten minutes. The rest milled around. Then we walked around while the others cantered in the field. The Bossman then spoke again, "Paddy, Joe, Paddy, Francis, Paddy, Paddy, you Jack, Tony, etc., take them to so-and-so (this was a particular name for one of the gallops). And Tony, don't be letting that f****rr idle with yer, now!" The thing that amazed me most was that a good half of the lads in the yard were called Paddy, and they didn't even have nick-names either! Whenever The Bossman gave "Paddy" an order, or whatever, the right Paddy always seemed to respond.

We went about 1½ miles on the gallops at a cracking pace all the way. "God," I thought, "how did Doorknocker stand up to all this?" Funnily enough, the horses weren't unduly sweating or a bit distressed. We rode them back to the yard. After work at Towton, we would have got straight off their backs, led them about for a while, and then given them a pick of grass. Here, within two minutes of everyone returning, the yard was deserted. Johnny Markham, who lodged with Paddy's mum, shouted, "Come on, Jack! It's breakfast!"

"I haven't done him up, yet," I replied.

"Oh, don't bother!" he said. "Just give him some hay from over there and a bucket of water – he'll be right."

I went back with Johnny to Mrs. Farrell's for one of the biggest breakfasts I have ever seen, apart from the ones made at Towton by Miss Haig. This was different, though – we had ridden out and were ready for it. Except for Tommy, who had gone off to his work as he wasn't employed by Mr. Sleator, we all sat round a beautifully-laid table which had been set by Paddy's mum. We were each served an egg, two or three rashers of bacon, a couple of slices of black pudding, grilled tomatoes, and two or three pieces of fried home-made bread. Piping hot tea was served in big china cups. "There's no way I can eat all that!" I thought, but I did, and what's more, I did it for another two weeks. After breakfast, we went back to the yard and went through the same procedure all over again with the next lot of horses.

Paddy and I didn't go to Naas. Instead he said, "We'll have a nice easy day at home today and we'll go to Thurles tomorrow." I wasn't bothered. I couldn't have been more suited with what I was doing. Paddy also promised to take me to Co. Kildare as soon as he got the chance to visit The Heron for the purchase of my eagerly awaited jodhpurs.

As we didn't go to Naas races we returned to the house around noon. The horses had all been ridden out and put away. About half-an-hour or so later, we had lunch, which was a properly cooked meal (I ate all that, too!). At about 2.00p.m., Johnny asked if I was going back down to the yard. "Love to," I replied. The lads got a head-collar, dandy-brush and a rubber from the tack room. They each led a horse which they had previously ridden, up the road into a field where they had a pick of grass. The majority of the lads had a fag in their mouth while they knocked them over with the dandy and rubber. They chatted away all the time and the horses hardly moved!

About half-an-hour later, they took those horses back and did the same thing all over again with the others. They had been chatting away all this time, and the horses never bothered. The Irish certainly have a way with horses – they are so natural.

Tony Prendergast and Johnny Markham were jockeys at Grange Con; Francis Flood (now a successful Irish trainer) was riding as an amateur. You might say he was doing so under false pretences, though, because he was as good as most professionals!

At about 5.10p.m., everyone said their goodbyes to each other. Then push-bikes (some with two people on!) set off in all directions. That evening, Johnny and I went to the local store. In the back was a room with a bar and stools in. Most of the other stable lads were there, and we had a really good sing-song. We had far too much to drink, but it was great. No sooner was the glass nearly empty than you'd have had another drink poured into it. These were great lads. What a difference working here was to back home, and yet the results were much the same. Both yards had plenty of winners.

The next day, I rode out the first lot then went with Paddy in his car to the races. Paddy took his sling off before we got there because he didn't want any owners and trainers to see that he had been broken up. The collar-bone was a lot better, and Paddy wanted to get a ride or two in Ireland, if possible, before going back to England. The sight of his sling wouldn't have been a good advert!

It was a brilliant and lovely day. Paddy knew most of the people there and they were all chuffed to see him back. In the weighing room it was electric: the crack was good. Mind you, that seems to be the case in weighing rooms everywhere. "Hi, Paddy! You're looking well!" the other jockeys were saying.

We had a most super time. We went to a dance, afterwards, at a place called 'Moon'. My Ullerskelfe apprenticeship put me in good stead, here. We danced to an accordion-band, every bit as good as Jimmy Shand, and it was absolutely brilliant. I had never seen most of the dances before, let alone done them, but the lads dragged me up for them. On reflection, I didn't need too much persuading, as I love dancing and music, especially Scottish, Irish, and Country music. It really was great. In the past, before going to Ireland, I'd only had a few drinks here and there, but at 'Moon' I got well and truly plastered! The next day, the boys told me I had even asked a priest for a dance, but I think they were kidding me on. I hope so!

Paddy's collar-bone got well enough for him to have two rides. One was at Limerick, the other was at Wexford. He didn't ride a winner, but that didn't bother him – he just wanted to be seen riding again, and to get back among his Irish pals for a change.

On another trip to the races, we went to a meeting called Bellewstown, up North in Co. Meath. It was fantastic – something like our own Cartmel. People were selling fruit and flowers, all good stuff, which created a nice atmosphere. On our way there, a gypsy lady asked me if I would give her a half crown for her baby she was holding. I gave her a half crown, but told her I didn't want her baby!

Paddy, as promised, took me to The Heron to get me measured for some new jodhpurs. A few days later, I went back to Kildare with Johnny Markham to pick them up. They were absolutely brilliant!

While I was in Ireland, I gave Paddy some money in exchange for one of his cheques, which I sent to Quants, of Newmarket, and ordered a new pair of jodhpur-boots to be delivered through the post to me at Towton, for when I arrived home.

We came back home from what was by far the best time I have ever had in my life. It had been my first proper holiday. All the money I had stashed away over the previous months to have a good time with, had been more than worth it. I have been back to Ireland a good few times since. The Irish are the nicest people you could ever imagine.

10

THEY COULDN'T MANAGE
WITHOUT ME

"Damn! I've got my calling-up papers!" I had already been deferred once last year, but now it was for real. "Shit!" I thought. "They've already got my elder brother, Harry, in the Coldstream Guards. Isn't that enough from one family? There isn't even a war on!"

It said in the letter to report to Oswestry Railway Station, and enclosed was a railway warrant. It was only a few days away. It all seemed to be happening, and at the wrong time, too. The 1957 season was nicely on the way. I had got myself a nice little bird called Mollie Summerton who was a school teacher living in Tadcaster, I was getting a few rides in races, and things seemed to be going for me – until this. They didn't give me much time to worry about it!

I had already had a medical a few weeks before that in Leeds. I lined up in a great big room with another forty (or so) men, bollock-naked. We had to file past some trestle tables with five to six doctors sat upsides asking us various questions. One guy at the end put his hand under our private parts and told us to cough. I had recently read that Michael Scudamore, Peter's father, had failed his medical because of his feet. "If there was a war," I thought, "he wouldn't have to shoot with his feet! They don't stop him riding winners!" Anyway, I had passed the medical A-1.

First, I had to get a train from Leeds, change at Manchester, then Crewe, and then go on to Park Hall Camp, Oswestry. At every station on the way, the trains were picking up these budding Field Marshal Montgomerys. There were lots of soldiers shouting and bawling. They rounded us all up, like cattle-drovers do cattle at markets, then loaded us on to the army-trucks with our little cases. The soft ones had big cases (you could see their mums had packed them up!). Destination: the Royal Artillery Barracks, Park Hall, Oswestry.

When we arrived, we were ordered into this big hall. "You lot stay there!" the N.C.O. in charge shouted. (He could have said it if he'd have wanted to, as we were all together and within hearing distance.) He came back, then (kind of) marched us to the stores to get some army-clothes. (I say "kind of" as we needed polishing up a bit!) The store-keeper was very good to us. He gave us boots, socks, vests, shirts, berets, blankets, bedsheets, pillow-cases, badges, a new suit with pockets in the breasts, a big overcoat, and lots more things – including 10s. In fact, the mummy's boys were now wishing they had packed their own cases! With our cases and new clothes, we marched down to the N.A.A.F.I. (a kind of café). "You haven't come down here for a cup of tea," the N.C.O. said. "You can have that later. They do sell things here other than tea. There are things you will require, so now is as good a time as any to get them."

We bought all the things the N.C.O. told us to, such as black polish, Blue Bell (to clean the brasses), blanco, dusters, etc. It all amounted up to 8s 10d, leaving 1s 2d change from the 10-bob.

"I'd better show you where your hotel is," the N.C.O. then said. "Some of you look as if you can't carry any more and could do with a rest! Don't worry if you drop anything – we have kit checks daily. Whatever you lose will come out of your pay. You have at least two years in which to pay it back!" So, off we marched. Even with all this gear, the N.C.O. kept us marching right up to our billets. There were the exact number of beds as there were men in his squad. The N.C.O. had a small room at the bottom of the barrack room where he slept. "Put all your clothes, etc., in your locker," he said, and he showed us how he wanted them putting in. "I'll be back in ten minutes, then we're going out again."

We new recruits had decided, while he was away, that we would prob-ably be going back to the N.A.A.F.I. for that cup of tea. True to his word, he came back in ten minutes and inspected all our lockers, but first told us to quickly go and stand to attention at the right-hand side of our beds, which we all did – only some got a bit confused and went to the left. When he got to the end of the line of beds, he threw a wobbler! He went absolutely berserk, and chucked all our clothes out of the lockers. "I told you this way, and so-and-so," he said. "In ten minutes, I'll be back to inspect your lockers again, and you had better do it right this time!"

He came back in ten minutes and bollocked about a quarter of us. "Now tomorrow, you will *all* do it right first time! Fall in!"

Then, he marched us off. Instead of turning left to the N.A.A.F.I., we did a right. "There must be another way, or maybe another N.A.A.F.I.," I thought. We arrived at a room, and were told to go inside two at a time. When the first two came out, you could hardly recognise them. It was the barber's. They were ever so quick. Mary wouldn't have had to chase Paddy off to the barber's so often if the barber in Tadcaster had given him a haircut like these fellows were giving us!

After our haircuts, we were marched into another room and told to hold a board chest-high with our own personal number on (mine was 23427695).

We were then photographed for our passports. We then had our photograph taken all together.

"Now you are in the Royal Artillery, you are a Gunner," the N.C.O. said. "So, before your name and number, you have to say 'Gunner' (like 'Gunner' Berry). I may stop you at any time and ask your name and number. Remember this, as after today, if you don't, I'll find you some fatigues!" (Fatigues were spare jobs).

This N.C.O. was a quick learner. He very soon got to know our names, especially the ones who weren't very fast at learning!

We then went on the march, back to our billet, to get our digging kit, i.e. our knife, fork, spoon, and mug. They issued us with mess tins, but told us that we wouldn't be needing them today, as the cookhouse had some plates. The cookhouse at Oswestry was like a giant kit form barn – it would have made a good indoor riding-school! It was very high to the roof, and there were thousands of sparrows in there. In fact, when we first went in, the new recruits who were already eating were leaning over their food. "They can't all be upset, surely?" I thought. "Or do they think someone will pinch it and they are guarding it?"

When we got our food I knew why – the birds were flying around and shitting on the tables, on the benches, everywhere! The menu, for what it was worth, was written in chalk on a blackboard screwed to the wall. The birds were a real problem. With our main course in one hand and our sweet and mug of tea in the other, it was a struggle to walk to the table without a sparrow plopping on it! If that had been a café in Civvy Street, the Ministry would definitely have closed it down! "When they give us our guns, I hope we have firing practise in here," I thought.

With that, our little N.C.O. came rushing in. "A and B sections – fall in!" he shouted. Most of us hadn't even started our sweet! He marched us down in pairs back to our billets for some kit cleaning. We had to do that until 4.00p.m. tea-time, after tea back to the kit cleaning, then he told us we could pack it up for the night.

At 6.00a.m. the following morning, there was someone blowing a trumpet waking everyone up. Our N.C.O. was up already! "Get up, get washed, get shaved, make your bed rolls, and put your denims on!" he shouted (denims are a kind of jeans for rough wear).

He gave us that much to do it was difficult to remember it all, let alone in what order to do them! When we got sorted out in our denims, the silly bugger yelled, "Right! Put your S.D. (Service Dress) on, and I'll inspect you in ten minutes time." He couldn't make up his mind what he wanted! He went back into his room. (I wondered if he had a bird in there, as he was always going back inside!). Sure enough he came back in ten minutes to inspect us. "Stand by your beds!" he shouted. Not one single person had got it right. "You're a f*****g disgrace!" he said.

If he'd have talked to me like that at school, or at Towton, I would have killed the little prat, but it's a different ball game in the army. "You three are the worst – you, you and you," he said, pointing. "I've a little job for you later on."

He marched us all to another room, like a lecture room or classroom. "Sit on these seats, and stand up when the officer comes in," he said.

Sure enough, a couple of minutes later, this officer came in. Our man in charge didn't give us a chance to get up of our own accord. He jumped up, shouted "Attention!", and saluted the officer. Then, he told us to sit down. The officer gave us a talk about the army being such a good life, and all that. "If he thinks playing around like this is a good life, he should have come with me to Grange Con, Co. Wicklow !" I thought.

Matey marched us back to our billet, yet again, to get our eating kit. Then we marched back to the cookhouse for breakfast and to see the birds. After breakfast, we went on to the square. Our N.C.O. left us with another N.C.O., who started to teach us how to march properly. "If I go marching into the paddock at the next meeting at Wetherby like this I'll look a right berk!" I thought. We were kept going, doing different things, until 8.30p.m. Then, our N.C.O came back to march us to the N.A.A.F.I. By now, we were definitely starting to dislike this little chap! He told us to fall in outside.

"You, you and you run and get your denims on," he said. He had us running on the spot until the three defaulters came running out. Outside, on one side of the path, was a big heap of coke. "I want that shifting to the other side of the path before you go to bed," he said, and that's what they did while we were living it up in the N.A.A.F.I.!

This is what we did for about a week. Then, we practised for a passing-out parade, which came on about the tenth day. When we passed out, we were being sent to our permanent army barracks, mine being the King's Troop Royal Horse Artillery at St. John's Wood, London. I was the only gunner going to the King's Troop from Oswestry.

I had to catch the train from Oswestry to King's Cross, then a tube on to St. John's Wood. By now, I was beginning to feel a bit like a soldier. My hair had grown to about an inch long.

When I arrived at St. John's Wood, Harry Wharton, my old pal from Wetherby, was actually on the tube station, on his way home having finished his National Service that very day. Jumbo Wilkinson and Stan Heyhurst, the jockeys, had also just finished their stint in the King's Troop. Harry and I shook hands, and he marked my card the best he could. He told me that the best job to have was a groom's job and also to keep out of Regimental Sergeant-Major Dove's way. Harry had been the groom of the C.O., Major Bill Lithgow (Eric Wheeler the Lambourn trainer had taken over from him). We wished each other good luck, and away we went.

The Troop consisted of three sections: Right, Centre, and Left sections. Each section had two sub-sections: Right section had A and B sub-sections; Centre section had C and D sub-sections; and Left section had E and F sub-sections. All the lads were proud of their section, and even prouder of their sub-section. I was told I would be in Left section, F-sub. I was shown where it was, then told to put my gear in the billet. After doing this, I went to get something to eat at the cookhouse. The food there was first-class, with different choices every day (and not a sparrow in sight!). I knew some of the lads there, and had seen many of the others before at race meetings. All the time I kept seeing more and more people whom I knew. This was better than at Oswestry.

"I'm in this man's army for two years," I thought, "They made me come – I didn't want to. The certain thing is that I can't get out of it. I might as well settle down and enjoy it!" So, that's what I tried to do.

Father drives a team to the Bramham Moor point-to-point in the 1950's.

Left: My first Guv'nor, Charlie Hall, going to saddle up at the races. Below: Mr. Hall's amateur Miles Baird-Murray on the gallops at Towton.

Jimmy Threadgold leads in Osborne Lad, ridden by Colin 'Shadow' Dukes, accompanied by Mr. Hall's head-lad, Ben Robinson.

Snapshots from the mid-1950's. Left: Paddy Farrell and myself in Ireland. Below: Me, riding out Stormhead at Towton.

Jumping the last for my first winner at Wetherby on Sarsta Gri, in 1956. Other jockeys in the photograph are Barney Cross, George Milburn, Jimmy Fitzgerald, Nimrod Wilkinson, Larry Wigham and Paddy Farrell.

King's Troop Days. Left:
Me, in the suit I bought
just before I was
demobbed. Below: On the
way back from Camberley,
giving the horses a break
near London Airport.

My old pal Scamperdale and Captain Thatcher at Stowell Park Horse Trials.

Left: Me, winning on Candy after refusing the last jump at Wetherby in October 1964. Below: Mrs. Poskitt leads me in after winning at Sedgefield in May 1966 on Moment's Thought ('The Coloured Horse').

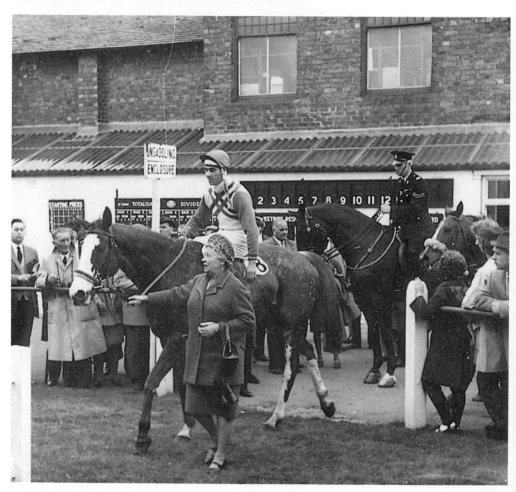

11

MY ARMY DAYS

The King's Troop was the cream of the Artillery. When The Queen took over from her father, King George VI, she didn't want the Troop's name to be changed. Therefore, a Yorkshire whipper-snapper like me wasn't going to try to alter things. People who had served in the Troop had been very proud to do so. I hoped that, at the end of it, I would also be proud to have served in the King's Troop R.H.A.

We chunkies (or "Red Arses", as we were called) had to drill every morning on the square to knock us into shape. The bit at Oswestry had just been to teach us some discipline – it was a collection point for everyone before they were sent to their permanent barracks in different parts of the country. The horses were kept in lines according to the sections, and these were divided in half for the sub-sections. All the horses were watered and fed at the same times every day by the call of the bugle, called 'Watering Order' and 'Feed-up'. When the bugler gave this call, all the horses were pulled out in unison to be watered, then later fed. These horses were great – they knew the time just as if they were wearing watches. When the bugler went out to blow Watering Order or Feed-up, the horses would whinny and stamp their feet before he had got the bugle to his mouth! There were some real characters amongst those horses. If someone hadn't fastened a horse up properly, the horse would stand there until there was no-one about, then walk to the feed-house, where the feed-man would have had all his feeds made up, and get stuck in.

Sergeant Strange was the man in charge of "Shiny F.", as we affectionately called our sub-section. We had the black horses in our section, so if anyone had a state funeral, our F-sub. horses would pull the gun-carriage with the coffin on.

There were some good lads in the Troop. There was Jimmy Uttley, the good hurdle-jockey who rode Persian War to win three Champion Hurdles; the trainers Eric Wheeler and Barry Hills, Eric Witts, who used to train; Brian

Delaney, who was Fred Winter's head-lad and is now Charlie Brooks' head-lad; Sammy McKeown, father of Dean, the jockey; and many more notable racing people. There were also some notable footballers in it – Cliff Jones, for one. They didn't work with the horses, though. They mainly had soft jobs in the stores.

R.S.M. Dove was a dead-ringer for Arthur Lowe from 'Dad's Army'! We called him "Dad" because, once, he arranged a muster parade (which every person on camp is compelled to attend) and told us that he had heard he wasn't liked. "I can't understand this – I'm like a father to you all!" he said.

At "The Wood" (as we sometimes called the Troop), there was a really old, civilian man named Jim. He lived in the boiler room underground and looked after the boilers and the gardens. He would take his own tin plate to the cookhouse, get his food, then take it back to the boiler room to eat on his own. At the top of the stairs, all his cats used to be waiting for him to return, so he must have fed them at the same time as he fed himself! Because he was untidy and smelt awful, whenever we had parades for any high-ranking officials, etc. (which was common practice), Dad used to round up Old Jim and tell him not to be seen outside until the V.I.P. had gone!

When I had been in the Troop for a few weeks, and got all my marching in, I was working in the lines, grafting my heart out, knowing full well that our Section Commander's groom was getting demobbed shortly and his job would be coming up for grabs. Fortunately for me, Lt. Thatcher asked me if I would like to become his groom. I said that I would be delighted to. So, next day, I packed up working in the lines and went for a couple of weeks as the assistant to his present groom, Gunner Kershaw, to learn the ropes. When he was demobbed, I was left as the Section Commander's official groom. I was so chuffed that I wrote and told Harry Wharton that I had got a groom's job!

This new job meant that I looked after my officer's chargers (which could be two or three horses), plus all their gear, tack, and everything that went on his horses. Officers' valets (or "batmen", as they were called) saw to all the parts of their personal clothing. It was great to see the Troop's horses together and watch them do the musical rides. It was a sight I never got tired of.

Being an officer's groom also meant I didn't have to do regular pickets (shifts at guarding the place at night), only fire-pickets. The two who were on duty would take their bed-rolls down to the education room and sleep the night there! If someone was on a picket and didn't want to do it, they could pay somebody else to do it for them. As it was expensive living in London, I did quite a few of these. We used to get £5 for every one. That was more than our wages, which, being National Service men, were 37s 6d per week. I also got £1 per month extra money for being staff-employed. Invariably, regulars would be selling their pickets, as they got a lot more money than us conscripts. Sometimes I would do someone's picket in return for their railway warrant, as we were only allocated one every three months.

One particular day, I was on a picket for someone when I saw Dad go up the N.A.A.F.I. steps into the T.V. lounge in the early hours of the morning. He was a bugger for creeping around to see if a section of the picket was asleep anywhere (me, in this instance). Anybody on picket-duty should close any open door, so, when he opened the T.V. lounge door, seeing as it was my duffy (turn to guard), I very quietly went up behind him, closed the door, and put the bolt on. For the rest of the picket, I never went anywhere near the T.V. lounge. When I had finished my stint, I spoke to the next guard on. "Don't go near the N.A.A.F.I. I've locked Dad in the T.V. lounge," I told him.

If anything unusual happened on a picket, we were supposed to report it. So, when the picket was over at 'Reveille', 6.00a.m., I told the Guard Commander that I had found the T.V. lounge door open and had closed it. Someone had let Dad out – the day hadn't been very old before he had started shouting and bawling. He would have known it was me – all he had to do was look at the picket list in the guard room. He never mentioned it, though!

Our stables for the officers' chargers was next to the main gate. Sergeant Ben Jones of Equitation, the senior riding-instructor, gave lessons to the officers, some of whom came from the War Office in Whitehall. One occasion, when I was in the stables, grooming, Ben was giving instruction to Dad on his horse, Savanak. Dad wasn't a natural horseman! "Your hands are like nigger's f*****g feet!" Ben was yelling to Dad. If I'd have been an M.P., I would have had to say, "Hear, Hear!"

Sergeant Ben Jones was an absolutely brilliant horseman and represented England in many international 3-Day Events.

The Troop used to have some good times performing the musical rides, and we went all over England and Wales. We grooms often went to civilian shows and functions, in addition to Troop activities that our officers took part in. We went to Badminton and Burghley Horse Trials, the Bath and West Horse Show, Bangor-on-Dee for camp, Fylingdales in Yorkshire for camp, the Earl's Court Tournament, Wembley, and Tweseldown Point-to-Point where we held the Troop race. We also spent some of the winter hunting at Melton Mowbray, where we stayed with the Royal Army Veterinary Corps.

"This old horse of mine, Scamperdale, is a cert. for the Troop race at Tweseldown," I said to the rest of the grooms during a N.A.A.F.I. break. "The only drawback is my officer (who had just been promoted to Captain). He's a fair rider, and very keen, but he rides two holes longer than Buffalo Bill! The old horse likes his jockey sitting up his neck and letting him go, not bumping about on the saddle!"

We decided to pull Captain Thatcher's jerks up a few holes, then cut the surplus leather off so he couldn't let them down again. I did this just before we saddled-up Scamp for the race. The first my officer would have known about this was when we gave him a leg up in the paddock, but by then, it would have been too late to do anything about it! The old horse made all, jumping like a buck. He never came off the bridle to win, and we had our few bob on.

When our officers didn't need their horses to take parades and rides on, we exercised them ourselves. On occasions, we took them for a canter round Hampstead Heath. It was really good, that. We would pull our jerks up, like we did at home. On the way back, one day, whilst riding the horses across the pond (as we always did when we went the Hampstead way), we decided to race across for a £1 sweep.

"Last one across pays for the N.A.A.F.I. break, too!" Scamp crossed his legs and fell down in the water. I was lucky I didn't get hurt – I was trapped underneath him and he was in no hurry to get up. The lads said it was such a funny sight to see just a peaked army cap floating on the pond, with neither horse nor rider anywhere in sight! I had to ride Scamp back to The Wood soaking wet!

The old horse loved a cup of tea. I found it out only by chance one morning when my officer led rough exercise, which meant that all the horses from the lines walked and trotted around the roads for two hours. This happened every Wednesday and Saturday. The lads rode on just a thick blanket with a surcingle round, and led a horse at each side of them. The sight of something like 100 horses out at 6.30a.m. in a town is worth seeing! The horses would follow the three in front, so some of the lads even had a doze while they were out. As I passed the cookhouse, always flat out, I used to dive in for my mug of tea. On this particular day, I put the mug in Scamp's manger as I was tacking him up. The next thing, he had his great big tongue in my mug, lapping the tea up. So, from that day on, I gave him a mug of tea every day, after I had had a swig, by way of tipping it into his manger.

Scamp competed at Badminton Horse Trials, ridden by Captain Thatcher. The old boy went really well: he was brilliant in the cross-country and the steeple-chase. His show-jumping was good, too. It was the dressage that let him down – he was too keen. He finished 7th. I saw Sue Wildblood there. She had come down with Mrs. Boon, the wife of Major Boon (one time Clerk of the Course at Doncaster). Mrs. Boon later got killed on a horse in an indoor school.

My Fair Lady was showing at the West End, and all the time I was in the Troop I never got to see it, as it was booked-up so far in advance; we were on emergency stand-by, because of racial tensions in Maida Vale and other places in London; my sister, Elsie, got married in Leeds; Pat Gulwell rode Sarsta Gri a winner; Paddy was still the North's leading jockey; Sally left Towton and went to her Uncle Sam's in Middleham; Colin Dukes had fractured his skull in a race; my young brother, Goff, had left school and gone into Hunt Service with West Percy. It was all happening!

Andy Barclay, who trained at Annan in Scotland, left a message at the Troop office for me to give him a ring. When I did, he asked if I could ride a horse at Kelso for him. I gladly accepted, and went to Kelso by way of trains and hitch-hiking. The horse finished 2nd, only beaten by a neck. It was nice to see the lads again and have a bit of crack with them. I had a 48-hour pass, so I went back to Towton and rode out the next morning.

In the army, my weight went up a bit, so on the odd occasion I had a ride, I sometimes had to do a stint in the Seymour Halls baths to sweat off a bit of flab. Barry Hills came with me on a couple of occasions.

It was a common practice in the Troop, that when any Red Arses arrived from Oswestry, or when someone was getting demobbed, engaged, married, or whatever, they would be troughed. Struggle as they may, they would be picked up (fully clothed) by several of the lads, put into one end of the water trough, and then dragged to the other. The lads only needed an excuse. A water trough was about twenty feet long, but we had three of them in a row. It looked like a furlong to the person being troughed! When our Adjutant, Major Andrews, was leaving The Wood, we caught him and troughed him.

"Well, Berry, that's the first time I've ever been troughed. No hard feelings, though," he said. "Shake." With that, he shook my hand, but didn't let go. "Come on, fellows," he shouted, "Let's have this bugger in now!" As I said, they only needed an excuse.

When we grooms rode out at Oswestry, as we did when we went to camp there, the new recruits often saluted us. As we were wearing peaked caps, they couldn't tell the difference between us and the officers. If no-one was about, we used to salute them back. Sometimes, we would say things like, "Straighten yourself up, man! Fasten your buttons! You could do with a haircut! When did you last have a shave? Report to the guard room at eighteen hundred hours in your best S.D.!" and so on.

Once every week, the Padré came to have a chat about religion. You would have thought the poor man had some terrible disease, as he couldn't drum up any trade at all. Dad went chasing around the Troop looking for staff-employed to send up to him (he didn't want to take lads from the lines, as they were always pushed). There were confirmation classes going on and, as I had missed out on getting confirmed (through galloping around Boston Spa at the time), I thought I had better put it right. So, I had the classes. I got confirmed at St. Paul's Cathedral, and Mollie came down to London for the ceremony.

Mollie used to write to me often – nearly every day, in fact. Then, one day, she wrote to tell me about a trip to Scarborough she had been on with Shadow, and enclosed was a photograph of the two of them holding hands. "Colin's looking after her well for me," I thought. "It doesn't look as if she's missing me as much as she's making out in her letters!"

On my twenty-first birthday, in 1959, I had a 72-hour pass. I went to the Rockingham first, and had a few jars with the lads from the yard. Then, I caught the 9.50p.m. bus to Tadcaster and went to Mollie's house. When I arrived, there was a deathly silence. Neither she nor her mother spoke, so I left after a couple of minutes and caught the bus back to Towton to rejoin the lads at The Rock. Apparently, Mollie and her mum had organised a surprise little party for me. They had got the biggest surprise when I hadn't turned up! Anyway, it had all been cleaned away before I got there. There's no show without Punch, but I'm not a mind reader! From then on, our love affair drifted apart. Mollie ended up marrying Shadow, but sadly they have since parted.

The F-sub. barrack room stood at the far end of the barracks near the gun-park, a sort of working museum for the Troop's guns and limbers. As a point of interest, there were eight of them at The Wood, all relics from the First World War. Six were used in the musical drive and for general Troop duties, one was a spare, and the remaining one was for funeral occasions.

The gun-park was also a regular area for the trumpeters to practise their art. The trumpeters, who spent the most of their lives sounding a bugle, mainly joined the army as school boys attached to The Boys' Battery at Hereford. Those fortunate enough came to The Wood on passing out at the age of eighteen. The whole daily operation of the Troop was run by sounding various bugle calls, from reveille, water-and-feed, boots-and-saddles, right through to last post at 6.00p.m., and finally lights out at 10.00p.m. Willing to try my hand at most things, and fancying myself as a budding Eddie Calvert, I borrowed a bugle from one of the trumpeters and slipped into the gun-park one evening, giving all to a rendition of a jazzed-up "God Save The Queen". Unbeknown to me, the Orderly Officer of the day, Captain Phipps, heard my efforts and promptly ordered the Guard Commander to investigate the keen musician, and add him to the duty-trumpeter roll for the next two weeks. The bush telegraph worked well – I was long gone by the time he arrived at the gun-park! Our compliment of trumpeters was six, which was quite enough – they didn't need me as well!

James Kearsley was Forage N.C.O. All our horses were supposed to be fed on a feed-poundage or ration: James made sure our chargers never wanted.

One particular day, from outside my stables on camp at Oswestry, James shouted, "Anyone in there?"

"Yes, mate," I replied, "I'm here." (I was grooming Scamp, getting him ready for my boss who wanted him to take the 2.00p.m. Parade).

"Oh, Berry. Come and sweep these areas outside the Officers' Mess."

"Bugger off!"

"Come and sweep these areas up right now!" he said in a sharp, stern voice.

90

I ran outside with my brush and curry comb, about to push them down James's neck. But standing there was R.S.M. Dove.

"You are on a charge, Berry, for insubordination to an N.C.O.!" he said.

"If I don't get this horse on the square for 2.00p.m., I'll be on a charge, anyway!" I replied.

Dad got Lance Bombardier Kearsley to march me to the C.O.'s office. I got three days C.B. (Confinement to Barracks). It wasn't James's fault, it was just the sort of thing Dad did. He was probably getting back at me for locking him in the T.V. lounge!

James and I were best pals in the army – we went all over in his Morris Minor. When we were at camp in Fylingdales near Scarborough, I passed my driving test in that car. Captain Chinn (our veterinary officer) took me for it, as officers were in a position to take driving tests.

We had some good times with the horses at camp. We were there for five weeks and never put a uniform on once. We had show-jumping competitions, cross-country, and all sorts. The line horses loved it: to get them out of town for a few weeks did them good. The sun shone nearly every day. One evening, as a few of us were having a ride in the car, we came across a village hall where a dance competition was being held. We all bullied James into entering, then asked a girl (who was with a local chap) if she would partner him. After she agreed, in order to take part, James had to borrow her boyfriend's shoes, as his own weren't very good! James was an exceptionally good dancer, and had no problem winning the competition.

One weekend James and I had off, we drove from Fylingdales to his house in Bolton, Lancashire, where we stayed. He had a girlfriend there, Christine, whom he later married. On the way back from Bolton, we were driving through the night, remembering how one of the other lads in our sub., Brian Cornel, had said that he had never seen a hedgehog. As I was driving the car, just coming out of Leeds, I saw one of the little chaps on the road. So, I stopped the car, picked him up, put him on James's lap (James was fast asleep), and thought no more about it. When we got on the dual carriageway between Tadcaster and York, my partner riding shotgun started flapping and yelling. I had all on to keep him in the car! To settle James down, I put the hedgehog on the back seat. What I didn't know was that hedgehogs have fleas – they were jumping all over! When we got back to the camp, at about 4.00a.m., I slipped the hedgehog in Brian's bed, waiting to hear some yelling in the morning when Brian met his first hedgehog. No sound. It can only be the hedgehog wasn't happy with his bedmate, and had got out and left (as we were sleeping in our beds but under canvas, it wouldn't have been too difficult to escape!).

When we got back from summer camp, we had a few shows to do at Earl's Court, back in London. Then, back to The Wood.

One of the tailors at the Troop was doing me a favour and making me a suit. I had only a few weeks left to do, and I wanted something decent to go out in (the army issuing troops with demob-suits was a thing of the past). I had just had a fitting, as the tailor had been waiting for me to get back from Scarborough. The suit was great. It was charcoal grey, and I was really chuffed with it.

"Come back tomorrow night and I'll have it finished," Mike said. When I went back it was really good – hand-stitched everywhere. He charged me £20 for making it up (I had bought the length of cloth weeks beforehand).

Finally, I got to my last pay-day. With all my extras, my demob allowance, and having had so much a week being put by, I got about £240. Just right. We had already had my party the previous night. I said "Cheerio" to my old pal, Scamp, thanking him for all the fun we had had together, and assured him that his new lad would bring him his mug of tea every morning (his new lad had promised faithfully that he would). I felt really bad leaving Scamp – he and I went back a long way. I'm sure he knew I was going for good.

12

MET THE BRIDE

On the train back to Towton, I started thinking. "Over twenty-one years old now, son. It's time you did something, or it will be too late!"

When I got back in the yard, working, things didn't seem quite the same; I had a few rides for The Guv'nor, and the occasional spare that Paddy had put me in for from other stables. One day, I had a ride for an outside stable at Catterick in a Novice Hurdle in a big field. The trainer told me to have him up in the first four or five. Anyone who has ever ridden in a big field in a Novice at Catterick will know that they don't hang about! My fellow was a bit flat early on. I was on the inside, quietly creeping past a few here and there, and hoping to get myself into the position the trainer wanted me to be in before he had time to find out where I was. Just passing the stands, I was a close-up 5th, having had a super run up the inner, passing about ten horses and probably upsetting as many jockeys in the process (one shouldn't poach that blatantly, especially approaching the grandstand!). Happy now, we were just starting to go round the back straight. "I hope this fellow can do what his trainer says he can," I thought. "I'm in a nice position, now, and I don't think I've burnt him up getting him here."

Just then, I got this almighty crack on my backside with a whip (this was before whips were shortened). My horse finished 3rd. When I was weighing-in, Dicky Curran leaned over the rail that jockeys put their saddles on when they have been weighed out. "Yer know what that was for, don't yer!" he said. It can't have bothered him too much, as I later rode for Dick when he started to train, and got myself in the winner's enclosure for him.

I bought a car from Tommy Lynch's father-in-law for £30. It was a Morris with a clock on the radiator. It was very old, but it was in lovely condition – he had owned it for years and taken a pride in it. His insurance company insured it for me. On its second day out, I went to see my sister, Betty, in Leeds. It went well on the way there, but got a bump at a minor crossroad just before York Road on the way home. "Just send me the bill. Just send me the bill," the piss artist who hit me kept saying. I would have done, except he wouldn't tell me where he lived!

Tom Walker was a permit-holder from Faxton Moor. His main business was farming, but he loved horses (his son, John, became a useful amateur). He trained a mare called Markeast. Three afternoons a week, I used to go in my car to ride the mare work. Afterwards, I would rush back for evening stables at the yard.

Going through York on my return trip, one day, I had just driven past the racecourse when an oncoming car made no allowances for me overtaking a bike and ran straight into me. "Oh, God! My bloody car!" I thought. One side of its face was bashed in, and water was leaking from the radiator. "Anyway, it's knackered now." Regarding who was at fault,"It was six and two threes," the other driver said.

I agreed, as I couldn't argue for too long – I was late for work already! The car struggled back to Towton. There was Ben, hands in the back of his trousers, waiting to welcome me at the yard entrance. "I wondered how long that would last, the way you drive it," he said. This was nothing compared to some of the things Tommy Lynch's father-in-law had been saying about my driving! There was a man in Sherburn-in-Elmet who dealt in scrap cars, so I sold it to him for £8 and cut my losses.

Not many rides were coming from Towton. Paddy and Pat Gulwell were both riding really well. Thinking of a change, someone told me that Roy Whiston was looking for staff. I thought I would just change the scenery a bit. The majority of the horses at Mr. Whiston's were ridden by Stan Mellor, Tim Brookshaw, and Roy Edwards (three of the best jump-jockeys around) when they were available, but I didn't go there expecting to take over from anyone.

"Have you given plenty of thought to what you're saying?" asked The Guv'nor when I told him I wanted to leave. "Give it a try elsewhere, if that's what you want, but you can have a job back here any time."

It was my last day working at Towton. A few regrets – it had been my home for so long and a lot had happened there. We had had some fun, some heartaches, some ups and downs, but this gave me the loneliest feeling I have ever felt in my life. The Guv'nor had been the best boss anyone could have worked for; Ben Robinson had taught me everything I know about a racehorse; I had worked with one of the best jockeys ever to jump over a fence – Paddy. "Surely, I must have stored *some* of it between my ears," I thought. "That might put me in good stead, one day. Who knows – I might even get to train The Ayr Gold Cup winner!"

So, on 2nd February 1960 I went to Nottingham Races with Paddy, as he had some rides there. I was getting a lift in Mr. Whiston's 'box from there to take me back to his own place. That day, Harry Maw, the Doncaster trainer, asked me to ride a filly in the 4-year-old Hurdle. The horse was called Fairy Loch, and she ran well to finish 5th. Mr. Maw was pleased, and asked me to ride one at Doncaster on the following Friday. "Yes sir," I said. "I'd be delighted."

At Whiston's, it wasn't anything like Towton. In the yard it wasn't busy. There was no rush – it didn't buzz. I lived in at Beech House, the home of my new boss. It was the small yard of the establishment. Mrs. Whiston was a really nice lady. They had a little girl called Candy. She once asked me if I would make her a doll's house (not that I'm a joiner!), and only a few years ago, Mrs. Whiston said that Candy still has the doll's house.

Roy, "the Boss", was a cattle-dealer as well as a trainer. He would buy lots of cattle from markets, fetch them home, and put them in the huge fold-yard he had. Coming from the cattle market, they all had numbered tickets stuck on their hind quarters. He could have one hundred, or more, delivered, as he dealt in cattle in a big way. "Would you mind giving me a hand to get these numbers off the cattle's backsides?" he would ask me. "I've a punter coming to buy them in the morning – it wouldn't be proper if the beasts still had market-tickets on." "Not at all," I would say (I thought it was a bit of fun).

We would tighten them up with gates, then I would climb onto their backs and jump from one to the other, scraping the tickets off with a curry-comb! They were so close together, they couldn't buck me off!

In the field, there was a lovely donkey called Noddy, who had a reputation that she couldn't be ridden. Over the field were two boxes with rough horses in. Every day, Doug, the head-man, gave me two feeds to take for them. So, every day, I got on Noddy's back, with a feed-bucket in each hand. She would buck and kick, whip round, and drop her shoulders, dropping me every time – she loved it! When the food spilt, she tucked in and had a feed. She used to wait for me to go over; whenever she saw me, she would bray. "That bloody donkey looks well," The Boss would say. "Are you feeding it? It shouts every time it sees you." "No, Boss," I would say.

If I'd have stayed there for another three months, I think I would have mastered her, as I was beginning to get the hang of her. Mrs. Anne Bevan, mother of Richard the conditional jockey, worked at Whiston's at the same time as me. She got a few laughs watching Noddy and me performing!

I got a few rides from the yard, but nothing much good. If anything improved, the horse went up to the big yard. Every time I had a spare ride, it was hard to get to the meetings as there was no-one around who I could get a lift with, and I couldn't afford another car, yet.

Although Percy Hinchcliffe had left Towton, he still went racing quite a bit as he worked shifts at a brewery. On 16th April 1960 at Manchester, he called for me from the weighing room:

"Mr. Watts, the Bridlington trainer, is looking for you, Jack," he said. "He wants you to ride a horse for him in the Handicap 'Chase. It's only got 10 stone – I told him you can do the weight."

"Great!" I replied. "Tell him I can. I'm only riding our two hurdlers here, today."

Sure enough, when I saw Mr. Watts, "Are you all right for Abershaw in the 2½-mile 'Chase?" he asked. "Here are the colours."

This was to be my first winning ride over fences. Abershaw won by a short head, beating Nobbutjust trained by W.A. Stephenson and ridden by Bruce Carr.

By now, I was riding all Mr. Maw's horses, and getting on well with him. So, after three months at Mr. Whiston's, I decided to leave. I left there on good terms, and still got the odd ride for Mr. Whiston. He even gave me a ride on his good horse, Fresh Winds, one day at Uttoxeter.

I went to join Mr. Maw as his jockey and head-lad, getting digs with a family named Parr at Carcroft, a mining village. Harold Parr worked in the pit, Mrs. Parr was a housewife, and they had a ten-year-old daughter called Avril. Harold's retarded sister, Annie, was also living with them.

Mrs. Parr really mothered me. She was a super lady, and we got on like a house on fire. If ever I was a bit pushed for time and went out to work without my breakfast, she would send Harold on his bike up to the yard with a flask of coffee and a bacon or egg sandwich for me. She was a really nice, genuine woman.

Harry Maw, an ex-racing car driver, trained at Owston Park, near Doncaster, where he lived with his wife, Millie. They were an oldish couple who were just about ready for someone like me to come onto the scene to take the hard work out of the job so the old boy could enjoy the fruits of the seeds he had sown, and get a bit of pleasure out of the game he had put so much into. He was a very proud man. Mr. Maw and his wife loved their small animals. They had two Yorkshire Terriers, four or five cats, and 'The Missus' fed the wild birds every day.

The stable yard was a beautifully cobbled, stone yard with twelve boxes around it. All of them were the cage-type. A loft ran all the way round the top of the stables, the large feed house, and the tack room. There were also a couple of big garages in the yard. I imagine that, in the past, they would have been used for horse-drawn coaches.

When I arrived, they had a couple of young lads working for them called Aggie and Bence: they had enough work to do. The lads travelled there by bus, so they couldn't go home for lunch as 'home' was too far away. Until we had got the place sorted out, I stayed on in the afternoons. We tidied the horses up and got them looking good, we mended rugs, we picked out all the grass and weeds from in between the cobbles in the yard, we cut down the dead wood from the trees, we cut the lawns, and we got the place all spick and span. All we needed then was a Doorknocker or a Stormhead!

Mr. Maw didn't pay up-to-date wages – he lived a bit in the past, and was very old-fashioned, but I rode all the horses we trained that went jumping. If I got hurt, he never rushed the horses to race until I was sound. "There's plenty of time," he would say. "There'll be a nice Hurdle that'll suit that one at least three times a week until the end of the season."

The old boy knew I was keen and wanted to get on – he wasn't going to stop me. He didn't give me much money, yet he had a heart of gold. Sometimes, he kept me talking in the tack room many hours after we had finished work, reminiscing about the past, often going over the same ground as the previous week. He might not have been the biggest trainer around, or have had the best horses, but he looked on me as a son, and I liked the old boy.

Soon, we got a couple more lads working for us, and a policewoman, called Ann Newstead, rode out and helped in the yard on her days off. The Guv'nor didn't ride out, so I took the horses round the roads before we worked them. I got them really well, and they were running out of their skins. The Guv'nor, though, being as old-fashioned as he was, wouldn't change the faces. The only 2-year-olds we had while I was there were Sister Aiston and Easter Bell. "Guv'nor," I said, "you don't owe these buggers a living. Some of them are getting a bit long in the tooth. Let's have some yearlings in, and some unbroken 3 or 4-year-olds." But, the old lad was set in his ways, so that was that. Doncaster Sales had just started again after a long absence, but on the days I managed to get The Guv'nor there, I could never get him out of the bar to buy any fresh horses!

The Guv'nor still drove his 'box. It was a bloody old banger he had bought years ago from Harry Wragg. It had no self-start, so, first thing in the morning when it was cold, I had to get it going with a starting handle. It kicked like a damned mule, and I hated it. I would rather have ridden round Aintree backwards than wind that handle! When I was in the cab with The Guv'nor, I sometimes got a bit ambitious:

"Guv'nor, why don't we sell this 'box and get another, more modern one? I'll drive it if you want. We can put an advert in our local paper, or better still, we can put one in the Life – 'Box for Sale, and 'box wanted with different numbers!"

"Good idea, Jack," he would say, but that was about as far as it ever got!

On one occasion, driving up the A1 on the way to Ripon Races, The Guv'nor passed an army tank-carrier and cut in far too sharply, putting the army vehicle in a ditch. Gordon Hill, one of the lads, was in the back of the 'box. The Guv'nor didn't even know what he'd done (or he didn't let on!).

When the 'box arrived at Ripon, police cars with sirens and lights flashing swooped round the 'box. The Guv'nor told them he didn't know what they were talking about. He finished up in court and got fined, though.

Whenever the 'box was going downhill, The Guv'nor used to knock it out of gear. Going to places like Manchester on the A57 would take pounds off me, free-wheeling for mile after mile. I could hardly see the bottom of the drops from my side! Sometimes, he would even take both his hands off the wheel, spit on his palms, then rub them together. On some occasions, whizzing round the hairpin bends on the way to Manchester or Haydock, he would start telling me about motor-racing and his days as a racing-driver. This always got his adrenalin going, which made him drive faster. It was far easier to ride in a 3-year-old Hurdle, or a Novice 'Chase, than to go to the meeting in the 'box with The Guv'nor! I got in such a sweat! Once, coming back from Ripon, he drove the 'box down the wrong side of the dual carriageway on the A-1 for about four miles. The drivers of the oncoming traffic were going mad! Lights flashed and heads were stuck out of the windows, cursing and swearing! "What's the matter with him?" The Guv'nor would say to me. "I'll get back over as soon as I see a gap. Can you see one, Jack?" I was sat there in a nervous sweat, with eyes popping out of my head looking for a way out! Every time we went out with him, either in the car or in the 'box, it was hairy. It was an even-money chance whether we got back home, or not! Whenever Anne was on point-duty at the roundabout in Doncaster, as soon as she saw the 'box approaching, she would make sure the traffic was flowing in his favour!

The horse-box was returning from Manchester Races in thick fog. We were getting a good lead from a grit wagon, gritting the roads. The Guv'nor never realised the wagon had stopped gritting and he followed it straight into a council depot!

Joe Sime rode our Flat horses whenever he could. There were more mixed meetings in those days than there are today – Liverpool, Ayr, Bogside, Haydock and other places. When I had outside rides, Joe used to give me a lift to meetings if he was going. At that time, I was getting quite a few rides for the likes of Billy Newton, Clifford Watts, A. Birch, Tony Doyle, and others. I was doing all right. The Guv'nor never moaned about me being away, or anything. Mind you, I went in first thing in the morning and got the horses out before I went racing, if possible.

The Guv'nor had never had a double before until 14th April 1961 when Prince Winter, ridden by Brian Henry, and Fairy Loch, ridden by Joe, won at Thirsk. I was dead chuffed for him. It was great to see a man of his age so pleased, it really was. The horses did well that summer – it was his best season ever.

One of our horses, Stunning, was bought after winning a seller at Doncaster for Sam Armstrong. He was a 5-year-old, full horse, by Stardust and out of Running Wild. His first win had been at Folkestone, ridden by Lester Piggott. Then, he won a couple of Handicaps at Windsor and Sandown. After that he lost his form, until he won the seller at Doncaster, where Mr. Armstrong was pleased to see him go for £250. Benny Lovett, a nice, kind man who owned and ran Stainforth Dog-track, bought Stunning from The Guv'nor. Every Sunday morning, he would bring his wife and daughter, Ann, to see his horse. He would also bring with him a big tin, full of packets of crisps, and a crate of pop for us lads to share. Stunning later won a race for us at Beverley.

At the bottom of the lane at Owston was a crossroad. A garage stood off the far side of one leg, which we often rode over to for sweets, and such. It was owned by a man called Sammy Sharp. "Sharp by name, Sharp by nature," we used to say, as he was a very keen businessman.

One day, it was very hot, so I bought one of those small bottles of pop from the garage. I drank about three-quarters of it, then bent over Stunning's shoulder, put the bottle in the side of his mouth, and poured the pop into it. He liked it! After this, whenever we went by the garage, I would bob off Stunner and give him a drink of pop. He really got a liking for it. One wouldn't dare do that today with all the rigorous testing done on horses.

1960/1 season Stunning ran a few times over hurdles, and he finished 3rd on his last two starts. The British Bloodstock Agency later bought him to go to The Highway Lodge Stud in New Zealand. As a sire, Stunning was to enjoy the sort of success which is impossible to predict. He sired the New Zealand 2-year-old champion, Darryl's Joy, winner of The Victoria Derby in Australia. He was then sold and sent to California, where he became one of America's leading sires. He sired Sledgehammer, who was to win twenty of his twenty-nine starts and who was syndicated for £150,000 in 1972.

Willie Carson was apprenticed to Gerald Armstrong at Middleham before he transferred his indentures to Sam, his brother. Willie came and stayed with us in my digs. We had borrowed him from Mr. Armstrong for a while to ride some of the horses. We called him "Scottie", in those days. I remember we didn't get a lot of work out of him, as he was always full of a cold. He was like me in my early days – a bit of a runt!

At the races one day, I met a girl; Josephine was her name. She worked for Pat Taylor. When I took our little sprinter, Silver Bug (or Billy Bugger, as we used to call him), he played about, bucking and kicking. He was always full of beans at meetings, but was as quiet as a mouse at home. All of us absolutely loved him. Once, as I was leading Billy Bugger round the parade ring at Pontefract, he was doing his usual messing about when he jumped really high into the air, whipped round, and kicked me in the chest, as I was still leading him round. What a lad he was, but he was great! He more or less clashed every week with a sprinter of Pat Taylor called Kessall and looked after by Jo. At the same time, Ernie Davey had a good sprinting mare called Granville Greta. She was very fast – our sprinters often saw her backside! Mr. Davey was a great man. He had an endless string of jockeys that he had got started as apprentices – Lionel Brown, Jimmy Etherington, Johnny Seagrave, P.J. Willet, Brian Lee, and a lot more. He had few equals when it came to buying cheap 2-year-olds and then winning races with them.

One day at Beverley Races, Jo told me about a party being held there that night, and asked me if I would like to go along. "Yes, I'd love to," I said, "but I haven't got a car, and I have to go home to see to the runners we've had here, today." In fact, we were talking in the horse-box park, and I was only waiting for The Guv'nor to come so that we could set off for home. That was the only thing I didn't like about The Guv'nor: we were always last to get to the races (we were always pushed for time with him not setting off till the last minute), and he was always last out of the bar!

One day at the races, Jo told me that the two best horses she looked after, Kessall and Moira Bia, had gone to stud. "Come and work for us," I said, as she was feeling a bit low. She knew what our Guv'nor was like, as I had told her before. Mind you, her guv'nor was a good trainer – he once had four winners in a day at his local meeting, Beverley. Jimmy Fitzgerald, the Malton trainer, did a stint with him, as did Brian Henry when he was riding winners. Jo did decide that she would come and work for us. I got her some digs next to mine with a lady called Mrs. Clark. The yard was only about two miles from our digs, so I used to go there on my bike and give Jo a crossbar until she bought her own bike.

In the summer, Jo went racing with The Guv'nor more than I did. This suited me, as it gave me more time to see to the horses at home. Jo wasn't used to riding in horse-boxes the way H.S. Maw drove them – she always insisted on travelling in the back so she couldn't see what was happening, but she still often came back telling me some hairy stories!

One day, while stopped at a set of traffic lights on the way to Nottingham, The Guv'nor set off to go and let the 'box roll backwards – straight into a car! Jo had pressed the bell in the back of the 'box for him to stop, but it had been too late. The driver got out of his car and started ranting and raving. "What's the matter with him, Jo?" The Guv'nor asked, looking at the man with the smashed-in car, "Has he run into me?"

The Guv'nor owned an old Bentley. It was really old, but instead of putting it away and bringing it out once a year for the London to Brighton Rally, he used it as his car for going places in. On Friday, 10th March 1961, I told him that I was going to Manchester to ride a mare, Happy Dene, in the 2-mile Trojan Handicap 'Chase for George Stanley. Just as I was about to set off, having started work early in order to catch a flyer and not to be held up, he said, "I wouldn't mind a day's racing with you, today, Jack. There's nothing spoiling here."

"Well, you're welcome to," I said. "Get ready."

So, I parked my car outside his house and waited.

"We'll go in the Bentley," he said when he came out.

"Oh, God!" I thought. "What have I done to deserve this?" Anyway, he wouldn't have it any other way.

On the way, he stopped at Sammy Sharp's garage to fill up with petrol, and ended up inviting Sammy along. When we got to the garage, Mrs. Maw phoned Sammy's, asking for The Guv'nor. While he was on the phone, I was in the shop, buying a few sweets. A new girl on the pumps filled the bloody car up with diesel instead of petrol! I pleaded with The Guv'nor to let me run back and get my car. "It won't take long to get things sorted out," he assured me. An hour later, we finished up going to Manchester in Sammy's

100

car. You would have thought that they were full-brothers – Sammy's driving was every bit as bad as The Guv'nor's!

When I had got up that morning, I had felt that Happy Dene would win, so I was really looking forward to riding her. I had ridden her in her previous race, The Princess Royal Hurdle at Doncaster. It had been a very competitive race and it had sharpened her up really well. When we finally got to Manchester, the mare won, so she must have been good.

Coming back from Manchester, The Guv'nor at the wheel was even worse than Sammy had been! The two prats in the car with me had been drinking at the races all day. Coming up to Hoyland Swaine, near Barnsley, there is a very low footpath – Stirling Maw only had his two near-side wheels on it! We whizzed past a man walking his dog on the path, and only just missed him. The poor fellow had to lean back against the wall, with his arms outstretched as though he was going to be shot, to avoid being hit (God knows where the dog went!). The Guv'nor never even saw him, I swear. What a day!

With Jo's digs and my digs being next-door to each other, our bedrooms upstairs were also next to each other. The windows were about four feet apart. They had ledges or sills at the bottom of them, about eight inches wide. Sometimes, late at night or if no-one was about (although preferably in the dark), we would open the windows and one of us climb into the other's bedroom. It was a bit hair-raising, to say the least!

On one occasion, at 3.00a.m., the police and Mr. Maw knocked on the front door of my digs, asking for me. Some horses had managed to get out of a paddock up at the yard, and no-one could catch them. They were running round the streets of Carcroft. My landlord, Harold, got up and answered the door. "I'll just go and get him up," he said. On this particular night, though, I was in Jo's bedroom. If they'd have gone round to the back door instead of the front one, I could have slipped into my own room without anyone noticing. As it was, if I'd have gone out onto the window-ledge while they were below, they would probably have thought that I was committing suicide! So, Jo and I got dressed and went downstairs. Meanwhile, Harold had found out that I wasn't in my bedroom. "I can't understand it," he told Mr. Maw. "I said goodnight to him at about 10.30p.m., and he went upstairs, but the bed hasn't been slept in." We eventually caught the horses and put them back in the field. Someone had left the gate open.

One of our horses, Duggan II, owned by our local doctor's wife, Mrs. Betty Adair, was a nice, thick-set, chestnut gelding (by Vulgan). I schooled him over fences, and he jumped well. His first race was on 16th February 1962 in a Novice 'Chase at Catterick on a very windy day, and he finished 3rd. There were two divisions of the Novice 'Chase, and horses were falling like nine-pins. One dead horse, Pappa's Pride, was still on the floor at the last from the first circuit. In the weighing room, the lads were all talking about what a rough race it had been, how they had done, and how difficult it had been with the strong wind. "Did you see my fellow hit that fence? Did you see so-and-so go?" they were saying, like they do. "Did you see that jockey's boot up that tree?" asked Mick Batchelor when he came in!

One day, we arrived late at Catterick with the 'box and three runners to find that all the boxes at the stable yard were full. This meant that all the horses had to be made ready in the horse-box on the car-park. I was riding all three, and had some other rides as well, so Jo had to get them all ready, lead them, wash them off, and do them up. As soon as The Guv'nor stepped off the 'box, it was the last you saw of him, except for in the paddock. I had to tack them up between races.

At Ripon, after racing, as usual we were the last horse-box on the park, waiting for The Guv'nor. Nearby, there was a caravan which The Guv'nor had to pass. He lingered near it for a few minutes, then walked on towards us.

"Everything all right?" he asked, as he always did. "Could you do with a sandwich?"

"No, we'll not bother," we replied, sick as parrots that we had been waiting for so long. "We'll get off home. We've got the horses in."

The Guv'nor always did his own thing, so he walked back to the caravan and asked the man what he was cooking.

"Just a few beefburgers," the chap said.

"Can we have three, please, and three teas," he asked, getting his money out.

"There's no charge," the man said.

It was only a private caravan – the man was making his tea after spending the day at the races. He thought it was so funny, The Guv'nor thinking his caravan was a cafe. We were there for another hour. That man ended up buying a horse, and sent it to us to train!

It was about this time that Jo and I decided to get married. After telling our families, I told The Guv'nor. He was a bit apprehensive at first, and asked me if I had given it plenty of thought. He then turned prophet, and said, "It won't last!"

That October in 1962, Jo and I got married at the Doncaster registry office. It was the very day before Fred, the husband of my sister, Betty, had a heart attack and died. He had just finished icing our wedding cake.

We arranged to stay with my dad at Potterton. By now, Joan was married, and Goff was whipping-in for The Belvoir at Melton Mowbray. Goff should have stayed here at Potterton to whip-in the Jack Russells that dad owned, as he had lots and they were running riot! Jo put a stop to that. She wouldn't let them in the living-room. They would stand in the doorway, all upsides, watching every move we made!

Jo packed up work at Owston, but I still carried on. I travelled to and from work (which was about thirty miles), and went racing as well. We had got another car, a second-hand Renault Dauphine, but I was already having trouble with it. So, in January, I also packed up work at Owston. I became a free-lance jockey, and still rode Owston horses whenever I could.

I had a horrible fall at Doncaster on 18th March 1963 riding Hypolytas for Freddy Wiles in a Selling 'Chase, which was brought down at the fifth fence. I was really shaken, and felt terrible, like my liver was in my mouth. In the ablutions attached to the weighing room, with my head down the toilet, I was sick. It wouldn't have surprised me if I'd have died, I felt so bad! Phil Taylor, the jockey's valet, came up to me and said, "Harry Bell wants a jockey for the next race. His jockey's been hurt."

"What?! You must be joking – I feel desperate!"

"Mr. Bell's at the door – go and tell him you'll ride the horse. Put these colours on, get weighed out, then have a wash and a cup of tea – you'll feel a lot better!"

So, that's what I did. Feeling so bad, I struggled with my 20 st. (or that's what it felt like I was carrying) to the scales to weigh out for a filly called Lady Of Kintail, owned by those fanatical jump enthusiasts, Mr. and Mrs. Leggat of Biggar, Scotland. The filly absolutely doddled up – she must have been Champion Hurdle material to win with me on board the way I felt.

The following day, Tim Thompson, Northerner for the Daily Express, put in his racing report from Doncaster:

". . . It's not much fun for struggling jump-jockeys to be waiting on the weighing-room steps, looking for spare rides."

If he'd have been an amateur jockey as well as a reporter (like Marcus Armytage or Charles Fawcuss), he'd have had access to the weighing room and could have witnessed me 'calling for Huey' with my head down the toilet! That didn't leave me time to be "waiting on the weighing-room steps, looking for spare rides"! However, it was a very lucky day for me. Lady Of Kintail was the first of a number of winners I rode for Harry Bell.

13

SETTING UP HOUSE

In the 1962/63 season, the weather got bad – really bad. Racing was abandoned throughout the country. Snow was feet deep, and there was a big freeze in general. We were snowed in at Potterton. It was hardly the time to be going as a free-lance jump-jockey! The poor weather looked as though it would stay for a while, so I got a job working in the piggery where dad worked (we had cleared a path that led to the piggery from the house). I bought Hotspur, my Jack Russell, from my dad, who had bred him there, at the pig farm. He didn't mind the terrible weather, as there were lots of rats about – possibly more than in a normal year, as they would have come into the buildings from outside to get a bit of warmth and food. Although Hotpsur was only about twelve or fourteen months old, he had plenty of practice at rat-catching. In the end, he got very good at it, though he would still be 3 or 4 lengths behind Fagin!

There were something like 4,000 pigs on the place. My job was mucking out sows with litters, before the young pigs were taken off the sows to fatten. It was a thankless job, cleaning those out every day. In the yard there, I had taken so much muck out of the pigs that the muck-heap had an avalanche! The sloppy, horrible shit swept half-way up the yard. We had to set to and clear it with tractors and muck spreaders to get into some of the bottom boxes.

During this exceptionally rough winter, there was only one race meeting held – Ayr. Getting there was going to be a problem, as some of our minor roads were still impassable. As I had a ride, I arranged by telephone to meet Johnny East (the jockey) at his house near Darlington, as we were having favourable reports that Ayr might be on. I dug the car out to get it to a road where the council had got through with their snow-plough and gritted. From Johnny's house, we would have a go at getting to Ayr by train. Racing took place but the horse I went for didn't run. Next day I was back with my old favourites, the pigs. Sometimes life's a bitch – but that's racing! Despite this, Ayr is my favourite racecourse; at a future meeting on 16th March 1964 I had four rides there and rode two winners for Harry Bell – Asian and Nirvaana II.

David Horner, the boss at the piggery, was a really good lad. He was always game for a laugh or a bit of fun. Once, we had two young boars in a pen, and David wouldn't use them. "If you don't use them," I said, "why don't you sell them?"

"I'll sell them to you for 6d (2½ new pence) per pound," David said. "I'll give you two minutes to make up your mind."

"You're on!" I said, after two seconds.

We weighed the two pigs, and I paid for them the next day. A pig-dealer I knew in Leeds bought them from me for 1s per pound if delivered to his place, just a few miles away.

Dave Bowes, a pal of mine who had a permit to train his jumper, Superscope (which I used to ride for him), was a joiner by trade. He owned a fairly new Ford van which he carted his tools around in. The Sunday after I bought the pigs, I went to Dave's house to ask him if I could borrow his van, or if he would take me and the pigs to the pig-dealer's house. After a lot of verbal about "putting smelly pigs in it", he finally agreed to take us, as he considered himself a more capable driver than me, and he didn't want anything to happen to his van.

Dave took all his tools out of it, and I met him at the piggery. We made a ramp for the pigs to walk up, and loaded them without a problem. There was still plenty of snow about. Going down the lane away from the piggery, we had to go steady, as the snow was compact and we had been getting keen frosts at night, making it very slippery. Half-way down, or so, we were talking away when Dave suddenly opened his door and jumped out without stopping the van. It hit the bank at the side of the lane and stalled. The pigs had been rummaging around in the straw that I had put in the back, and one of them had turned round and shat down Dave's neck! He went absolutely crackers!

"Any minute now, this fellow is going to have a heart attack!" I thought.

"Get the b*****ds out!" Dave yelled as he tore his clothes off.

"Settle down, Dave," I said.

"Settle down!?" he said, "I must be f*****g mad listening to you! Why couldn't you get a cattle-wagon to do the job? You're that f*****g mean, trying to save a few bob, you bear no regard to me and my job! I'll have to drive around, now, with the van stinking rotten of pigs! My clothes are bloody ruined!"

He stormed off towards my dad's house. Once he was out of sight, I drove the van to the pigs' destination myself! When I got back home, Jo said that Dave had been really upset, and she had lent him my car to go home in. I washed and cleaned out the van really well with disinfectant and water, but when I returned it, he still complained that it stank of the pigs!

That winter was so severe for such a long time, I actually sawed up two apple trees we had in our garden, to make logs for the fire. I know we all go on about the bookmakers being mean, but in all fairness to them, they had a country-wide whip-round for us jump-jockeys, for which we were extremely grateful. We were paid the money on a scale of how many predicted rides we had lost during the bad weather.

By now, Jo was expecting Alan. Life with father wasn't great, as the old boy was set in his ways and too old to change, so we moved back to Carcroft as a temporary measure, getting digs with Don and Margaret Jackson who we had previously made friends with when we worked at Mr. Maw's. We hoped to settle somewhere around Doncaster, as it is nice and central for racing.

Harry Bell was putting me up quite a bit. I then got a job working for Walter Wharton at Wetherby. Mr. Wharton gave me a wage for riding out and doing horses when I wasn't racing. I wanted to get back into a yard to keep my hand in, as I didn't want to just be a bum, spivving around race meetings.

Now that Jo and I had moved into digs, it wasn't easy keeping Hotspur at Margaret and Don's. Mr. Maw said that he would look after him until we found a house. The Maws, like us, were into animals. My old Guv'nor used to let Fred, the estate gamekeeper, take Hotspur for walks. One day, Fred said that Hotspur had been chasing sheep. He took him back and told The Guv'nor to keep him tied up, but Hotspur got loose and went after the sheep again. Fred shot him.

While I was working for Walter Wharton, I bought a house at Wetherby from Messrs. Thomlinsons, the firm who ran Wetherby cattle-market. "I'll be up tomorrow with the deposit," I said.

I had to go home to my Doncaster digs to get it. The next day, when I returned to the office, I was told by the staff that Mr. Hill, the boss of the firm, who was dealing with the sale, wasn't in and no-one knew when he would be back. I knew that was a whopper, as his car was parked outside: I wasn't amused. The top and bottom of it was that the prat had sold the house for more money, and now didn't have the guts to face me. Grandad, who had bought hundreds of pigs from Wetherby Market, wouldn't have been pleased with Mr. Hill. I bet grandad never welched on any of his deals!

On 30th May 1963, in Balby Hospital, Jo gave birth to our first son while we were at Carcroft. We named him Alan Warwick. Shortly after that, we bought a terraced house at Askern, near Doncaster, which we made really nice and cosy. It was our first home. It reminded me of grandad's house from years back.

After we had bought the house, we had to furnish it, of course. On a shopping spree at Doncaster, we saw an Oxfam shop with all sorts of junk in it. In the window, there was a T.V. for sale, with a '£5 – FOR SALE' ticket on it. Looking at it, it must have been one of the first made. I gave them £10 for it, seeing as it was for a good cause. Earlier on, Jo and I had been admiring a lovely colour television in the Comet shop, which was giving £20 in part-exchange for any T.V., any condition, so we took our newly purchased possession to Comet and did the deal. That is how we acquired our first T.V.

Our first three-piece, we bought from Snowy Wainwright when he trained at Flockton. Enid Baxter, a hairdresser in Askern, whose son worked for Snowy and now works for Michael Stoute, said, "Snowy is getting a new three-piece. His old one isn't bad – he wants £14 for it." David Baxter Snr. brought it up from Flockton in a van for us. At the time, we were a bit stretched, as I had just bought my first brand-spanking-new car. All my many others had been second-hand and kept breaking down, which is where David Bowes probably got the idea that I wasn't a very good driver – no mention on them being knackered to start with!

On the first racing day out for my new car, Jimmy Fitzgerald and I arranged to meet in Tadcaster, where Jimmy left his car, then we drove to the meeting in mine. At the races, I had a fall, breaking my shoulder, and Jimmy had a fall which aggravated his ankle (it had just got better after breaking). On the way back, I drove my car and Jimmy changed the gears. When we had to go our separate ways from Tadcaster (Jimmy to Flaxton Moor, me to Askern), it was very difficult for me to change the gears, as it was my left shoulder that was injured. For most of the way home, I drove it in third-gear, making the occasional change, with the gear-box stiff and having to lean right over. Driving like that was very painful and it didn't do the gear-box any favours either!

When Jo and I went to Liverpool to see the 1964 Grand National (which was the year Team Spirit won, ridden by Willie Robinson, trained by Fulke Walwyn) my shoulder still wasn't better. I drove the car and Jo changed the gears, as she hadn't passed her test at the time. We stood down by The Chair to watch the horses jump. My old pal, Paddy Farrell, took an awful fall there on Border Flight which was to end the great man's career as a jockey. It was a cruel blow for Northern racing, but even more cruel for Paddy's wife Mary and his young family. Having checked with Mary, there was nothing we could do to help. We could tell Paddy's fall had been a bad one. We went home feeling very depressed, without even stopping to eat! It was ironic: Paddy was the third of W.A. Hall's jockeys to break their backs. The first was Matty Hogan, who was riding Wolfhound at Catterick Bridge in a 2-mile Selling 'Chase in October 1950, and the second was Lionel Vick. Lionel's fall at Sedgefield in March 1951 was from a horse called Feathered Fisher, trained by Joe Paisley, which, unfortunately, had a fatal fall and put Lionel in a wheelchair. Lionel had ridden the winner of the Scottish National, Magnetic Fin, owned by Mr. Willis, a Malton farmer, and trained by my old Guv'nor, Mr. Hall.

Paddy was taken to Walton Hospital in Liverpool, then transferred to

Southport. He also had a spell at Stoke Manderville and York. He had a lovely bungalow built for him in a village called Strensall, north of York. Paddy named it Port Luna after the first winner he rode.

One day, I rode a winner of the seller at Southwell for Tony Doyle. The horse was owned by Mr. William Chapman, father of David the trainer. Although the Chapmans are a very nice family, they are very keen regarding financial matters. Instead of giving me 10% of the original stake, which was the custom of that time, Mr. Chapman gave me 10% of the money remaining after buying back the horse, which came to £7. Dave (Dandy) Nicholls, the Flat jockey, must have pleased Mr. Chapman – when he rode Higham Grey a winner, he gave him a dozen eggs! Being involved in more and more paperwork, and with these sorts of goings on, it's no wonder I had to engage Lionel Vick as my accountant. Sadly, Lionel was killed in a car crash in the late sixties just before we started to train.

I was now getting quite a few rides, adding Ben Bielby of Worksop and Russ Hobson (who had a very good horse in Rackham) to my trainers list. I rode a few more winners for Mr. and Mrs. Leggat of Biggar, who had horses trained by several trainers up in the North, and also trained some themselves on a permit. In 1964, the Leggats gave me a retainer to ride for themselves and their daughter, Jane (who is now married to Jimmy Fitzgerald).

Meanwhile I was riding for Pat Ferris, the Lockerbie trainer, at Carlisle. Pat thought that everything he ran would win – he had the most wonderful imagination! That man was a star. Dessie Hughes, the Irish trainer who used to work for him when he was a jockey, can tell a few stories about Pat! Pat is the funniest man I have ever met. He once made a record called "I Know A Little Girl With Pigtails", and he got Kit Patterson (then a prominent Northern Clerk of the Course before he retired) to play it over the loudspeaker at a race meeting at Carlisle!

Pat was the host of Lockerbie House Hotel, and trained about eight or ten horses. He had one horse that was supposed to have finished 4th in the Irish Derby, but Pat used to romance quite a bit, so I'd take that excellent form with a pinch of salt! What I do know is that the horse was a bigger rogue than Al Capone!

One night, Pat rang me up bubbling with confidence, as was his usual self, to tell me about a device he had had made for this Derby horse. He said the horse really went for his new invention. Pat had entered him at Perth and wanted me to go and have a sit on him before the race. Gullible as I was, I trudged off in my Wolseley Hornet to Lockerbie.

In the yard, Pat put round my waist a wide belt which had batteries fastened to it, a switch on the front, and wires running down from the batteries (to be fastened to a pair of spurs I would be wearing)! On his gallop, which was a thirty-or-so acre field, I got aboard the horse and he told me to turn the switch on. Well, I have never gone so fast in all my life! At

Left: 'Bertha', and our two children, at Arksey, near Doncaster. Below: Alan, Sam, me and Bambi. 1967.

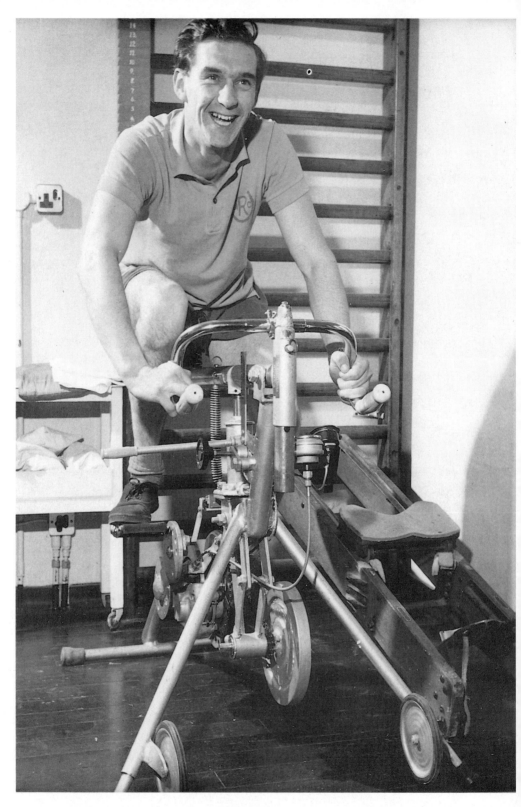

Me, at the Rehabilitation Centre at Camden, in 1967.

Jo riding Fiona's Pet, our first Flat race winner, at Wolverhampton in May 1974.

Two of our best Flat race horses.
Left: So Careful winning a match at
Haydock in August 1988, just before
his victory in The Ayr Gold Cup.
Below: I hold Bri-Eden, ridden by Jo.

Michael Dickinson, being led into the winner's enclosure at Wolverhampton, on one of our best 'chasers, Duffle Coat, in December 1974.

The Moss Side Team in 1980

Almost Blue, ridden by J. Carrol, winning The Molecomb Stakes at 'Glorious Goodwood' in July 1988.

The whole family (myself, Jo, Alan and Sam) with O.I. Oyston – we all rode him in races at some stage of his career.

this stage, I would have believed him if he'd have said the horse had won the Irish Derby! The big field we had set off in now looked like a small garden. My style went to pot, I can tell you, as I fumbled for the off switch!

Pat loved a bit of fun. On another occasion, he asked me if I would bring one of the "jockey-boys" (as he called the lads) up with me and stay the night, so we could have a good schooling session the following morning. So, I got John Doyle (who later took over training at Wetherby from his father). When it was bed-time, having just had a super meal with wine, Pat said to me, "Let's have a bit of fun with John. Tell him I'm queer."

John and I were drawn in a lovely, big, twin-bedded room at the hotel. As we were going to bed, I was telling John, "Watch this fellow, John. He's as bent as a nine bob note, you know!"

"Is he?" asked John.

"Yes, he is," I replied, "And he could come in anytime!"

"Let's lock the door, then."

"No, there's no need for that. I'll tell him to bugger off if he comes in here."

Just as we had settled down, Pat came into our room, wearing just his underpants. "Is he ready, Jack?" he said in a convincing voice. With lightning speed, John jumped out of bed, dived straight out of the open bedroom window (which was two storeys up!), and landed on the gravel outside. Pat laughed so much, tears rolled down his cheeks! John wouldn't come back up to the bedroom until Pat had gone back to his room. When he did, he made me lock the door! Every time I see John now, I ask him if he's seen anything of Pat Ferris recently!

In 1964 season, Pat invited Jo and me to the Dumfries Hunt Ball as it was being held at Lockerbie House Hotel. Our eldest son, Alan, was only about twelve months old. He was standing up in his cot as Jo and I were changing. The hired suit didn't look as good on me as it had done when I tried it on in the shop – the cummerbund was far too big and the trousers looked as though I had been weighed for them! So, I tied a knot in the back of the cummerbund.

I had forgotten my black shoes, so I rang down to Pat to ask if he could lend me a pair. He said he only had the one pair, and he was wearing those himself. Jo and Alan were cracking up – they thought it was so funny! I was getting more and more annoyed. I rang Graham MacMillan, the amateur jockey, to see if he could lend me a pair, but he had already set off to come to the Ball. Then, I rang his brother, Charlie, also an amateur jockey. "No sweat!" said Charlie, in his Scottish brogue.

When he arrived with the shoes, I was already sitting at my selected position at the table, as it was a knife-and-fork do and we hadn't to be late. Charlie handed me the shoes under the table. They were about size 10 or 12, and I took size 6½! At the first chance I got, I went to my room and put my brown jodhpur boots back on. I had lots of dances – not one person said they liked my boots, or even remarked about them! It's a pity I hadn't taken the girl from Walter Wharton's with me instead of Jo!

14

UPS AND DOWNS

I had a ride in the three jump races held at Bogside mixed meeting on 18th April 1964. All three had a squeak and I honestly thought they could win. They were Lady Of Kintail, for Harry Bell, in the Redburn Handicap Hurdle; Candy, for Bill Jones, in The Scottish National; and Safe Approach, for Pat Ferris, in the 2-mile Handicap 'Chase.

Lady Of Kintail obliged in the Hurdle. Candy, cantering down to the start, felt brilliant. In the race I popped him out, as he was a front runner. Going to the first, he stood right back, hit the top of the fence and came a cropper, giving me a pretty bad fall, breaking my nose, cutting my tongue very badly, and giving me concussion. That put paid to my potential treble! He was normally a good jumper; I think he felt so fresh and well that he wanted to get on with things! But, he was too keen and he paid the penalty. Johnny Haine won the race on Popham Down trained by Fulke Walwyn.

Later that year, on 3rd October 1964 at Wetherby, in the Otley 3-mile Handicap 'Chase (which was the first race of the season the B.B.C. televised) Candy made amends. I was coming to the second last fence upsides Peacetown, when Peacetown fell leaving Candy in the clear. Candy ran out at the last and I took him back to jump the fence, this time successfully. Roy Edwards was remounting Peacetown whilst Eric's Star (the only other survivor), who had been tailed off a fence behind, was closing up on us both. It wasn't a close run affair, just chaos for a few moments, because we won by a distance, causing Peter O'Sullevan to comment afterwards on T.V. that if all races had as much incident as that we were in for an interesting season.

That 1964 Bogside meeting, Jo had come with me and we had brought our next-door neighbours with us. They had never been racing before and we had promised them a day at the races. Travelling to the meeting, I had also committed myself to buying them a slap-up meal on the way back if I rode a winner. So, true to my word, I did. While they ate steak with all the trimmings, I struggled away with soup and blood!

The 1964 meeting was in fact the last time I rode at Bogside because the following year on 10th April 1965 (when Jimmy Fitzgerald rode the Scottish National winner Brasher) the course closed. Ironically I had three rides at another course which closed on the same day, Rothbury. At this meeting I rode a winner for Dennis Yeoman, Royal Guard, in the Craigside Selling Handicap Hurdle.

Around about this time on one of my visits to see my old Guv'nor, Mr. Maw, he asked me if I fancied training. "Yes," I said. "One day – but not yet." "Think about it," he said. "The owners would like you to take over."

I felt very touched by this gesture. All I had to do was pay the rent for the yard, as he had to do. Everything else, he would give me absolutely free. The Guv'nor's place was no Manton, but the thought was there. He had never got over me leaving the yard. Jo and I really had our minds set on training one day. In fact, we had started to buy tack here and there. We had bought some rugs, saddles, bridles, and all sorts for the day when we would hopefully make a start. If I had a regret for not taking over the yard it would have been not being able to scrap that horrible horse-box that kicked me so many times and in which I had countless hairy journeys.

On 8th of May 1965, I had a nasty accident at Market Rasen. The saddle of Saint Nicholas, trained by Russ Hobson, slipped and, unable to get free from the irons, I went underneath the horse's belly. As he was galloping, I was bumped on the ground several times before finally parting company. It was an awful fall, very messy. The racecourse doctor had sent me straight to Lincoln Hospital in the ambulance. I had broken two dorsal bones and three vertebrae. The next day, I was taken to the plaster room to have a plaster vest put on me.

It was a warm, sunny day. Some patients had been wheeled out in their beds, onto the lawn, to take in the sunshine. Not to be outdone, when I was being wheeled back to the ward, I asked the nurse if she would push me out for some sun as well. With all the heat, my pot dried too quickly. This caused a bit of a panic, as it was so tight that I could hardly breathe. I had to go back to the plaster room fairly sharpish and get the pot changed.

"I don't like this place at all," I told Ben Bielby when he came to visit me, one day. "Last night, the poor fellow in the next bed died."

That hospital was an awful place. Of all the hospitals I have ever finished a day's racing in, I can safely say that Lincoln is the one I disliked the most. The wards were like Nissen huts – it was so cramped! A lot of the injuries were traction cases, and some of the inmates' fractures were infected. No hospital is nice, but this one was really awful. I couldn't settle there at all. Getting to sleep was impossible, as I was compelled to lie on my back and just look at the ceiling.

The first few days lots of people were coming to visit me. I wasn't well enough to be talking to them for any length of time, so I told the nurses not to let anyone in except Jo. One of the family's best pals, Jack Allen, came on trains and buses from Pontefract to see me. He wasn't well himself. The nurses wouldn't let him in, telling him they had been given strict instructions not to let anyone in. He later rang Jo that night, very upset.

Jo, being a non-driver, relied on Paddy and Mary Farrell, Pat Gulwell, and the lads to pick her up from home and bring her to visit me. It was hours of a job with the hospital being so far away. She was hardly in a fit state to be travelling all that way, every day, as she was only a few weeks off expecting Sam. My old Guv'nor, H.S. Maw, brought Jo on one occasion. Even then we had a laugh about his driving!

Looking towards the future, I had always fancied training, although at the time I didn't have nearly enough money to start. That was something I would definitely have to get over and work at – I had a wife, one youngster and one on the way. So, I thought of ways to make money if I was ever lucky enough to train, like by putting adverts on horse-boxes. Lots carry adverts on their 'boxes nowadays, but I was the first.

I began to plan our yard in pencil (as the biro wouldn't work upside-down!). Drawing the yard, it consisted of twenty-one boxes, a feed house and a tack room, and two passages to walk through to get the hay and straw. I ran the water pipes under the edge of the verandah in the horses' stables, so the heat of the horses would help prevent the pipes from freezing-up. "Paint the stables black and white . . . . racing colours – red, white and blue . . . paddock sheets – the same colours, only in my own design . . . all our stationery the same – red, white and blue . . ."

Doodling away for hours, I gave lots of thought to the idea of training – what type of horses I would like (always wanting speed), how I would work them. I designed round stables to stop the horses getting cast, a mixture for shy feeders, all sorts of things: time was on my side at Lincoln. I even came up with the idea of having grades of staff – muckers-out, yard men, a set of lads and lassies to ride out the horses and a different set to take them racing. For evening stables, the yard staff would come back to groom, etc. In years to come, this won't seem so far-fetched. I got lots of ideas, some of which I haven't yet put into practice, but I hope to some day.

Every Wednesday, the main doctor in charge of operations used to come round. If any patient could be discharged, this chap broke the good news. One of these Wednesdays, when the doctor came round the ward, I got out of bed, sat in my 'chair (like a prisoner hoping to be released), and resisted the nurses' appeals for me to get back into bed as they said I wasn't ready to be discharged yet. Anyway I gave the doctor such a story about the wife expecting and all the travelling in her condition – I got out! I rang Mr. Bielby up, as he was the nearest contact, and he came straight away to take me home.

Once at home, an ambulance picked me up every week day and took me, along with others, to the out-patients at Doncaster for physiotherapy. On these trips to physio, I met a man called Bill Auty, who was recovering from a car crash. He and his brother, John, had a farm at Norton, about three miles from Askern. We became firm friends. The ambulance picked us up at 7.30a.m. to get us to the physio at 9.00a.m. It travelled all over the district, picking people up at various places, so Bill and I decided we would make our own way there in my car, as we were only half an hour away from the hospital.

Jo had our second son on 13th June 1965. He was christened Martin Stratford. When he was born, he had a chubby face and looked a dead ringer for Sam Hall, the trainer, so we nick-named him Sam. The name stuck. The 'Stratford' part and the 'Warwick' part (for Alan) are after racecourses. If we'd have had a girl, we would have named her Wetherby or Beverley.

After a few weeks, I went in the car to hospital to have my pot taken off. It must have been 'pot-casting' day, as lots of people were having them removed. When it was my turn, I went in the plaster room and the man told me to lie down on a trolley. He cut down both sides of the plaster vest and took the front away, leaving me in the bottom half-sandwich.

"Where's your wife?" he asked.

"At home," I told him.

"Who are you with?"

"I came by myself."

"You should have had someone with you! How are you going to get home?"

"In my car – it's on the car-park."

"You can't drive a car!"

"I'll be all right!" I said, "I drove it here."

Then, he went to get a doctor to see if he should put the pot back on or send me home in an ambulance. While he was gone, I tried to sit up, but felt dizzy and weak. Attempting to lie back down, I couldn't get the cast in the right position. When the man came back with a nurse, I was still struggling with it. "Normally, when people try to commit suicide, they take pills or cut their throats!" he said. In fairness to the fellow, they were busy enough without me creating more hassle. The nurse wheeled me off on the trolley into a side room. After an hour of exercises – putting my feet on the floor then back on the bed, sitting up then lying down – I was released. Gingerly driving my car home, I arrived in a muck sweat!

Jo and I went to Devon for a holiday, leaving Sam with Jo's mum and taking Alan with us. We stayed at the hotel of Ian Cocks's parents (Ian was then an amateur rider, who I actually put in for a couple of rides for Pat Ferris – he now works for Weatherby's at the races). We stayed in Devon for two weeks, and had a lovely time. The weather was beautiful, and we came home with super tans – just like berries! After that, I was all right for Market Rasen in August, exactly three months after getting hurt.

Alan was now about two years old, and travelled everywhere in the car with me. He loved it. Even as early as 6.00a.m., he would come into our bedroom and ask,"Where are we going today, Dad?"

121

One Sunday, a trainer was sneaking a gallop on Doncaster Racecourse. As I was to ride the horse, I discreetly planted the car and waited for the 'box to arrive. When it did, I went to get on the horse and left Alan with his bag of sweets and the radio on. While we were on the course, 'matey' started turning the lights on and off, and blowing the horn. He had also turned the radio on full blast and opened the windows! That particular trainer still calls Alan, "Hornblower"!

Mad Mick left Towton. He had taken a job with Mr. Longdon, a permit-trainer from the village of Sutton, near Tadcaster, who also owned the village pub. Mick had a licence to ride – before coming to Towton, he had ridden a couple of winners on the Flat. The first mount I ever saw him ride was at Sedgefield, when I took along a friend of mine from Tadcaster, Walter Parsons, who also knew Mad Mick. Mick was riding longer than John Wayne! I laughed when Mr. Parsons said, "Doesn't Mick look like a bag of you-know-what!" "My day will definitely come, now," I thought. "I can see Mick's not in love with being a National Hunt jockey."

Sure enough, on 29th January 1966 at the next Doncaster meeting, there was Mick, not the same man now that he had a jump-licence out. "He must have a ride for his new boss," I thought. That day, there was a spare in the Burghwallis Novice 'Chase, Red Perion, one of Alf Watson's (of Earby, near Colne). I had been known to send his colours back through the post from hospitals! On one occasion at Sedgefield in a Novice 'Chase, I rode a horse for Mr. Watson called Elfingate, who buried me, breaking my right collar-bone. A fortnight later, making my come back at Bangor-on-Dee, I was riding Elfingate in a Novice Hurdle (I had told Mr. Watson that he would be better over hurdles, as he didn't jump well enough to be going over fences). He was in with a good chance, when he fell at the last. In trying to avoid falling on my sore collar-bone, I kind of twisted in the air, landing awkwardly and breaking two ribs on my other side! Mr. Watson was a nice fellow, but he always had one or two bone-breakers around! Whenever I asked him how the horses were, he would always say, "They're in fine fettle, fine fettle!"

Mick came up to me in the weighing room:

"Oh! Jack!"

"Hi, mate! How you doing?" I asked.

"I've taken a spare in the Novice 'Chase from a fellow you sometimes ride for."

"Oh, yes? Good. Who's that?"

"One of Alf Watson's," he said.

Unbeknown to Mick, Mr. Watson had already told me about his ride. I thought this would be my chance to get a bit of my own back on this ex-piss taker.

"I don't believe it! Honestly? Oh, Mick. I hope you know what you've done! Are you insured? See if you can get off it! I can feel it in my water – it's a brush and shovel job! These Doncaster fences take jumping; they make Wetherby's look like dandy brushes!"

"What's it like?" he asked. "Is it bad?"

"Well, you know me, Mick," I replied, "I would tackle most things – but not that! It's bad enough if you think they might fall, but when you know they will? Phew! The lads at Alf's said the other day that the crab didn't jump over hurdles well, and this is his first time over fences!"

By now, Mick was a nervous wreck.

Down at the start, Mick's horse was not very big, and it was lathered. Sweat was dripping from the surcingle buckle.

"That's not a good sign, Mick – it sweating like that," I said. "You should have put some gloves on – I hope you can hold it all right. Ask the starter if he's got a spare pair, Mick!"

When we lined up, Mick was on the wide outside. He wouldn't give that position up for anyone!

"Keep a good hold of his head, Mick!" I shouted to him as we jumped off.

I never saw Mick in the race. I think he fell off at the first, hurting a bone in his neck, probably not letting the horse go fast enough to jump the fence. He went to the hospital, where they gave him a 'collar for a bit of support for his neck. He wore it for so long that one would have thought he was the local vicar! After that, poor old Mick didn't ride any more. I was told he went to Butlin's to work as a Red Coat!

Red Perion's next race was at Haydock Park on 22nd February in a Novice 'Chase, ridden by P. Jones; he fell. On 7th April 1966 at Southwell my turn came in a Novice Hurdle where I pulled him up.

In March 1967, I had a few rides booked at Wetherby. The first was in a Selling Hurdle, riding Big Star for J. Richardson. As I was cantering down to the post, an ambulance was making its way down the course. On the side of it were the words 'J. BERRY', just like on the number boards in the paddock. I closed my eyes, then opened them again. There it was again. Walking round at the start, as they do, I told one of the lads about it. "I've just had a dream without even going to sleep," I said.

Sure enough, the horse fell and I broke my leg. As I lay near the hurdle, a young St. John's Ambulance lad came over in a bit of a flap.

"Are you all right?" he asked.

"I've broken my leg, mate. There's nothing you can do about it, just give me a fag. I'll hold on to my boot, you put your arms under my shoulders and pull me under that rail on the inside of the track, out of the way of the horses next time round."

After being brought up in my ambulance, the doctor cut my boot off in the first aid room. He had the scissors out and was half-way through one boot before I realised what he was doing! I was very upset because they were nearly new!

An ambulance was going to take me to Harrogate Hospital, but I told the doctor that we had two little kids and Jo couldn't drive.

"She couldn't travel all that way to visit me," I said. "It would be more convenient if I went to Doncaster."

This, he immediately arranged for me.

"You'll have to wait until after the last race," he said.

"That's O.K.," I replied.

I smoked a couple of fags. In between races, the lads kept popping in to see me. They wouldn't give me a cup of tea, in case I needed an anaesthetic.

On arriving at Doncaster Infirmary, the X-rays they took showed that I had broken my right leg in five places around the knee. I was operated on that night, then put in plaster. The comradeship in National Hunt is brilliant – Doug Barrott drove my car and parked it for me on the hospital car-park, then one of the other lads picked him up. (Later Doug was killed in a fall at Newcastle on 28th April 1973 from a horse called French Colonist in The Whitbread, the year it was transferred there from Sandown. It just goes to show that, in National Hunt, one never knows what's around the corner.)

I was allowed home after a few days. The ambulance used to come and pick me up, periodically, as an out-patient to get the leg looked at. The first time it came, after I had been put inside it, Jo and the kids said, "Cheerio!" When the kids realised that I was actually going, I could see them through the darkened windows. The poor, little mites were crying their eyes out, running after the ambulance, shouting, "Don't take my dad! Dad! DAD!"

I was on The Jockeys' Council. One Joint Committee meeting we had was held at the White Post Inn, on the way to Nottingham in May 1967. My leg was still in plaster, and Jimmy Fitzgerald was bandaged up around the head after a fall in a Selling Hurdle at Doncaster. It was a bad fall – in fact, it finished Jimmy; a good jockey he was, too. With all our injuries (and alcohol!), we struggled to get into the car. Jack Boddy was driving, as he was the only one of us who was sound! Two policemen, in a police car parked on the nearby roundabout, were laughing like hell at us. I bet they thought we had escaped from a hospital!

When we got to our house, Jimmy and Jack rang up places that they thought had answering machines (or 'robots', as Jimmy called them!). They had just come on the market, then. The messages and jokes they put on them was no-one's business!

The following day saw my first attempt at driving the car with my pot on. It also saw me get my first speeding offence. I was taking Jo and the kids out for a picnic. With all the time in the world, I just passed some old boy in a village to get by him, as he was loitering. I got fined £20 for doing 46mph in a 30mph zone.

While I was off with my leg, Jo and I went in the car, one day, to Harrogate Horse Sales to buy some more tack (getting ready for the big day when we started training). While we were there, a smart little pony was going through the ring whom we liked the look of, so we bought him for Alan and Sam, then spent even more money buying tack for the pony. The kids named him Bambi. Bill Auty said we could keep him at his farm with his daughter's pony. The two boys had lots of fun with Bambi. Jo took them to horse shows for the leading-rein classes, as I did when I had the time.

Pat Ferris sent me a horse down to ride, which we also stabled at Bill's. He was a grand old horse called King's Crusade, who had won point-to-points. In the past, he had been ridden by Graham and Charlie MacMillan. When I rode him, I had my full-length pot on: young Sam would sit in front of me in the saddle while Alan rode upsides us on Bambi. We covered miles like that, sometimes even popping over little jumps.

When we were in our car going shopping, while Jo was in the shops, Alan, Sam, and myself would play "I Spy" and things. Sometimes, we would make up little songs and sing them. One day, I sang:

"Poor little Jo, out in the snow,
Nowhere to shelter and nowhere to go;
Jack Berry passed by
And she started to cry;
Poor little Jo, out in the snow.

He gave her a shilling to buy her some bread,
When she got back, poor Jo . . ."

That's about as far as I got, as Alan suddenly started to cry – he wouldn't stop! When Jo came back to the car, she asked, "What's the matter with Alan? Why is he crying?"

Martin Hines owned our local garage where I had an account for petrol. Sometimes, I took Martin racing with me, as we were quite friendly. One day, I filled the car up with petrol, then Martin said, "Are you coming in for a coffee, Jack?". I got my crutches from the rear seat and went inside. Martin had a parrot flying loose in his house. What a laugh we had – as soon as I got through the door, the parrot flew onto my shoulder. "He's never done that before," Martin said. "He must like me," I said. He must have thought I was Long John Silver from Treasure Island!

I had an appointment at the hospital to get my pot taken off. After it had been removed, my leg was very weak – there was a lot of wasting and very little bend at the knee. I had a manipulation, a minor operation to give it more bend.

The cubicles in the recovery room at the hospital were only divided by a curtain. Punters having similar minor operations occupied the other cubicles. "What's your name?" the nurses were asking us as they slapped our faces to bring us round. They asked it over and over again. Every time I heard them, I replied in a long, drawn out drawl (being under the anaesthetic), "J . . a . . ck

B..erry". I asked Jo, who I had brought to the hospital with me this time, "Why does she keep asking me my name?" "She's not asking you," Jo said, "she's asking them!"

I was still having treatment for my broken leg. One day, the doctor at Doncaster said, "The only thing that will get the leg right, now, is time and exercise."

"Will you sign me off, then?" I asked.

"Your own doctor will."

"Are you sure you're ready?" asked Dr. Adair (my own doctor).

"If I don't start again soon, I won't have anything to ride."

So, he signed me off, even though I only had half-bend in the leg. When I announced myself fit to ride again, Dr. D'Abreu, the Jockey Club doctor, asked to see me. "This is a bad leg," he said. "How do you expect to ride like that?" He would have been quite happy to rough me off there and then.

For the next six months, I went to Doncaster Hospital every day for physiotherapy. After this treatment, the leg was a lot better. I had about seven-tenths bend in it, but it was very thin and weak.

One day, I got a phone call from Jeff Summers, who worked at the Levy Board close to Lord Wigg. They were promoting a scheme to enable injured jockeys to recover more quickly, and asked me if I would like to be part of it. Great! – I jumped at it. Jeff later went on to become secretary of the Jockeys' Association.

Dr. Somerville and his staff at the rehabilitation centre in Camden Town were brilliant. I was the first jockey to go there. Lots of jockeys have since taken advantage of the facilities at Camden Town. Dr. Somerville and his dedicated staff spent hours and hours working their butts off to get us all better. Although it took fifty-four weeks for that leg to mend, only twelve of them were spent at the centre. If I hadn't gone, I honestly believe that my leg would never have got right. I used to ride a stationary bike at 30mph with 40lb. of pressure on to strengthen my leg. Lord Wigg came to see me at the rehabilitation centre while I was exercising on my bike. He brought with him a photographer and a reporter. My photo on the bike ended up in the Levy Board annual magazine.

15

NATURAL TRANSITION

My old Guv'nor, Harry Maw, isn't well. He's asking for me. A nurse has been coming every day to see him. They want him to go into hospital, but he won't. After a few days, he is saying, "If Jack will come with me, then I'll go."

Mrs. Maw rings me up to tell me this at about 5.00p.m.

"Is it the best place for him?" I ask.

"Yes," she says.

Off I go, straight away. They call an ambulance and put him in. I assure him I will follow in my car.

When we got to the hospital, the young doctor on duty was messing about, doing tests on him. The Guv'nor was cold, and shivering.

"Doctor, I'm not trying to tell you your job," I said, "but can't we put him to bed in the ward? You can do your tests on him, tomorrow. He's so cold."

By now, it had gone 9.00p.m.

"Let me do my job," he said.

"Jack, don't leave me!" the old boy said, then he died.

That doctor definitely shortened his life. He had died of pneumonia, so surely he should have been put to bed. He could have done that at home. Mrs. Maw was in the waiting room. It was awfully sad having to tell her, as they were very close.

Carlisle, Easter Saturday 13th April 1968 was the day of my return to the saddle after breaking my leg. The 13th wasn't my lucky day. I had a fall in the 'Chase on Oban Bay and broke my wrist. Later on in the season my wrist was still niggling me – I felt it especially at Catterick on 19th October 1968 when I rode Slang Cottage in the 3-mile Handicap 'Chase. He was a big, numb bugger that pulled my arms out for most of the way. My next ride was a horse called Basket in the Novice 'Chase for Tommy Sheddon. Cantering down to the start, he was very nearly carting me. I had my full-nelson on him, with my feet somewhere round his ears! When I finally got him anchored at the start, I said to the starter, "Either I rode two pullers today, or I'm getting weak."

Basket proved to be one of the hardest pullers around. Later on, Ernie Fenwick rode him on one occasion at Sedgefield. The horse nipped off going to the start, doing an extra circuit of the course, and ended up in a ploughed field before Ernie regained control. Then, after three or four fences in the race, a distance clear, Basket fell. Ernie, who used to stutter quite a bit, said, "I w-was never s-s-so pleased for a horse to f-f-f*****g fall! He n-ne-needn't b-b-bother a-asking me to ride that f-fu-f***er no more, either!" Basket went on to break the course record at Sedgefield in 1973 for 2 miles over fences, without the assistance of Ernie. He probably still holds the record for going down to the start, too!

Riding at Southwell, one day, in the first race (a Novice Hurdle), the horse threw its head up and hit me in the face, breaking my nose. It didn't hurt much, it just felt kind of numb, but blood was pouring out of it! In between races, I went to the ambulance-room to get it plugged. In the last race, I rode a nice, little, grey horse of Ben Bielby's. Of course, as soon as I jumped off in the race, the plugs came out! The grey was all red down his shoulders when he came in, finishing 3rd. When I went to weigh in, the vet went to the horse in the unsaddling enclosure to see where all the blood was coming from!

Around this time, Jo and I started to give more thought to the possibility of training. We decided to look around for a yard to rent. In the past, I had ridden a few horses for Freddy Taylor, who trained at Low Farm, Almholme, near Arksey (where Peter Ward also trained, before his untimely death in a car crash on the way to the races), and I had also been down there to ride a bit of work from time to time. Remembering that John Masserella (the show-jumping man who owned the great Mr. Softee) was the landlord of Low Farm, we went to see him. I knew him fairly well, anyway, as I had ridden for him when he had runners trained by Freddy Taylor, and I had also seen him hundreds of times at shows when I was a kid.

"Mr. John", as he was affectionately known, could not have been nicer. He went out of his way to help us. The place was run down, as it hadn't been used for such a long time. In fact, pigs had been in since the horses, rooting up the floors and chewing the doors. When the owners of the pigs took them out, they must have forgotten to take the muck with them – the boxes were three feet deep! We set to and threw the muck into the yard, then Mr. John's men carted it away with a tractor and spreader. Next, we mended, washed, and painted all the boxes. My pal, James Kearsley, sent me two lifts of wood and two of his men to underseal the roofs. As the roofs had red pan-tiles on, by undersealing them the boxes became warm and cosy. They also wood-panelled the tack room out for us.

While we were doing all this, a young man came to the yard looking for a job:

"What's your name, mate?"

"John Spouse."

"When do you want to start?"

"Now."

So, he did, and a really good lad he turned out to be. John now works in Newmarket as travelling head-lad for Clive Brittain. At the time, he didn't know anything about horses, but he was very keen and willing.

On one occasion, I was giving John a leg-up onto a young horse we were breaking. Just as I threw him up, he shouted, "Let me go and change my trousers!" "Don't be so bloody soft," I said. "You should come to work in the right clothes to start with!" I was in a rush, as I was going racing. When I drove past him riding down the road, I thought he looked a bit like Quasimodo, the way his back was bent. "I wonder if the lad's messed himself?" I thought, seeing him like that, "And that's why he wants to change his trousers." When I was out of sight, he went back to the yard. Apparently, he had split his trousers, and he didn't have any underpants on!

We worked away and got the place looking good. Mr. John, being the decent fellow he was, never charged us rent until we started getting some horses in. For the first few months, we just broke horses – a good half of them Mr. John's. In fact, we broke Law Court, who was in the British show-jumping gold medal squad in 1978-79, ridden by Malcolm Pyrah.

Mr. John once sent a grey 3-year-old for us to break in – it was the worst wind-sucker I have ever seen! "Do you really want this breaking?" I asked him. "We'll have to do something with it, so you may as well hack on and break it," he said. All night, as we were in bed, we could hear this thing gulping air. Never have we put in so much time breaking a horse – we gave it hours of lunging and driving. After three weeks, so we could send him back, we had broken him to perfection. Monty Roberts would have been proud of us!

Ginger Powell, the Irish breeder and vet, also sent us yearlings to look after, before they were sold at Doncaster Sales. In trying to drum up any work we could, we had an advert running in the local paper:

'HORSES AND PONIES CLIPPED. RING J.BERRY ON DONCASTER 54126'

I was still riding in races, but cut all the unnecessary travelling to ride work unless I was forced to. Nimrod Wilkinson, Paddy Broderick and I arranged to meet at The Scotch Corner Hotel to go to Perth together. At the races, Nimrod had a fall, breaking his collar-bone. We went to the ambulance-room to see him after the race, but the ambulance had already whipped him off to the hospital in the town. So, when Paddy and I had finished riding, we went to Perth Hospital. There was Nimrod, in bed, happy as a sand-boy, with all these little nurses fussing round him. We had a heck of a job getting him out! "You'll have to let him out," we told the staff. "It's only a broken collar-bone. We live getting on for 200 miles away – we can't be coming back for him!" Anyway, they let him out.

Coming back through Newcastle in the early hours of the morning, I was at the wheel and my two colleagues were dead in the back. There wasn't a soul in sight. I was really trapping, meeting all the lights in my favour, when, looking through my mirror, I saw a police car with its lights flashing for me to pull up. When I stopped, the policeman walked up to the car. I rolled down the window. "Was he speeding, constable?" asked Brod. Luckily, the policeman wasn't concerned with that.

"A patient has escaped from a mental hospital with a butchers' cleaver. Have you seen him?" he asked me.

My 'friend', Paddy, told him, "There's no chance of Jack seeing anything, officer, the speed he's driving!"

The policeman was a good old boy. I told him, "If we see the man, and I hope we do, I'll make sure I throw Brod out. Hopefully he might shut him up with his cleaver!"

As a jockey, of all the miles I travelled riding, only twice did I get speeding fines: the first, as previously mentioned, when I took Jo and the kids out for a picnic; the second when I was on my way to Ayr to ride a horse called Vittorio. This horse made me get the only riding fine I ever got in all the time I had a riding-licence. He also got Harry Bell and David Sheddon suspensions. Knowing Vittorio, though, I'm not sure they deserved it with this particular horse!

The first time I rode Vittorio on 12th April 1966, was at Wetherby in the Montagu Hurdle, a race I had previously won for the same trainer, C. H. Bell, on Too Slow. Vittorio was a bit of a lad, always bucking and kicking in the preliminaries. He had very big ears – almost like a donkey! This day, at Wetherby, the horse was in mid-division. When entering the straight, his big ears started rolling around. "Look at this fellow's ears," I said to one of the lads in the race. "I wonder what's the matter with him? Why's he doing it?" I picked the stick up and, with the flap, just fiddled about with his ears. He grabbed his bit and started to motor. He absolutely trotted up beating Rigton Prince, ridden by Kit Stobbs by 1½ lengths.

At a future Kelso March meeting in 1967 I rode him. He wasn't in the first eight jumping the last. All the beating in the world wouldn't make him go until he was ready. Half-way up the long run-in, the ears started to roll. I gave him his usual twiddle with the end of the flap: he turned on the gas and went on to win by a couple of lengths.

When I rode Vittorio at Ayr in the Milsington Handicap Hurdle on 19th May 1969, he didn't get his ears going until he was just approaching the last. He finished 4th, but got hampered by a horse that fell; otherwise he would have won. I got fined £20 for "excessive use of the whip", as the stewards called it: they appreciated that I wasn't hitting Vittorio, but I shouldn't have had my whip near his head, fiddling with his ears. It would have been nice to have kept a 100% record. Mind you, the authorities are far more vigilant now. I don't know what modern stewards would have said if they had seen jockey's like Tim Brookshaw riding a horse in with a squeak going to the last.

Our jockeys come in for lots of criticism nowadays regarding the misuse of the whip. The authorities have recently compulsorily shortened whips to thirty inches long and half-an-inch wide, so that they won't hurt horses as much as they did. If they want to stop all this nonsense about "misuse of the whip" for good, then they should act again and stop talking so much about it! Shorten the whips a further ten inches, and keep them half-an-inch thick. In doing this, one couldn't hurt a horse – you'd be hard pressed to give a dog a good hiding with a pencil!

Instead of suspending jockeys a couple of days for trying too hard, I would suggest taking the whip off them for a week, and making them wear white boots or black breeches, so everyone will know what they have done. That's surely punishment enough, but it's not fair to take their living from them – some of them have wives and kids to support. Often, it can be difficult for them to get back on their mounts when other jockeys have done well on them in their absence. It's a pity some of our stewards aren't magistrates, as child or women beaters and muggers often get off too lightly! When they are guilty of reckless or dangerous riding, by all means suspend them.

The next day, 20th May 1969 at Ayr, I rode a 4-year-old novice hurdler Koh-I-Kan for Eric Collingwood, who now trains in Hong Kong. He told me, "This fellow's dead lazy, Jack – you'll earn your fee! Chase him all the way." Fortunately for me, the horse must have been having a good day, as he won without me being hard on him (I didn't feel like visiting Col. Greig and company two days on the trot!).

In the half-hour between races, there isn't a lot of time for jump-jockeys. Imagine a race gets off at 2.02p.m., finishing at 2.08p.m. If a horse falls, the jockey often has to run back to the weighing room, tell the connections what happened, see the doctor to be passed fit to continue riding, get washed, change colours for the next ride, adjust the weights, pass the preliminary scales, then the official scales, give the tack to the trainer, and get back in the paddock for the next ride at least five minutes before the race, so to save a minute anywhere helps.

In a race at Catterick, one day, my horse fell at the second-last fence. When I got up, Chris "Kit" Stobbs was hacking up behind. His horse had fallen too, at the third last, only he had kept hold of his. "Give me a lift, Kit," I said. "I've a ride in the next." "Hop on!" he said. So, I vaulted up behind him. He was steering and I had my feet in the irons.

Just approaching the stands, we were going faster and faster. "Can you hold this fellow, Kit? He's changed gear – not one side of him."

"He's away!" Kit said.

"Get hold of him and stop pratting about!" Kit was trying to tell me how unlucky he was falling, as he thought he might have won. The people in the stands were cheering.

"It's time I got off, mate! Thanks for the lift!" I then slipped off the horse's back, doing about six brilliant somersaults, to add a few more bruises to my already battered body!

In 1969, I applied for my trainer's licence. I travelled down to London for an interview with the stewards of the Jockey Club, then got it! I was now officially training at Low Farm Stables, Arksey, near Doncaster.

On the way back from London, a message awaited me: David Horner from the pig-farm at Potterton had been killed in a car crash.

Boxing Day, 26th December 1969, we had a horse called Pollibrio (by Con Brio) who we ran at Wetherby. He was owned by Mrs. Poskitt, who was a lovely woman: her son, Mark, and I were very good pals, and used to go hunting together with the Badsworth. Her other son, Ralph, is married to John Masserella's eldest daughter, Penny (Mr. John's other daughter, Diane, is married to Norman Gundhill, the Pontefract Clerk of the Course).

Mrs.'P' also owned Moment's Thought, though he was affectionately called "The Coloured Horse", as he was a chestnut with a lot of white all over him. A most super jumper, it was a pleasure to ride him – he didn't know how to run a bad race, and very seldom made a mistake. We jockeys should have been paying Mrs.'P' to ride him, he was that good! He was trained by the late Tommy Sheddon, the father of my pal from Boston Spa School and ex-friend of Vittorio. Luckily for me, I rode the old boy three winners, or should I say, I sat on him three times when he won!

It was pouring down at Wetherby on Boxing Day 1969. When the trainers were in the paddock, with all the owners in their little groups, Mrs.'P' was on her very own, as Jo was leading her horse round and I was riding him. There and then, I decided: "Do one or the other, Son. There's not a lot of pleasure for our owners standing on their own on days like this." That night I went home and took stock. My riding must be the one to go – forty-six broken bones (about the same number of winners), a few operations through injuries, and concussion countless times. That night, I handed in my riding licence. Very sad, but there you are – one cannot go on forever.

16

FIRST TRAINING SUCCESS

James Kearsley bought a horse-box from Jack Hanson and left it with us at Almholme to transport our horses. I charged the owners and credited James's bill, as he had four horses with us. It was a very big 'box – massive, in fact. It could carry six horses, and could really motor. We called it "Bertha".

One Sunday afternoon, I was doing a little job, locally, with Bertha. There are some very narrow lanes near Almholme. This day, I met a car. The driver wouldn't back up. I got out of the cab and said, "You don't honestly expect me to reverse this great, big 'box? Come on, man! Don't be a prat, just back up."

"I'll stay here all day if I have to," he said. "I'm not going to back up just for you. If you can't reverse it, you shouldn't be driving it."

With that, James Kearsley came up in his car, as sometimes he stayed with us at weekends. "What's to do?" he asked.

"This fellow is being a bit difficult," I told him.

James (who, in those days, was quite a big fellow and very fit) walked up to the man and said, "If you don't move that toy, I'll throw it, and you, over the hedge!"

The poor man ran into his car to reverse it away!

Sandown Sales were on. James had a horse entered in them, so I drove Bertha down there with the horse, taking John Spouse with me to lead him up. We sold the horse. At the Sales, there was one of the nicest looking 4-year-olds you ever did see.

"What's he like?" I asked the lad with the horse.

"He's all right."

"Has he a turn of foot, mate?"

"He's all right."

"Does he jump well?"

"He's all right."

"He is sound? No vices? He doesn't weave? Wind-suck? Crib-bite?"

"He's all right."

That's all he said, just like a record. Anyway, I liked the horse so much that I bought him for 800 guineas. It was a fair price at the time – just as he stood, with breeding I had never heard of and no vet's certificate. The man who bought James's horse asked me, "Would you take the horse back to my place, somewhere near Leicester, only a handful of miles out of your way?" He gave me £20. "Great!" I thought. "I have to go back anyway. £20? Money for old rope! Like taking sweets off kids!"

John and I loaded the horses up in the 'box-park at Sandown. I was reversing Bertha, when a man came running up to the cab, shouting and screaming. He was in a right state! I got out of the cab, "What's your problem?" "My f*****g problem? Look what you've done!" Since we had loaded our horses, the goon had only gone and parked his trailer behind our 'box. I had reversed into it, making a real mess of it. It must not have been very strong – it folded like a match-box! The man was furious! "Settle down," I said. "I'll kill you, you so-and-so," he said, in language not fit for ladies to hear. After a while, through pressure from him, we decided that I would take the two horses he had bought to his home, free of charge (believe it or not, he lived in Winchester – miles in the other direction), and I would pay for his trailer to get mended.

Dropping the horse off near Leicester wasn't as easy as the man had said it would be. When he'd said "a handful of miles", I hadn't looked to see how many times he'd put his hand up – by the time John and I got home, it was 4.00a.m.! My eyes were like pee-holes in the snow. We put our new purchase away, then went to bed. I was so excited, thinking of the new horse, that I couldn't sleep. At 5.30a.m., I got up and put a saddle and bridle on him. What a good feeling he gave me – he was a beautiful mover! We walked and jogged down our lane to the gallops to have a little canter. We jumped off and cantered for a furlong, or so. "Come on, Son," I said, just asking him to quicken his stride. Nothing. He just stayed at the same pace. Dead slow – that was his problem. A big, good-looking, slow bugger.

At 9.00a.m., I put my tack back on him and rode him round to see my landlord. "What's that, Jack?" he asked.

"A young horse I recently bought," I replied. "God it's a good sort."

"Man, it looks capable of winning The Yorkshire Show!" he said.

This was music to my ears because Mr. John was a great judge of a horse. "How much have you got in him?"

"Anything over a thousand is a bonus." I replied.

"I've got the very man for him."

He sent a man down at lunch-time. I sold the horse for 1200 guineas to go showing – he did all right, too. The profit at least took the sting out of the repair bill for the trailer I crushed at Sandown!

At Almholme, we were short of somewhere to put up some fences. Down the lane was a paddock, very long but not very wide (about three acres), only it had dozens of felled trees and old tree-roots in it. They had been put there, and had been there for years. On one of my regular whinges to poor old Mr. John regarding improvements to our lot, I asked, "For a minimal fee, would it not be possible to rent that paddock so we could make it into schooling ground?"

"It wouldn't be much use to you with all that rubbish on," he said.

"No, but I intend to get rid of it."

"Okay – you can have it. You don't have to pay me anything, either. It'll be a bloody long while before we see horses jumping in there."

John North and I were good pals. He was a cattle-dealer and a farm contractor. So, I rang him up that night and asked him if he and his wife, Coral, fancied coming out for a meal, as I wanted to have an important chat with him regarding this paddock. I told John all about the trees and roots. "Would it be possible to collect them all up in a heap? We'll have a barbecue afterwards, inviting all the people we knew – friends, owners, etc." "I've the machinery to do the job," John said.

One weekend, John, David Bowes, and a couple of farm lads who John knew, dragged these great big trees into a heap. John had a big tractor with a front-end loader. "It isn't a problem," as John said. We put a few bales of straw in it, then got all the burnable rubbish that we could find from around the yard. With five gallons of red diesel ready, we sent out the invitations to our party.

One of our owners was a dentist – his wife did the sweets! Rosemary from the village, Coral, Shirley (David Bowes' wife), and Jo barbecued portions of chicken, beefburgers, sausages, etc. We had a barrel of cider and people brought bottles of spirits. It was fantastic – we had a great night! It was the biggest bonfire I have ever seen, I've never seen a fire like it. It was going strong for two days. Mr. John put some bullocks in to tear off the old grass, then we harrowed and rolled it. That paddock made a brilliant schooling ground.

The first winner ever trained by us was Camasco, on 16th December 1969, at Kelso, in the Earlston Handicap Selling Hurdle for conditional jockeys. It was ridden by Tony Potts and owned by James Kearsley. The 1.30p.m. race was the first on the card that bitter cold day. Tommy – as we nick-named him – in a field of seven, was always prominent. He took up the running going to the last hurdle and drew clear to win by 3 lengths, beating Botum. His starting price was 8/1 and for his effort, the winning prize money was £137. On the owners behalf, I bought Tommy back for 280 guineas.

Stuart Oliver, Ken's son, did the auctioneering that day for us. Stuart was also a capable amateur rider. When conducting the auction, he said:

"Ladies and Gentlemen, Camasco won very easily today and looks the type to go on and win over fences."

As Tommy was a very small horse, at this statement by Stuart, I said, "When he runs over fences, I will ask you to ride him!"

It was a brilliant day; I was over the moon we had trained a winner. The little fellow had been good to me – I had also ridden him a winner at Wetherby when he was trained by my mate Colin (Shadow) Dukes.

On the way back, I gave a horse a lift to Derek Bestiman's, who trained near Wetherby. Leaving Bestiman's yard at about 9.00p.m., we had to go over some crossroads on the Leeds-Wetherby road. Bertha started coughing and spluttering. The old bag air-locked right across the main road and stalled. Within minutes, it was impossible to see the end of the traffic on either side of the road. Wetherby police came and sorted us out. They were really good – they got Vaudby's Garage to tow us to their place in Wetherby and free the air. The mechanics there worked like demons to get us going. We finally got home at about 3.00a.m., but it was all worth it. We had had a winner. The next day, Pat Ferris sent us a telegram, reading:

TRAINER EXTRAORDINAIRE JACK BERRY,
LOW FARM,
ALMHOLME
ARKSEY,
NR. DONCASTER.
THE GOLD CUP AT CHELTENHAM OR NATIONAL, TOO,
WILL NEVER MEAN AS MUCH TO YOU:
TO GET YOUR FIRST ONE PAST THE POST
IS THE THRILL THAT YOU'LL REMEMBER MOST;
I'M SURE A PARTY YOU WILL THROW,
BUT DON'T FORGET TO TOAST KELSO;
CAMASCO YOU'LL REMEMBER BEST
SO GIVE HIM LOTS OF GRUB AND REST;
AND AS YOU LOOK ON HIM WITH GLEE,
GIVE HIM AN EXTRA PAT FOR ME.
EX-OWNER, TRAINER, POP-STAR, NOW CURRENTLY APPEARING
AT THE MINISTRY OF LABOUR
PAT FERRIS.

I went to Ascot Sales and bought Gameone for 310 guineas, who used to be trained by the great Fred Winter, then trained by Ken Payne. The horse had lost his sparkle – he used to drag himself around the roads, listless. When I brought him back home, I couldn't sell him to any of our owners – they didn't want to know him. Bit by bit, though, the old fellow started to enjoy life, again. He'd give a buck and a squeal. His first run for us was in The Bishop Auckland Handicap 'Chase at Sedgefield on 23rd February 1971. He ran a cracking race to finish 3rd, beaten 2½ lengths, 3 lengths by The Celestial Traveller and Glenkiln (in a fast time).

His next run, on 3rd March 1971, was in The Border Selling Handicap 'Chase at Ludlow. Glenkiln was running in a Handicap 'Chase at Wetherby on the same day. In the morning papers, Glenkiln was 2/1 favourite. Our fellow at Ludlow in the Selling Handicap 'Chase had 10st. on his back, and wasn't in the betting. Just a few days earlier, I had sold a half-share in him to Peter Parkinson from Leeds. Gameone absolutely hacked up by 10 lengths ridden by Tony Potts, who used to ride our jumpers (he now trains a small string near Doncaster). On the race, I won £1,600, which to me was an absolute fortune! Glenkiln, trained by Ken Oliver, was 3rd in the Wetherby race.

Bertha was expensive to run, plus there was the fact that she belonged to James Kearsley: it was time I bought my own 'box. With my newly made fortune, I bought a second-hand one for £1,400 from a firm near Wetherby who made 'boxes. They had taken this one in part exchange. It was a Bedford and a bit old, but it was a good runner. It had a wooden body and a funny-shaped cab.

The following week, we ran Gameone at Huntingdon in another Selling 'Chase. The race came just a bit soon for him, as he liked to run fresh – the three races in the month had just taken the edge off him. He won by a head, but had to fight for the win, not like at Ludlow where he doddled up. At the auction, we were let off the hook – we had to buy him back, but not for much. The auctioneer told my girl to stop as she was walking him round in the winning enclosure while he felt his legs, although he had been fired. He then got on his rostrum and announced the horse had got good, sound legs without a blemish on them. I didn't say anything at the time, but I thought, "I wouldn't like this banana to vet a horse for me!" In the rule book, I don't know whether this practice is permitted, but I thought he had a neck!

Johnny Kenneally, the ex-jump-jockey, was about to pack up training. He told me he had a set of starting stalls for sale for £750, so I bought them from him that same day at Huntingdon. On seeing Ken Payne at a Catterick meeting shortly after, Ken asked me if I was "pleased" with the old horse! I used to keep looking in the sales catalogues to see if he had any more like him entered!

Alan Mactaggart, then an amateur rider and permit-holder (now a Northern Steward), rode a horse of his at Sedgefield which broke down. Alan asked me if I would mind giving the horse a lift to Kirkby Fleetham on my way home, "There's a lady with a livery yard who'll look after him," he said. "And Mr. Ashby, a man who treats such injuries, can see to him." When we put the horse into our 'box, he was sweating quite a bit with the pain. "Make sure the rug goes out of the 'box with the horse," I told John.

When I got to our destination, I found a nice bit of grass to let the 'box ramp onto, rather than use the rough gravel on the lane, so the poor horse could have a bit of cushioning as he was very, very lame. A military-looking man came flying out from the yard. "Put that horse back in that 'box, boy, and bring it round the back!" he yelled. He came right up to me, within inches, his face as red as a beetroot.

The next day was Sunday. When I went to clean the 'box out and give it its

"Do you own this place?" I asked.

"Yes, I bloody well do!" he replied.

"Take him where you like," I said, wrapping the shank of the head-collar three or four times round his neck. His face had now gone blue. Then, a young woman came onto the scene, frightened to death after seeing this animal-hater wrestling with a rope with a horse on the end of it. Apparently, she rented the yard from this man!

The next day was Sunday. When I went to clean the 'box out and give it its weekly hose-out, I found Alan's horse's rug inside. John was still having his breakfast (it was his day off, but he lived-in with us). "When you've finished your breakfast," I said, "take that rug you left in the 'box to the yard in Kirkby Fleetham where we dropped that horse off yesterday." He hitched forty (or so) miles to deliver that rug, but his memory improved on account of it!

The summer of 1971, James and Chris Kearsley, Anthony and Pip (their two children), Jo, Alan, Sam and myself, all went to Majorca for a week. Except for going to Ireland with Paddy and Mary Farrell, that was the only time I had been out of the country. On the Sunday, I went to Palma, as I couldn't wait to see a bull-fight. The minute I saw inside the bull-ring, my adrenalin got going. After watching the bull-fight, I still had that gut feeling: I would have loved to have had a go.

The opening day of the 1971/72 season, 31st July, Tony Potts broke his leg on Roger's Bet, one of our horses, at Market Rasen. It was a bad break, and poor, old Tony had to pack up riding on account of it. When I went to Lincoln Hospital after racing to see him, he was in a lot of pain. On the way back home, I felt so bad for Tony that I even stopped at a pub and had a couple of drinks – a thing I had never done before or have done since (not on my own at least!).

17

TIME FOR A CHANGE

One day, I said to my pal, James Kearsley, "Arksey, here, may be all right to start training from, but I wouldn't like to spend the rest of my days here, training. There's a lack of facilities. The ground gets baked up. So it will never be ideal."

At that time, James lived at Windermere with his first wife, Christine. As I didn't have much money, I wanted to form a partnership, if possible, to buy a farm, make some good gallops and some schooling grounds, and build the yard I had designed when I was doodling for hours lying on my back in Lincoln County. I wanted to train some more winners.

"Let's keep an eye on farms for sale," James said. "They'll be advertised in *The Farmer's Guardian*." So, that's what we did. We went to see a farm for sale near Harewood, Yorkshire. It had some very nice buildings which could have been converted into boxes, and a beautiful house. The land was stony, though, so that put paid to that. Then, James rang up. "Get in your car and come to Forton Services, junction thirty-three on the M6, going towards Carlisle (In those days, they called the M6 'The Preston Bypass'). There's a farm near there for sale."

He had seen it advertised in the Lancashire Evening Post. Keen as mustard, I met James at Forton Services. I followed him through a sleepy, little village called Cockerham, which consisted of a village hall, a pub, a school, and a small police station on the shore-road towards Blackpool. We took a left. Now on Crimbles Lane, about a mile down, we came to the most dilapidated farm you ever did see. The land was all grass, just short of 100 acres. The farm was owned by a very nice family by the name of Hunter. Mr. and Mrs. Hunter had bought another, bigger farm, as this one was a bit small for them now that they had a grown-up family.

The whole place wanted pulling down and rebuilding. Personally, I liked the land (or most of it). It had potential. The house was awful, and the buildings were no good. The Hunters told James and me that the farm was coming up for public auction in about three weeks time. James and I went back to Forton Services and talked about the farm over a cup of tea and a sandwich. "If you wouldn't settle for the farm near Harewood, I hardly expect you to go a bundle on this run-down, wreck of a place," James said.

"On the contrary," I replied, "I like it."

"You're joking!"

"No, I really do like it. Well, I like the land. The buildings were all useless. Most of them were wood, and absolutely rotten, damp and very depressed."

We were also training for Colin Nutter and David Hall, both Lancastrians, at the time. James and I called a meeting with the two of them to see if we could buy this old farm between us. Colin, David, and James would be sleeping partners, then I would buy them out as we went along, or something like that. We all decided we would have a go at it. Three or four days before the auction, James and I went back to see Mr. Hunter. We bought the farm for £46,000 so he took it off the market.

We settled up with the Hunters. James arranged with a demolition firm to take all the buildings down. There was no go in them at all though – they were messing about, just taking the slates off the roofs and the best of the timber, etc. I went down and told them, "You've got till the end of the week to take what you like. On Monday, we're going to burn the rest of it, and I don't want you on the place."

On the Monday, builders started to gut the house. I left Jo to run Almholme Stables. We bought two second-hand caravans, then I moved into one, taking two of our lads from Almholme, John Spouse and Rob Henshaw, who moved into the other. For two whole weeks, it rained all the time. We did nothing but burn – all the buildings, cow mistles, pigsties, garages, huts. All the metal – an old car, washing machines, bits of tractors, all sorts – we put in a big heap. Colin Nutter took it away for us, as Colin was in that trade. We just wanted rid. After our burning spree, all we had left standing was the house and one barn.

The first job we did was erect a pre-fab in the orchard for the staff. Next, we raised the whole area of the stables three feet to the level of the house, by buying tons and tons of hard-core. A lot of it was bought cheap from a contractor pulling houses down in Lancaster, who was glad for somewhere local to tip it. All the natural stone that was mixed in with the bricks and rubble we kept on one side to build walls and face stables with at a future date. Wagons were queuing up down the lane, waiting to come up to get tipped. We hired a caterpillar to track the hard-core in, then we got tons and tons of crusher-run to level everywhere up. We then sent the designs for the boxes off to Harlows of Loughborough for them to make up. We put the concrete base down, put new drains in, then the yard was tarmacked by a firm called Harbour & General. Unfortunately, this all happened at a time when the whole of the building industry was on strike. Anyway, the firm kept sending us some workers. It was a struggle with the labour they sent up, as the key people weren't allowed to come because of the strike.

Harlows came and put up the twenty-one boxes, feed house, tack room, and two passages. They were really good – all in a few days. We got an electrician from the village to wire them all up and put some lights under the verandah, then brought our horses, dogs, cats, bantams, and kids to Cockerham. My old pal, Harry Wharton, took Almholme over. He gave me £1,000 for leaving things for him, in way of valuation. At least it was in a lot better nick for him than it had been for us when we went there!

Jo, Alan, Sam, and Bouncer (our Labrador) moved into the caravan, as the house was being done up. The dog hated it and left home. We never saw him again, after endless hours of searching. At the time, we also hated it because it did nothing but rain – we were never out of wet clothes. Jo had to take young Sam to Beverley for her mother to look after, as he had an awful cold. The highlight of our week was Sunday, when we boiled the kettle to get washed with, got changed, then went to Forton Services on the M6 for a good meal.

Every other night, Jo and the lads would mix up a mountain of cement, by hand, after stables. I would turn the verandah lights on and work right through the night, stone-facing the boxes. In my spare time through the day, I would get my stone ready for the next night. We bought some slates and hired a slater to put them on the roof. This took six weeks to finish.

At Almholme, we had trained about fifteen horses, but most of the owners didn't come over with us as the move was such a long way. We brought seven horses with us. There were no record-holders amongst them, either – with all their abilities added together, they would have struggled to win a Selling Hurdle around Sedgefield! David Hall bought a horse out of the *Horse and Hound* for £600 called Casualty Call (by Bleep Bleep). We called him Stan. The beggar was a savage, though as bad as he was, we all liked him. On 2nd September 1972, he was the very first runner we had from Moss Side Racing Stables, ridden by Pat Buckley, the jockey who rode the 1963 Grand National winner, Ayala, trained by Keith Piggott, Lester's father.

Stan won the Shylock Novice Selling Hurdle for us at Stratford. This was confined to 3, 4 and 5-year-olds, and the prize money was the same as Camasco had won at Kelso in 1969. The prize money hadn't altered at all in low grade races. We had fancied him a bit, so I had told David Hall to have a few quid on the horse, especially as the race was a seller. He had had £5 each way. He returned 5/2 second favourite. While I was bidding at the auction to get Stan back, David, the professional gambler, was standing behind me. "You've gone far enough (the bidding was around 400 guineas). If you bid any more, you'll own him yourself!"

Anyway, I bought Stan in for 500 guineas. To celebrate our first Cocker-ham win (I was absolutely over the moon!), we went to the bar and I ordered a bottle of champagne. David was telling me it didn't make sense having to buy back your own horse, to win a race and cost him money. He finally agreed to still be the proud owner of Stan and pay for the champagne. For this, I was relieved and grateful as I couldn't afford to be writing out cheques for horses, buying champagne, or boozing and paying owners for the few horses we had! This was also David's first win. Had it have been my first win, I think I might have got a bit more excited than this fellow, though! It takes all sorts.

I ran Stan again the following week at Worcester, in another seller. I was justified running him in sellers, as he was a 5-year-old, entire horse who had been fired, and we had a soft-palate operation done on him for his wind. He would rather eat people than oats! Getting David to allow me to run him in another seller was a work of art. "The old boy is only good for a seller," I told David. "If anyone bids for him this time, it'll be a good way of selling him, as it isn't easy keeping him sound."

Stan duly won again. This time, there was no bid. It never happens when you want it to! David sold Stan shortly afterwards, but he never ran any more. At least the old boy had got us off the mark with a couple of wins.

Ted Briggs, a local farmer, owned a horse called Gay Como in partnership with another farmer, Ernest Pawson. Como was trained by Snowy Wainwright in Malton, but Mr. Briggs and Mr. Pawson wanted their horse nearer to home, so one day Mr. Briggs called at the yard to ask me if I would train the horse for them. Thrilled to bits that someone had actually *asked* me to train a horse, needless to say I did not need asking twice!

The horse duly arrived, looking good. At the time, it was very wet and this horse couldn't go a yard on the soft. Mr. Briggs came down to the stables most Sundays to see Como – he and his partner were looking for a touch. Every Sunday, it was beginning to sound like a record: "It's too soft. Be patient; let's wait until the better ground comes." Added to the fact that he acted best on right-handed tracks, it meant our chances were limited.

Sometimes, we took Como to the beach at Fluke Hall near Pilling to work. On the sound surface, he went like a dream. We had him well entered up, as it was the three-week entry system then, not the five-day one like now. Carlisle was coming up and the going was good – I told Mr. Briggs we would run Como there, in a conditional Selling Hurdle. "The horse could fall, get up, and still win!" I told him, after seeing and studying the entries in *The Sporting Life*.

He made me swear secrecy – I wouldn't tell a soul about this horse, and he would have a real go on him (I didn't have to back him, as he would look after me!). I thought it a bit unfair not to let at least our other few owners in on the fact that we fancied Gay Como, seeing as Mr. Briggs always wanted to know when *their* horses passed wind!

Anyway, the big day at Carlisle came, on April Fool's Day 1974. When I got to the races, the first people I saw were Mr. Briggs and his son, Jim.

Reassuring Mr. Briggs that the horse was as well as when he had phoned up that morning and that I was still as confident, he went on his way, leaving me with my new-found friend, his son (who followed me around like a dog follows a bitch on heat, right up until the race had started!). In *The Sporting Life* prices that morning Como was 10/1.

Thankfully, ridden by Kevin Grey the horse duly won by 8 lengths, opening up 4/1 in the betting and returning 2/1 favourite. Messrs. Briggs and Pawson kindly invited me to the bar for a drink and the big pay-out. We found a table in the corner as Mr. Briggs ordered the drinks. We were huddled in that corner as if we had just robbed a bank! Mr. Briggs pulled out a wad of notes that would have choked a donkey! "God," I thought, "If he gives me that, our chickens certainly won't need to worry for a bit – I'll fill the freezer up with proper meat! Should we struggle on at Cockerham or buy a yard at Newmarket?" Heart in my mouth, he peeled me four tenners off. It's true one can spoil people giving them too much too early. On this occasion in my opinion Mr. Briggs didn't overdo himself. I don't want to sound ungrateful, but Mr. Briggs didn't get where he is today by throwing his money around!

Gay Como's next outing was at Perth on 23rd April in a handicap, with third top weight of 11st. 10lbs. There were sixteen runners and again, ridden by Kevin Grey, he won.

We then put an indoor-school up, building up a very good schooling ground, with some lovely hurdles and fences. We worked away, trying to fill the yard up. We had lots of people coming round to see what we were doing, as racing was then unheard of in this neck of the woods. It wasn't easy getting local owners.

Desperately trying to improve the quality, I went to Doncaster Sales. I went through the catalogue so many times, trying to cut out the deadwood and see which horses I thought might improve, etc. Reading through the vendors remarks about their horses, one sees such things as, "Sure to make a top-class hurdler . . . will make into a nice 'chaser . . . this fellow looks like going to the very top . . . has been corn-fed since birth.." What rubbish! What would one expect to feed it on – nuts and bolts? It's like when some farmers are seen feeding their sheep in winter. It's pouring down, blowing a gale, freezing cold, and he walks into the field with a sack on his back with half a bucket (or so) of sheep-nuts in it, to feed possibly sixty to seventy sheep. They bleat like mad as they follow him, and have just about eaten the nuts before they drop into the trough. When people see this, they think, "Don't those sheep love that farmer!" Nothing to do with the poor sods being hungry!

At the Doncaster May 1972 Sales we bought Glenzier Lad, formerly trained by Barney Cross. He was to be a great horse for us. I sold a half-share in him to Harry Arundel at the sales (as he couldn't afford the whole share). We advertised the other half-share in the local newspaper, then Mr. and

Mrs. Sam Vernon bought it (Sam was a retired chemist). We nick-named the horse Barney, after Barney Cross. What a character Barney was! When we used to turn him out for a couple of hours every day in our orchard, he would roll in the pools of water getting really plastered in mud! He won some nice 'Chases for us, on a couple of occasions ridden by my old pal, Jonjo O'Neill. When Barney retired, we gave him away to someone to hack about on.

Mr. and Mrs. Vernon proved to be first-class owners. In the September St. Leger Sales that year, they asked us to buy them a yearling. We bought them a filly, who they named Fiona's Pet. Ironically, she was by the same sire as Stan, Bleep Bleep. She was a very fast filly, but just a bit of a short runner. When jockeys rode her in races, she gave them such a good feel that they hung on to her instead of letting her run the 5 furlongs and poach a couple of lengths. Fifty yards out, she would fold up, just not getting home.

On 6th May 1974, at Wolverhampton, Jo rode her in an amateur race, just short of 6 furlongs. Jo popped her out and let her run. She was clear half-way, then, shortening her stride inside the last half-furlong, she held on to win by a short head, beating My Eagle, ridden by Merinda Frieman. A further short head away on Regal Bingo was Merinda's sister Katherine. Twenty-five ran. She was our first winner on the Flat. It was nice that Jo rode our first Flat winner, as she had worked so hard; she so richly deserved to win.

We had had a bit of luck getting her there that day. Jo was going racing with Mr. and Mrs. Vernon in their car as they only lived at Garstang (a few miles from the yard). I was driving the 'box down to Wolverhampton when the fan-belt broke. I pulled in at Keele Service Area on the M6, where, fortunately, there was an A.A. man. "I shouldn't touch Commercials," he told me when I approached him. He didn't have a 'belt to fit, so he went in his van to a nearby garage, got one from there, and fitted it on his return. After paying him for the 'belt, he wouldn't take anything for his work. I managed to persuade him to take a fiver, telling him to put it on the filly – if I got there (as time was ticking on and she was in the first race). The man assured me he would have the bet on, as he had a bet every day anyway. The filly's starting price was 20/1. I sincerely hope that A.A. man put the fiver on – he was one of life's gentlemen, and without him, we would never have got to the races!

We were quickly starting to get lucky. A young horse we had bought privately, called Duffle Coat, for Peter Parkinson & Partners, had just started to get his act together over fences. The previous season, 1973, he ended on the floor three times on the trot when he looked like having a winning chance, each time ridden by Tommy Skiffington, who now trains successfully in America. One day a man came into the yard and asked me if I would buy some big beams from a church that was being demolished in the Manchester area. We built a stiff schooling course alongside a hedge in one of our fields, with the fences at varying distances apart. Every day of that summer, we put boots on all four of Duffle Coat's legs and I rode him over the beams before turning him out for the day. We also gave him lots of schooling over our normal brush fences which we stiffened up. The horse became a brilliant jumper and in the 1974/75 season he won first time out at Sedgefield over fences and again seven days later at Bangor-on-Dee. He went on to win five of his first seven races that season scoring also at Wolverhampton, Doncaster and Ayr.

At Cockerham bit by bit, we drained land and put better perimeter fences up. Always up against it financially, our partners didn't sleep for long and wanted out. We got George Leatham and Alan Binns, two of our Doncaster owners, to arrange a deal on our behalves so Peter Moores could buy the land from us, then lease it back on an agricultural tenancy. Moores weren't interested in the house or buildings, just the land as an investment. We sold the land for exactly the same price we had paid for the farm and land. We just kept the house, the buildings and three-quarters of an acre in order to expand them.

We arranged a meeting with our shareholders at Colin Nutter's office in Bury, where we concluded the deal and paid back all the partners who had invested in Moss Side. All the negotiations were done in a friendly manner, and we continued to train their horses for them. After terminating that partnership, I formed another one with Jo. Then, we got a mortgage from the bank. It was a real struggle, though. Afterwards, the bank manager hardly missed a day ringing us up, asking when we were going to give him some money. Every cheque Jo or I wrote, we had to ring the soft sod up and ask him to honour it.

Jo and I never paid ourselves a wage, and we worked all the hours God sent. Jo led most of the horses up, and I drove the 'box. On race days, as soon as it was light, Jo and I would ride and muck out three or four horses each, to give our staff a bit of a start.

We always tried never to owe money to individuals – it's the bank's job to lend money. This is why I am so grateful to Willie Stephenson and Ken Oliver, who always gave me a bit of credit and let me buy horses at Doncaster Sales. They knew I wouldn't rest until I had sold them, and that the minute I did, they would get the money.

On one occasion, I rang a publican in Preston, called Don Goodfellow (who, someone told me, was interested in horses) to see if we could arrange a meeting in his pub with all the landlords of Preston (and there are dozens of them!). I told him I thought it would be a good idea if we could get them together to form a syndicate in a cheap yearling I had bought. Don told me the likely ones.

We arranged a meeting at Don's for 7.00p.m., thinking it would take an hour, or so. I think these landlords thought it was a good idea to have a piss up. They were drinking all night. I was laying up with them, as I wanted to conclude a deal, though it isn't my style to drink so much. Most of them got paralytic, but I got my cheque for the ten shares and all the relevant forms that needed signing, signed. The bad head the next day was worth it!

I sold them a pretty, little, grey filly (by Abwah) that we had bought for £500 at Doncaster Sales. Up The North was her name. She won a race for them at Hamilton, on 17th June 1982, ridden by our Sam. She was also placed a few times, and they had a lot of fun with her. It just goes to show: everything has a time, and there's a time for everything!

Although I was a jump-jockey, I love 2-year-olds and sprinters – they are so innocent and unspoilt. When I rode out for Tony Doyle at Wetherby, I often rode his 2-year-olds. Be fair with them and give them plenty of love and care – if they are sharp enough and have it in them, they will repay you. Darryl Sherer, a racing reporter who writes for the *Thoroughbred News* in Australia, calls me 'King of the Kids', and Dr. Cornelius, a stud owner in Holland, refers to me as 'Mr. Two-Year-Old'.

One day Jo and I called into Robinsons, the shop on the way to Haydock, to buy some grooming kit and odds and ends. In a particular part of the shop a man was waving a lunging whip (sometimes called Long Toms). We weren't taking a lot of notice of him but when we arrived at the cash desk to straighten up, this fellow was there in front of us weighing in. His goods consisted of two Long Toms, several whips and a pair of spurs. At the sight of this Jo and I cracked up laughing, I said to Jo, "I bet this fellow doesn't give his 2-year-olds much love". I wouldn't fancy Olly would be keen on a vacation at his place either.

We had a lad working for us called Simon Shaw. He was supposed to be able to ride, but there's riding and riding – at the time, this fellow wouldn't have been safe in a brand-new car with its doors locked! He was so slow and useless that his parents actually offered me money to employ him!

His mother, Barbara, sent us her 11-year-old jumper, Blue Nip. A nice old horse, but not gifted with a lot of speed. As a 7-year-old, he had won a point-to-point. We ran him in a Novice 'Chase at Carlisle on 19th September 1977, in which he jumped well and finished 3rd of the four runners, ridden by Jonjo O'Neill. The next time he ran, 27th September in a 3-mile Novice 'Chase at Sedgefield, he won very easily, ridden by Michael Dickinson. The following morning, at 3.00a.m. Jimmy Shaw, Barbara's husband, rang me up from Germany. "What right have you to run the horse while I'm away? I'd have liked to have had a good bet on him!" Anyway, galloping downstairs, bollock-naked, to answer the phone at that time of the morning just to take all this ear-ache was too much for me. I said, "If you haven't got your useless lad and your horse out of our yard by the weekend, I'll turn the pair of them out!"

The following day, he rang up again, full of apologies, so we kept both of them. The horse never won again, and the lad didn't top the jockeys' list! But to be fair to Simon, he did improve. When he left us, he went to

Maryland, U.S.A., where he rode seventeen winners in his first season. His career was cut short with a bad fall in which he received head injuries. He now works as an assistant trainer in California.

Dick Gibbons, one of our owners, was a farmer who lived near Carlisle. Dick loved his racing. On the way back from an Ayr meeting, I called at The Dunwoody Lodge on the A74, where racing people used to congregate for a drink and a bite to eat after the Scottish race meeting. Dick was already there. When we had finished the meal, he invited me to his house for a coffee and something stronger – he wouldn't take no for an answer! At his house, Dick showed me a sheep-dog pup. "His mother's a champion trial bitch and his father's the best dog around," he said. The bitch had only had two pups, and most of the sheep-men in the area wanted one. Dick, the nice fellow that he was, didn't want to upset anyone so he kept one and gave me the other. At past 3.00a.m., when I finally arrived home, in the car with me I had a sheep-dog pup, a whole ham, four kittens in a basket, and some bantams in a cardboard box. When Jo saw this lot later on, she blew a fuse!

Poor old Dick was later involved in a car crash and died a few weeks afterwards in hospital. I named the pup Dick after Dick Gibbons – we still have him.

18

IN LOVE WITH OUR JOB

Lancaster Auction Mart is held every Friday for the store cattle. Most Fridays, if I was not racing, I would be rushing about trying to get finished so I could pop down there, as I still love going to markets to have a bit of a banter with the local farmers. Most of them only go for the crack – in fact, I think it's the only time some of them go out!

No-one had to tell Jo that it was Market Day, as she would say to me, "If you buy anything, make sure it doesn't eat!" She would say it, but I never took too much notice! Invariably, either I came back with something, or it/ they followed me up in a cattle-wagon; and livestock *do* eat!

One Sunday mid-morning, after we had done the horses up, Mr. Briggs came to the yard on one of his visits. I was in the field, admiring my herd of eleven cattle. They were of various sizes as I had bought them in ones and twos, on different days, at the Lancaster Auction Mart, when I had considered them cheap, or as the farmers would say, "worth their money".

"They look well, Jack," Mr. Briggs said, as he himself must have admired stock countless times. "What sort of money are they?"

Mentally, I valued them at £280. "Two hundred and eighty-five pounds, across the board," I said.

"Don't seem too far out at that," he replied. "I'll have a think on it."

I wasn't keen on selling them, anyway. Then, I thought that if he did buy them, I could buy some strong calves or small stores with the money, and virtually double my total.

Next day, I went racing. When I came back, Jo told me that Mr. Briggs had been, taken some of the cattle, and left a cheque. "Didn't he take them all?" I asked. "No, just some." Needless to say, I went straight to the field. There, were left my smallest five, worth about £220 each. I never screamed to Mr. Briggs, but I hope he buys this book!

In our jumping days, we trained some good horses, Glenzier Lad,

Canonbie Key, Red Earl, Duffle Coat, New City, No Commission, and Bold Warrior, to mention a few of the best ones.

From Peter Easterby's, we got Vascar, owned by Albert Waring. Albert was a very nice fellow who used to play rugby for Wigan. He rang me up, one day. "Would you give a horse a lift back from Catterick, which has been in training with Peter Easterby, and is now coming home for a rest?" Albert said he would meet our 'box at our yard, with his trailer, then take the horse on to his home, Freckleton (on the way to Blackpool).

The following season, Albert sent Vascar to us to train for him. We had intended to run him in The Schweppes Gold Trophy at Newbury. Prior to the race, Jimmy Jack (one of our Scottish owners) and others, all went and stayed the night at a hotel in Newbury. In the early hours of the morning, the fire alarm went off. People were flapping, shouting and running about like mad things. One part of the hotel had an open-air balcony where everyone was being directed. "Come as you are. Leave everything," the Tannoy system kept repeating. People were in night-dresses, gowns, pyjamas, and the like, panicking like mad in the bitter cold. Our man, Jimmy Jack, strolled up in his suit, case packed, just as if nothing had happened at all! Luckily, it was a false alarm. They later abandoned the races because of frost.

Albert fancied a yearling that year, so we went to Doncaster St. Leger Sales. We didn't stay at The Punches as we normally do because it was booked up. We got in at The Post House, on the A1 at Selby Fork (near Ferrybridge). In the lounge, we had a few drinks and looked through our catalogue for a bargain.

Albert was a very big man – I mean BIG! He weighed possibly 20 st. or more, but he was the nicest fellow one could ever wish to meet. I am very proud that I was one of his best pals (I say "was", as poor Albert died in Preston Hospital a few years ago: he was only forty-eight). When we went to our rooms, Jo and I were drawn in the next room, where Albert and his wife Sheelagh were. Albert said, "I'm going to have my breakfast in bed in the morning."

For breakfast, in bed, we had to order on a chart, then put the card on the outside doorknob to be collected, so the staff knew what to prepare for the next day. When we had all gone to our rooms, I went to see what Albert had ordered for his breakfast. His card read:

2 boiled eggs

Toast and marmalade

1 pot of tea

So, I swapped his chart for mine. On the chart that I hung on Albert's door, I put:

A generous helping of porridge

6 fried eggs

10 rashers of bacon

1 tin of tomatoes

1 tin of beans

mushrooms

2 rounds of fried bread

Half a loaf of toast

A pot of tea

Can this please be brought to the room at 7.00a.m.

When morning came, before we set off for the sales, Albert told me, "I like this place. Do you know, two waiters brought me my breakfast on a trolley at seven o'clock this morning, and I couldn't eat it all! I only ordered a couple of eggs and some toast!" Well, I couldn't hold it – I burst out laughing! "It was you that ordered it, you bugger, wasn't it?" said Albert.

At the August York Race Sale at Doncaster, a lovely 3-year-old (by Deep Run) came. I loved him; I had been to see him in his box four or five times. Anyway, he didn't fetch his reserve. Ken Oliver knew how much I liked the horse, as I was having a bid at him in the ring. Also, he was Supreme Champion in the show, the Sunday before the Sale. Ken may have seen me on one of my several visits to the horse in his box. He rang me up when I got home, "Jack? That horse, lot number so-and-so. You liked him very much."

"Guv'nor," I said, "that's putting it mildly – I loved him!"

"Come back tomorrow – see if we can do a bit of good."

"You realise that I haven't got a client for him?"

"Get yourself here tomorrow and we'll see what we can do."

The owner of the horse in Ireland would take nothing less than 6,000 guineas, bearing in mind that the horse was half-brother to The Dikler, winner of The Cheltenham Gold Cup in 1973, ridden by Ron Barry. Ken, being the great man he is, worked and worked on the owner until he got me the horse for 4,600 guineas. "Pay for him when you've sold him," Ken said. I later sold the horse to Geoff Dawes, and he was named Kas after the owner's son, Keith, and our two sons, Alan and Sam.

The first time Kas ran was at Wolverhampton, on 27th December 1975, ridden by Richard Evans. He finished 3rd, beaten by a short head and a short head. He was 6 lengths in front, jumping the last, then started to look about because of the crowd shouting for him. "He'll never be beaten by the likes of these, again," said Richard. It was a good performance; he had only been broken in just over three months.

We lost Kas soon after, as Geoff had angina and, living near London, couldn't face the long journeys to the North. Kas went on to win countless other races, including The Saddle Of Gold at Newbury in 1977, when trained by Peter Ashworth of Epsom.

Before Kas's time, Geoff came to stay with us. I was going racing, Geoff and Jo were going to Doncaster St. Leger Sales. Before they went, I said, "If you buy anything, make sure it's sound. Don't buy any cripples."

They came back with a leggy, bay filly (by Swing Easy, out of Va Beni bred by Claude and Caroline de P. Berry in Scotland) which had cost 520 guineas. Looking at the breeding, I asked, "What's wrong with her?"

"She's a bit straight in front," I was sheepishly told by Jo.

When I saw the filly, I said to these two, "Were you drunk, or what?"

Geoff ended up giving Jo the filly. Jo named her I Don't Mind. I turned her out in the fold-yard with some bullocks we had. One day, when I had fed the bullocks, not one of them came near the tumbrel to eat. They all stood in a corner while she ate their food – they were frightened to death of her! "At least she's got some bottle!" I thought.

So, I brought her in and we broke her. When we put a roller on her – buck? – you never saw the like! She turned herself inside out! You wouldn't have believed that when we got her going, she was really lazy and laid back.

Before the Flat season started in March, we took our four 2-year-olds to Carlisle for a gallop. Those days, Eric Apter rode our Flat runners when he could. "You had better ride this filly, Eric," I said, "to give her a bit of a chance. You're the lightest." She beat the other three out of sight.

At the next Beverley meeting, on 10th June 1976, I ran her in a seller. It was an absolute doddle for her – she trotted up, in a time on a par with the Robert Massey winner, Jameson, the same day. I had had £20 on her at 4/1. At the auction, it was like Doncaster Sales when Harry Beeby is selling a good horse – everybody came to see the action:

"You won't want it back, will yer," said Mick Easterby.

"Yes I will – the missus owns her."

"I've a job for it, that's all" he said. "It'll be lucky to win again, tha knows? They're a bad lot – mine's ner good, ner good at all!"

Bill Marshall set the bidding off. The auctioneer was taking bids from all directions. Mick was breathing down my neck, "Have yer finished?" I hadn't even started, they were going that fast! Jo was next to me, giving me a hard time – every time it was my turn to bid, she would say, "*You* put her in the seller, so *you* can get her back!" I bought her in for 3,700 guineas, which was then a record for Beverley. The Clerk of the Scales gave me a blank cheque, as I didn't have one with me. I put our bank's name and address on and signed it, then, next day, I rang and asked our bank manager, "Please honour this cheque until Friday, as I might get warned off if it's not paid. I'll sell my cattle to pay for her (which I did)."

At Cockerham we seem to be like the Masai tribe in Kenya: our wealth is shown by the amount of cattle we have in stock!

I Don't Mind didn't win again as a 2-year-old. She won as a 3-year-old, then as a 4-year-old. I entered her in The Ayr Gold Cup, my dream race, in 1978. By now, we had sold her to Messrs. Oyston, the estate agents as a deposit on a house in our village that fell through.

The day before The Cup, the going at Ayr was good to firm, which couldn't have been better – she loved fast ground. Selsby Oyston (father of Bob and Owen) and myself stayed overnight in the Station Hotel. It started to rain. It rained all night, and was still raining the next morning – so much so, the ground was very soft. My hopes sunk – I had fancied her so much. I was sick.

The filly ran her heart out for us; she ran the best race of her life to finish 4th to Vaigly Great, ridden by Greville Starkey and trained by Michael Stoute. Only beat by 3½ lengths. "Don't worry, Jack" Selsby said. "You'll win it one day."

I Don't Mind ended up winning ten races for us. She also went on to breed some good winners, including Swing It Gunner, the horse that won the 1987 November Handicap by half-a-length at Doncaster for trainer Colin Tinkler, beautifully ridden by Mark Birch.

Like most yards we have had our ups and downs with horses coming and going. The majority of owners are great. Most are easy to please. Some are not so good; some are impossible. It reminds me of a poster I once saw while staying at a guest-house down South. It read as follows:

"We the willing, led by the unknowing, are doing the impossible for the ungrateful. We have done so much for so long for so little, we are now qualified to do anything for nothing."

As I have previously stated, it wasn't easy to get horses in our early years at Cockerham. However, in April 1977, we had a stroke of luck. Billy Greenwood, a retired Isle of Man businessman, who used to live in Blackpool, came to Cockerham. He sent us some horses he had in training in Yorkshire with Bill Haigh. That's not all. He also said he fancied some young National Hunt stock. Off we went to Doncaster May Sales. There were some lovely young horses there. We finished up buying three cracking 3-year-olds: by Deep Run, who was later named Deep Sound; by Harwell, later named Wellfort; by New Brig, that got named Braven. We broke them in and got them going really well, just ready to run, when Mr. Greenwood, who was a real nice fellow, listened to someone's advice and took all his horses to Gordon Richards of Penrith.

Mr. Greenwood moved them again from Gordon before he won with them. Braven finished winning nine races; Wellfort six; and Deep Sound won two. One of his was a Novice 'Chase at Cheltenham, but in his next race, also at Cheltenham, going like a winner, he unfortunately had a fatal fall. Martin Tate, who trained him, told me he was probably the best horse he had ever trained.

We don't make hay at Cockerham any more, as my philosophy is that if one makes hay and it's poor, one is stuck with it; if one's buying hay, though, one only buys the best. In the second year we were at Cockerham, we made about a thousand bales. After a few days, it started to smell – it was in the barn, steaming away. What a worry! An old farmer, when he came to look round the yard, said, "You've got hay that doesn't seem so good about, lad. It's a bit sickly. The last time I smelt hay like that, it went up in flames."

The next day, Rob (one of the lads) came running round. "Boss! Boss! The barn's smoking!" We promptly called the fire brigade then just kept pouring water on with a hose until they came. It was lucky for us that Rob had seen it. The firemen put it out, helped by our local farmers. We took all the hay out of the barn, put it onto trailers, dumped it in the middle of one of our fields, then burnt it!

One particular year, we made some hay which wasn't brilliant, as it had had too many showers on it. I made a deal with Tom Bibby, a local dairy farmer and a friend (to whom, for years, I have let a field for grazing his cattle). I agreed to swap him a big load of hay and two Hereford bullocks for a yearling of his, by Warpath and out of a mare that had never won or even looked like winning (Warpath wasn't the best sire in the book, either!). I then sold him the rest of the hay for very little money.

We named the horse after a folk group I like in Lancashire (I have since got to know them well) – the Houghton Weavers. On 15th April 1981, the first time we ran Houghton Weaver, he won the seller at Hamilton, only to lose the race when he was tested positive for theobromide, from Pegasus horse nuts. The feed manufacturers reimbursed the owners with the prize money, as did Spillers when we lost another race for the same reason with Lucky Boardman.

I swapped Houghton Weaver and £2,000 for half of Solares as a yearling from Henry Zeisel, the owner of Rheingold, runner-up in The Derby to Roberto in 1972 and who went on to win the Prix de l'Arc De Triomphe, trained by my Army days sauna pal, Barry Hills. Houghton Weaver went on to win three more races for Henry, including the Derwent Nursery at Redcar. Solares, in return, won thirteen races for us on the Flat, over hurdles and, as the jump-lads would say, "proper racing" (steeplechases) – he won no less than eight of these.

Tom Bibby works very hard. He has a milk round and bottles the milk himself. When Tom wants a day's racing, he rings me up. He either comes to our yard or I pick him up at a prearranged place on my way to the motorway. When he goes racing, he starts his milk round at 2.00a.m. or 3.00a.m. to get finished so he can go.

This particular day, we had a jumper running at Southwell. Tom rang the night before to say he would like a day out. I arranged to pick him up from a bridge on the M6 motorway. Tom said he would be looking out for the car – but I completely forgot about him! He rang that night to have a whinge about me leaving him, "When you passed the bridge, you were doing at least a ton!"

Poor old Tom. He went home, got changed, and went back to work on his farm. Since then, he mainly goes racing with John Brown, another of our owners. He doesn't trust me any more!

19

OLLY AND BRIAN

We began to get more Flat horses. Frank Carr, the Malton trainer, rang one morning to say Mr. Sangster had a horse with him which he would like us to train, a 3-year-old called Lightning Tour who had never run. Frank said he would get him over to our yard as soon as he could. True to his word that same afternoon his box arrived driven by his travelling head-lad, Derek Holmes. Derek told us to be careful with the horse as he hadn't been out of his stable for a while.

After the horse had dumped every person in our yard, gone through every hedge in sight and up every road on its own around Cockerham, we decided, for a change, to take him down with three other horses to the beach. (The beach is only fifteen or so minutes away from the yard in a horse-box).

When we arrived the tide was starting to come in. We cantered the horses on a gallop we had there that a local farmer used to rotovate and look after for us. After their exercise we paddled the horses in the sea – they used to love it. Lightning Tour, the daft bugger he was, crossed his legs, fell down, depositing his lad in the water, and took off out to sea. He swam towards the Isle of Man, perhaps wanting to see his owner. We chased after him on horseback until we dared not go out any further. The horse was getting further and further away until he looked the size of a grey-hound on the horizon. We quickly loaded the other three horses in the 'box and I drove round the coast road to Fleetwood. Fortunately the horse had turned and was swimming back towards the shore. He was absolutely knackered. We put him back in the horse-box and took him home. That next morning when I fed him, he was as fresh as new paint and ate every oat up.

We persevered with him and ran him at Teeside Park, a course that is now closed. The horse ran very mulishly. So, I rang Mr. Sangster, who over the years has had every type of horse through his hands so he understands that everything doesn't always tick like clockwork. After I told him the horse had no future in racing at all Mr. Sangster said, "Give him away to some girl to play with". I told him I didn't know one I disliked that much and the horse was an absolute nut. When I explained in more detail how he really was, we both agreed the only future he had was to feed some dogs and so I'm afraid we had to have him put down.

Touch Boy, owned by Gary Mullins, came to us from Dick Peacock and won the 1981 Portland Handicap at Doncaster. He was favourite for The Stewards Cup with Lester Piggott on board, the year Soba won, in 1982. I ran Touch Boy in The Ayr Gold Cup in 1981, but he never really saw the 6 furlongs out.

Ironically, in 1981 on 30th May (Alan's birthday), the whole of our family rode in races. Jo rode Lilac Star at Ayr for the late Derek Leslie, finishing 5th to Jose Collins, ridden by Maxine Carvalho (Juster). Russian Winter was 2nd and 3rd was Solar Grass, ridden by George Syvret (who has a good filly, Lyndseylee, in training with us now). Alan rode Montazem in the same race, finishing 7th; Sam rode Miss Chessy on the same card in another race. I rode Sailord in the trainers' race at Kempton, finishing 8th. Stan Mellor rode the winner on Kinnigger for Merrick Francis (Clive Brittain was 2nd).

At the July 1982 Ayr meeting, Willie Carson rode Touch Boy for us carrying 10st. 8lb. and won, beating Little Starchy, which must surely have been a weight-carrying record at the time. We started to get a few more winners, and put everything (as we still do) back into the firm to try and better our lot. We bought a new horse-box, made for us by Jeremy Glover. It was a smasher. We sent out dozens of letters, asking firms to put an advert on our 'box, just as I had thought of doing whilst doodling away at Lincoln County Hospital.

The first person I asked whether he would put an advert on the 'box was Willie Stephenson. He thought it was a brilliant idea. He put 'Doncaster Sales' on, along with his saddlery business. We got *The Sporting Life* on the back ramp, getting £1,000 per year for the advert. We had eighteen other boards, three feet by two-and-a-half feet, at £250 each. We had these boards painted with whatever the firms wanted, then screwed them to the wooden 'box – it was unique.

I have never told Jeremy before, but that 'box was too heavy and used to wear tyres off at the front for fun! My arm muscles got like Geoff Capes's, pulling it round bends on the way to the races. The next 'box we bought was a really good one – a Mercedes chassis with Smith body.

By now, other people were putting adverts on their 'boxes, so I went for a change. With the assistance of Stephen Jack, one of our owners' sons who designs his father's coachwork, we set about putting more of my Lincoln Hospital thoughts down on paper again. "All my life, I've been patriotic, so let's have the 'box red, white, and blue." We streamlined the 'box. It was a revelation compared to the miserable, drab colours of most other horse-boxes that went racing.

Mel and Sheila Haughey own an antique shop and a café in Kirby Stephen, which we call into for a cuppa on racing days. They also owned a horse in partnership with a farmer called Nelson Robinson. Mel used to be Tommy Robson's head-lad when Tommy trained up in Cumbria. I got to know Mel well, as I had had a few rides for his guv'nor.

One day, when we called into the café on the way back from racing at Catterick, Mel asked me if I would go and see his mare and the yearling from her. "I'm not impressed with the yearling," I told him. "It's round-jointed and has long pasterns. Sell him on. He looks like being an old man before he gets on a racecourse!" I didn't mind a few faults, but he had more than I care to live with.

He sent the horse to Eric Collingwood to train, who pin-fired his joints. He didn't run as a 2-year-old, but ran in several races over all sorts of distances as a 3-year-old and a 4-year-old. He never ran a bad race, always finishing within the first half-dozen. When Eric went to train in Hong Kong, Mel asked me if I would take his horse to train. Seeing as he had been placed, I agreed to take him, even though he was a 4-year-old maiden. It looked as though Mel had forgiven me for (or forgotten about) my earlier not-very-complimentary remarks.

Working the horse at home, he was laying up with most of our sprinters. I rang up Mel and told him, "He appears to be a sprinter. Eric has been getting the trips wrong." "If that's what you think, you're wasting my money," said Mel. "He needs at least a mile. He was 3rd in a Hurdle at Kelso."

I made a compromise and ran him in a 6-furlong race at Carlisle. He finished 4th, ridden by John Lowe. "If it had been 5 furlongs, he would have won," John said.

So, we started to run him in 5-furlong sprints, even on sharp courses like Edinburgh and Wolverhampton. That season, he won no fewer than six races. The horse I'm talking about, of course, is Bri-Eden.

He was a real character, "Brian". He didn't like men (he had bitten every man and lad in the yard at sometime or other!), so Jo and Chris Glenn (now the wife of Stewart Morris, the jockey) used to do virtually everything with him.

In the first race he won, Jo rode him and he dead-heated with Tim Easterby on Broon's Secret at Ayr on 3rd June 1978. He won The Bovis at Ascot for us on 9th August 1982, and he was our 100th Flat winner when he won £5,000 in The Paddock Stakes at Epsom, ridden by George Duffield, on 31st August 1982. As good as he was, Brian still had a lot of problems – he used to take off down the roads. On occasions, he used to run away with jockeys down to the start. Several times, after winning races, the jockey hasn't been able to pull him up and he's done a lap of honour (even carrying 10st. at Carlisle, one day, with Kevin Darley!). After finishing 3rd in a sprint at Catterick, Brian kept going and did another circuit. As I was waiting for him to finish, I heard two race-goers talking. One said to the other, "That bloody Jack Berry couldn't train pigs to be dirty! If that had been a 2-mile race, the horse would have pissed up!" That season he ran sixteen times; he won seven races and the old fellow was placed four times. What a horse!

When Willie Carson rode Brian at Hamilton, in 1980, he had the race sewn up; but, Brian broke down, so we had to have him fired again. When he came back into training, the old boy had gone in his wind. So, we had him hobdayed. When I told Mel that he was going through a difficult phase, he came to ride him out – Mel thought he could straighten Brian up. He must have been flat out around our gallops for ten minutes (Brian must have done this with him at home before we got him, giving Mel the impression that he stayed).

The Middlebrook Mushroom firm kindly sponsor The Northern Trainers' Invitation Stakes at Catterick. On 23rd June 1982, Brian won it, with the burden of myself on board. In the same race, the late (and I may say, great) Steve Nesbitt had a ride. He was the nicest man who ever walked in a pair of shoes – never have I heard a bad word said about him. Steve always had a minute for everyone, and always had an ear when we wanted a moan. All of us in The North loved the little guy. He had trained at Middleham; when he died, the yard was taken over by his successful son-in-law, George Moore.

When we were getting changed for the race, and Steve put his colours on, we pinned a notice to the back of them: 'WIDE LOAD – PLEASE PASS'. Steve went marching out into the Catterick paddock with it on!

For winning the race, all concerned got lovely glass trophies and a basket of mushrooms (no money). Poor old Brian got a 6lb. penalty in his next race, The Brandling Handicap at Newcastle (which is a very competitive sprint), that took his weight to 10st. 2lb. He was beaten a head by Gill Richardson's grand old campaigner, Rambling River, (trained by Arthur Stephenson) who carried 8st. 11lb. I rang Weatherby's regarding the penalty. "Was it a mistake, seeing as the horse didn't win any money?" But, those 'Rods of Iron' in London stood by their rule book. Yes, he should carry a penalty (until they could have a meeting to say otherwise!). For the record, they don't have penalties for such events, now.

In 1983, the year of Teenoso's Derby, we won the Surrey Stakes at Epsom with Clantime, ridden by Willie Carson. The Derby that day was worth £165,000 to the winner. The Surrey Stakes was worth £3,830 – bit of a difference. With it being Derby Day we were all dressed up in top hat and tails. Mine I hired from Moss Bros. Willie Stephenson had his own. By the look of Willie's hat he had owned it for a long time, possibly from the days he rode for King George VI or was it King George V? In the car-park before I drove home I discreetly changed into something more casual. Willie tried my hat on. "Fits like a glove," he said, "we'll have a swap." Not taking too much notice as I'm changing, I said cheerio to Willie.

When I went to take the gear back to Moss Bros, sure enough in the boot of my car was a ringer for the hat I had hired. They were so different Stevie Wonder could have told them apart. In the hire shop the man was in shock. The hat box lid was perched on top of the hat as the hat was a good three inches taller than the box. When the poor fellow got his breath back he said he would have a word with the manager later on and that I'd probably get a bill for a new hat. I never did though. You never know, the manager may have liked it.

We retired Bri-Eden in 1985. The last race the old fellow had won was The Ballyogan Stakes (Group Three) at Leopardstown in 1983, ridden by Steve Craine, which had brought his total to nineteen wins in all. Thanks pal.

Brian and O.I. Oyston were very good pals. They were so close, we often said that they were a couple of poofs! When Brian and "Olly" were turned out for a rest in summer-time, we used to bring them in at night and put the pair of them in a very big box we have at the end of our passage boxes. One day, we heard a banging and clattering, so we went down to see what they were doing. They must have had a kicking match, as Brian was stood in one corner and Olly was stood in the other, with their backsides to each other. The pair of them sulked like that for about a week – they must have had some row!

Every year, for his summer holidays, we sent Brian for a few weeks to the farm where he was born. On 1st September, 1988, the old fellow had a heart attack and died. Thankfully, it was peaceful – he just lay dead in the field, without a mark of a struggle. Pity, though; near our all-weather gallop we have a spinney where we had always promised to bury both Brian and Olly. However, with Brian passing away at Kirby Stephen, it wasn't feasible for us to move him. So, we had him buried on the farm where he was born. It was a sad day when he went, it was like losing one of the family.

We bought O.I. Oyston (by Martinmas, out of Last Lap) for Messrs. Oyston at Doncaster Sales for 2,600 guineas. I liked the way he walked – although he turned his feet in quite a bit, he looked like a racehorse in the making. Bob Oyston liked him. He was named "O.I." after Ian Oyston, Bob's brother who had recently died.

When we broke Olly and got him going, he looked like running in The Brocklesby at Doncaster as he showed us plenty of speed. "The best early 2-year-olds will be in that," I thought. "We'll go for The Greyfriars."

As it happened, The Greyfriars was the better race. In it, we came up against Schweppeshire Lad, trained by Ryan Price and bought by Jack Doyle (that astute, Irish Bloodstock agent) for a competition for the you-know-who firm. Olly led the race till a hundred yards from the post when a few horses went past him. Schweppeshire Lad won and proved to be one of the best 2-year-olds around that year, 1978.

The next time Olly ran, he was 3rd at Pontefract to Touch Boy. Then, he ran in a 6-furlong event at Catterick, jumping out very fast to beat a 2-year-old filly of Sir Mark Prescott's, A Star Is Born. I read in the papers before the race that A Star Is Born was "possibly the best 2-year-old Mark had trained" (Mark's filly went on to finish 2nd in The Cherry Hinton at Newmarket, which was good form).

"Make sure he has a good look around this winning enclosure," said Lindsay Charnock, the jockey who rode Olly when he won his first race, at Catterick. "I don't think he'll be in to see another one – he's a right shit!" meaning that he was a rogue. Lindsay and I often have a laugh about that.

As a 3-year-old, Olly ran a few times without winning, but always knocking on the door. The jockeys told me, quite rightly, that he wasn't doing his best. That I already knew, as I have always ridden him myself from being a yearling. At home, he could catch pigeons!

Willie Carson rode him at Haydock. He was a short price. I'm not going to write in here what Willie said, but he finished it off with, ". . . send them to me and I'll eat them for my breakfast!"

So, we had Olly cut. Since then, the old fellow has won in every season except one. He is a great pal – I idolise the old horse. I know I have said it before, but if it was possible to make him a stable in our house, like the one Mr. Ed had in the pictures, I would. When Jo and I go on our holidays, we send Olly somewhere for his. At the moment, while we are here in Tenerife, Olly is walking round the roads of Yorkshire. He now has twenty-two Flat wins and two hurdle wins to his credit. He hates it when he isn't in work. Twice, we have tried to retire him, but he just walks up and down the field after he has had enough. He has won the seller at Ayr's first Flat meeting for the last three years.

After Olly won at Ayr on Monday, 30th March 1987, James Lambie of *The Sporting Life* wrote this for his Ayr report:

"It would have taken a soulless fellow to bid for O.I. Oyston after the grand old veteran had made all in the Ravens Park Selling Handicap at Ayr yesterday. The 11-year-old gelding, who knows more about racing than Phil Bull according to his trainer Jack Berry, was winning his twentieth Flat race of his career, and auctioneer Harry Beeby left no-one in doubt that he would not be looking too hard for bids. 'It would be a crime for him to be changing hotels at his time of life', said Beeby as O.I. Oyston – 'Olly' to his friends – was led round the unsaddling enclosure. He added 'I am sure you will all agree with me that the best thing to do is to give him a nice round of applause and hope we see him back here soon.' So saying 'No bid' and O.I. Oyston was led out of the ring."

Olly is a star; he went on the last leg of a marathon trek around the country's racecourses with Brian Goodwill, from Haydock to Liverpool, to raise money for Cancer Research and the Jane Thompson Memorial Fund. He was the star of the show on one of our charity days for the Royal Manchester Children's Hospital on Sunday, 13th August 1989 when we divided an acre of land into yard squares. Olly was turned loose into the acre. The yard where Olly deposited a set of droppings won £1,000. He has been to lots of event for good causes but not as many as Red Rum.

The crowd absolutely love him at Ayr. Last year, he got a reception as if he'd won The Ayr Gold Cup. Two people judged him to be their Horse of the Year – they're not bad judges! If I'd have had a chance to vote, I would have made it three!

I must be one of the luckiest men in racing to have had the privilege of being associated with this gentleman for all these years, and sincerely hope that he lives for another fourteen years in retirement. It's just too bad that his old pal, Brian, isn't here with him to enjoy his retirement.

As a point of interest, we all rode my old pal, Olly, in races at some time. Sam did the best on him when he rode him a winner in an apprentice race at Doncaster in 1982. At Newmarket in the Dickins Invitation race for Lady riders against jockeys on 6th August 1988 The Princess Royal rode Olly to finish 4th.

Old Mr. Oyston was, and still is, a super old boy. Ninety-six years old, he is. Until recently, I often used to take him racing with me. Someone from The Oyston Group would bring Selsby down to the yard and he would sit in the front of my car, puffing away on his pipe (Bob wouldn't let him smoke in his car), and reading the papers. The faster I drove, the more he liked it!

When we got to the races, I would get him a badge and race-card, take him to a seat somewhere near the Tote and tell him I would pick him up at a given time. The old boy played away, having a few bets, and he really enjoyed his day – he would talk to anyone. We used to stop on the way back for something to eat, as he lived by himself and I didn't want him to be getting food ready when he got back in.

One day at Chester, when Olly was running, Bob said to his dad, "Will you put me £50 on Olly?" and gave him the money. One bookie had Olly at 7/2, so Selsby put £50 on at that price. Then, the old horse went to 5/2, so he had another £50 on. Olly won. Selsby told Bob, "I had two £50 bets on at two prices. I got yours on at 5/2!"

Jonjo O'Neill is one of life's gentlemen. We have had some fun together. One day, he and I went hunting with the Cumberland Farmers. I took Jo's horse, Babbling Brook, in our 'box and met Jonjo at his house. We picked up Keith Darby (the amateur), then set off in Jonjo's 'box to meet The Hunt. On the way, a cattle-wagon had turned over and blocked the road up. So, we went another way, and the great man got us lost.

We finally came to a grass verge with lots of horse-boxes and trailers parked up nearby. Jonjo (who must have been practising for Mastermind) said, "It looks as if they started from here." It was pouring with rain, and we were just in our hunting clothes. We rode for hours, looking for The Hunt and got absolutely soaked to the skin! I have never been so wet and cold in my life. When we finally found The Hunt, they were just ready for packing up!

On the way back, we dropped Keith off. At Jonjo's, I had a bath, and Sheilagh (Jonjo's missus) lent me some of his clothes. They were miles too small – in them, I knew how trussed-up chickens feel! I left Babbling Brook and the horse-box there, and went back to Cockerham in Jonjo's car, as time was getting on and I had to go to Preston Snooker that night. In his car, there was a tape of Susan McCann – it was the first tape I had heard of her singing. Jonjo and I have since been to see her live, and she's great.

Jonjo had a cracking little Jack Russell terrier called Pigeon, named after Sea Pigeon, on whom he won the 1979 Tote Ebor Handicap and the 1980 Champion Hurdle. I sent my little bitch, Bonny, to Jonjo's to get mated. Here is the bill he sent me for the bitch's keep, etc.:

BONNY. – JACK RUSSELL BITCH 3.11.82 – 17.12.82

6 weeks & 3 days @ £35	£225.00
Stud Fees	£ 50.00
Vet Fees	£ 35.00
Transport	£ 40.00
	£350.00
VAT 15%	£ 52.50
TOTAL.	*£402.50*

Not surprisingly, I never sent a cheque!

Bryan McMahon (the Tamworth trainer) and I have been pals for years. We are both game for a laugh and have been known to play a prank or two on each other. One day at Wolverhampton Races, I was sat down eating a meal before racing when Bryan picked up the trilby next to me and kicked it into the air. It landed about three tables away, on a gentleman's lunch! Bryan made his apologies to the man, then grabbed the hat off his plate, threw it on the floor, stamped on it, and sat down at a table! All our table (and most of the people at the other tables) were amazed at the antics of this hooligan. When I finished my meal, I picked up *my* hat and binoculars up from under the table, put my hat on and walked out. "See you, Bryan," I said. Bryan's face went as red as a beetroot! The hat he had been kicking about belonged to Mel Haughey, the owner of Bri-Eden whom he didn't even know!

20

VERY NEARLY BLEW IT

The St. Leger Yearling Sales at Doncaster are unique. Of all the sales anywhere in England or Ireland that is where we buy the majority of our 2-year-old winners. Whether it's luck – call it what you want, but that's where they come from. None of the others have the buzz or atmosphere of Doncaster. It is brilliant.

The sales were set up in 1962 by Willie Stephenson and Ken Oliver. Previously there had been sales there, at Glasgow Paddocks, but they were let go.

Willie was one of the very few men to have trained a Derby winner (Arctic Prince in 1951, ridden by C. Spares) and a Grand National winner (Oxo in 1959, ridden by M. Scudamore). In fact, I think the only other person to do so since the War is Dr. M.V. O'Brien of Ballydoyle, Ireland, who won the National three years on the trot: Early Mist in 1953, Royal Tan in 1954, and Quare Times in 1955; and the Epsom Derby six times.

Most people at the sales stayed at Punches Hotel, on Bawty Road. Every night, after the sales, we had a marvellous time there. We met up with lots of Irish people, including the likes of Timmy Hyde, Ginger Powell, Jack Doyle, Micky Browne, Paddy Prendergast, and my old bloodstock agent pal, Jack White, who always said, when looking at the horses, "Have you see anything you like better than yourself?"

It was good at Punches – we had great sing-songs. Willie Stephenson's party piece was to walk around with a bottle on his head. One night, as he was doing this, I picked an apple out of the fruit bowl and threw it at the bottle. What a result – the apple knocked the bottle clean off Willie's head! Racing lost a real character when Willie died in 1989, and I lost an old pal.

Willie was one of the hardest men in racing – he never had any time for anyone who was soft. I never knew anyone who loved small animals more. At home, he had his dogs, lots of hens and bantams. Willie would get up in the middle of the night to do a deal. One Sunday, when I was at Willie's

162

house, he said, "Let's go for a run in the car." We went to a pal of his, called Johnny Graves, who owned a smallholding and market garden in a village called Reed. Johnny had some young Canada Geese.

I bought six of these geese off him. He lent me a crate and I put it on the back seat of my car. When I got them home I put them in a hut in our orchard. On the third day, I let them out. They wouldn't go back in at night. The next day, they had gone into the next field; the day after that, they had gone a bit further. "Those geese are for going, mate," I said to Neville, our feed man. The next day, they were nowhere in sight.

About six months later, when Neville and I were in Royston, we called in to see Willie and Auntie Bobby, his wife. Willie, with a twinkle in his eye, said, "Come on, let's go for a drive in the car."

We went to Johnny Graves's place where I had previously bought the geese. He was laughing like mad when he saw me. "Recognise them?" he asked. The geese had flown back to Reed!

Neville Hill had been an apprentice to Willie for years; when Willie retired (that's over eight years ago), Neville came to us for a week's holiday, and he's still here! Once, in an apprentice race at Ripon, Neville rode a horse for Willie, which Willie thought would win. Neville gave the horse a bad ride to finish 2nd, beaten a neck. The winner had been on the other side of the track, and Neville hadn't seen him. "You'd break the Bank Of England!" Willie told Neville. "You can walk back to Royston (only he used a bit stronger language!) – it'll give you time to realise what a cock up of a race you rode! And don't be late for work in the morning!" When Willie was out of sight, Neville got himself a lift to Six-Mile Bottom with Geoff Littlewood, the jockey, then hitch-hiked the remaining ten miles!

Ken Oliver is an ex-jockey, and now a National Hunt trainer. He once trained five winners in a day at Wolverhampton. Ken's speciality was falling asleep at dinner. In between dozes, the waiters would take his food away to keep it warm: when he woke up, they would bring it back. He could fall asleep and wake up six times an hour!

Harry Beeby, the current Managing Director of the Doncaster Bloodstock Sales, is the son of the late George Beeby, who was a successful trainer. Harry has got to be one of the best auctioneers around: sell rice to the Chinese, Harry would!

The first thing Harry's son, Henry, sold at a public auction was one of my red shirts. That was at Punches in aid of some kiddies charity that Liz and Frank Barry were collecting for. Henry squeezed every last drop out of everyone. David Brown, the ex-Warwickshire and England fast bowler, bought the shirt for £70. I had to take it off and give it to him there and then. David is a very good pal of mine – he, Trish (his wife), Jo and I own a greyhound between us (quite a good one, too!). What kind of cricketer David was, I don't know. Once, at our house, when we were playing about, throwing an egg to each other, Dave dropped it on one of his turns.

Someone said that when Trish had her babies, she wouldn't let Dave nurse them! I don't know how true that is, though!

I bought my first red shirt when I was about twenty, while shopping just before racing at Ayr. At the time, it was quite a gaudy colour to wear – all the lads took the juice out of me on account of it. The next day at the same meeting when I wore the shirt, I rode a winner! From then on, whenever I rode a fancied horse, I put the red shirt on as a lucky omen. Even when I started training, the red shirt was worn on the same basis. It began to arouse suspicion that when we had a winner, I was invariably wearing a red shirt. People often ask me if I've only got the one: this was once the case, but I've got lots now. In fact, people actually send me them. These days, I always wear a red shirt at the races, as we seem to be running more and more fancied horses. Besides, the owners would be upset if I didn't have one on!

When Clantime won The Surrey Stakes on Derby Day, 1983, I wasn't wearing one of my red shirts with my top hat and tails. On television, Brough Scott said, "Jack Berry isn't wearing his red shirt today, but he's got a very big, red carnation in his buttonhole!"

In addition to red shirts, '8' is my favourite number. It came about when we rode work at W.A. Hall's. When Mad Mick and I went on to win a gallop, as we passed the leader we would say, "Number 8, judge". Just like the judge does when he announces the winner at the races ie. "First . . . number 8 . . . . . ." All our stationery has a horse and jockey printed on it and even the horse's saddlecloth has the number 8. Our horse boxes have number 8 on them too!

One day when Jo took our travelling head-lad, Martin, to the painter's to pick up a 'box that had been repainted, the man had painted number 6 on the saddlecloth. They wouldn't bring the 'box back till he had sorted the number out.

On 16th May 1983, Alan 'Manny' Mercer and I were travelling to Wolverhampton. Manny was driving (as it was his car), half dozing off, when there was a whacking bang. I looked out of the side-passenger window and saw that we were half underneath a wagon. Sparks were flying and metal was screeching. Manny, after a struggle, got the car out from underneath the wagon and pulled it up onto the hard-shoulder. It was a right mess! Manny was a bit in shock. While we were there, admiring the mangled wreck, someone I knew stopped and gave me a lift to the races. Manny was going to ride the 2-year-old that we were running in the first race, but he was in no fit state to be riding. He also had to sort out the accident with the police and arrange to get his car towed off the M6 motorway.

When I arrived at Wolverhampton Racecourse, I saw Joe Mercer and asked him if he would stand in for his namesake. This, he willingly did. The 2-year-old was a big, strapping, lovely-looking colt called The Manor (by Manor Farm Boy) and it was his first time out. He was owned by the North

Both our sons rode well. Left: Sam winning an apprentice race at Doncaster in March 1982. Below: Alan riding work in 1983 in Florida.

Willie Carson rides Clantime into the unsaddling enclosure at Epsom on Derby Day 1983, having won The Great Surrey Stakes.

1988. Left: Watching work on our gallops at Moss Side. Below: HRH The Princess Royal with Jo and myself before riding O.I. Oyston at Newmarket in August 1988.

A lovely shot of Robert Sangster's Distinctly North at Sandown in 1990. He won us The Flying Childers at York, but that was after I had finished writing this book.

West Racing Club, and was the first horse the club had owned. They were at Wolverhampton in full force.

The Manor had the worst draw – on the wide outside – in a field of fifteen. He jumped out fast, always up in the first half-dozen, and ran a great race to finish 5th. "What a lovely horse," Joe said. "He knows his job and stays well. He'd probably be even better suited to a stiffer track."

We were all thrilled to bits with his run. The following week, attending a meeting with the N.W.R.C., I was asked what I thought his chances would be of winning a race. Brazenly, I said, "If this horse doesn't win a race by the end of the season, I'll show my backside on the Town Hall steps in Black-pool!" It shows how they can let you down! The next race The Manor had was at Carlisle. Everything was just right for him. He jumped out fast, but wouldn't put his head in front at any price. He finished 5th, but he never tried a yard – he'd used up more energy eating his breakfast than he'd done in the race! "Let's cut him," I said. "The season's early – we could run him again in six or eight weeks time."

Most of the members, though, wanted to see how he did on his next run. So, he escaped the operation, but got worse instead of better. We sold him at Doncaster Sales and some of the members bought him back. What gluttons! They ran The Manor for quite a while on the Flat, then over hurdles, but he never looked like troubling the judge. Every year, now, when I attend the N.W.R.C. Dinner, my Blackpool threat always gets a mention!

At the September Yearling Sales, 1983, I bought a nice colt by Martinmas, a sire I am particularly fond of as he sired Olly (we have trained over a dozen horses sired by Martinmas, and there have only been a couple, or so, that we haven't won with!). A gentleman, called Mr. David Harrison, was very busy buying yearlings and placing them with different trainers. However, that evening at the Punches, Mr. Harrison asked me if I had an owner for this colt, as he said he was the underbidder. "No," I said. "You can have him for the same money I paid for him, providing I can train him."

We shook on the deal. Then, I asked one of the auctioneers if he would transfer the yearling from my account to Mr. Harrison's. The job was a good one – nice horse, new owner. We took the yearling home, broke him, and had him ridden upsides, doing nice work. A phone call came from Mr. Harrison's secretary, "He's collecting all his horses up and sending them to Newmarket, to Alan Bailey's yard."

Two days after the horse had gone to Alan's, Harry Beeby sent me one of the 'fan-mail' letters he sends when someone's in his ribs for any length of time. Mr. Harrison hadn't come up with the necessary and seeing as I'd bought the horse at auction, it was my responsibility. I rang Alan up and told him I would send our 'box down the next day for the horse. "You may as well," Alan said, "because it's no f*****g good!" Most of Alan's sentences start with that word, or have it in at some stage! "Well," I thought, "if Alan says he's no f*****g good, I've a lot more here that's no f*****g good!" as I thought that he was one of my best early ones.

Anyway, I paid Harry for him, then later on sold the horse to Tony Williams, a Yeovil bookmaker, for his wife Carol. We had met on holiday in Mombasa. After telling Tony and Carol the horse's story, they appropriately called the horse Timewaster.

First time on the racecourse for Timewaster was 30th April 1984, at Warwick, on firm going, ridden by Kevin Darley. Kepagi, one of Walter Wharton's 2-year-olds, ridden by his son, Wally, jumped off and made the running for 3 furlongs. Just as our chap was making good headway, Kepagi started to weaken. As he got swallowed up, slipping backwards through the field, Timewaster bumped him and Kepagi hit the rail. But to be honest, it made no difference to the result, as he was legless and going nowhere. Timewaster went on and won easily (Wally finished 4th on Kepagi, beaten easily). A Stewards' Enquiry was announced. "They may give me a bollocking for his bumping," said Kevin, "but these 2-year-olds do hang and run around, sometimes, on firm ground."

One has got to remember that 2-year-olds are not machines – when a horse hangs, it's nearly always for a reason. They will invariably hang when the ground is very firm – it's their way of trying to get out of galloping on it. We've trained and worked enough 2-year-olds to know that! "The knock cost my horse a length," Wally said at the enquiry.

The Stewards, in their infinite wisdom, took the race off Timewaster and gave it to Thalberg, ridden by Lester Piggott and trained by Michael Hinchcliffe. They placed Timewaster 4th, behind Kepagi, moving the rest of the placed horses up a position. The beauty of it was, the Stewards sitting on the panel didn't even wear masks – Dick Turpin put one on when *he* robbed people! Many times I have watched the race on video, and no way should that little fellow have lost it. Anyway, to prove my point, I named one of the next season's yearlings, "Warwick Wallys". I entered and ran her at every Warwick meeting I got the chance to. The Warwick Stewards *must* have known I wasn't impressed!

Don (Ginger) McCain, the trainer of the famous Red Rum, winner of three Grand Nationals, rang me up one day. Could I meet him at Forton Services on the M6 with a view to giving him a lift to Ayr as we had a runner there? Being a great lover of Country'n'Western music, I was playing my Billy Jo Spears, Kenny Rogers, Johnny Cash and Foster and Allen tapes whilst chatting away to him. For no apparent reason, he said, "Will you pull this bloody car up and let me out. I don't like music at the best of times, but you can't call that crap even music. Just because it's your bloody car doesn't mean I have to put up with all that rubbish. Come on let me out and I'll walk."

To settle Don down I turned the music off and we started talking about his favourite subject – Red Rum. I'm a very big fan of Rummy's (whose name incidentally spells 'murder' backwards). During the conversation Don invited me to go down to his place for a sit on the old fellow. I went down to Southport in April 1984 and had a ride on him on the beach. Rummy has been to a couple of our Open Days; he is always a favourite with the punters.

One August day when we were busy in the yard, Jo asked me something I thought was stupid. I bit her head off, like I had done many times before, telling her if she couldn't do better than that she may as well not be here. To my amazement she packed up some of her things and off she went in her car.

On the tenth day she rang. Blimey, was I pleased to hear her voice. Another shock . . . . . . she wasn't for coming back. In all our years, together except once when she left to stay with her mum for a few days, this was the only time we had been apart. Remember our job isn't a nine to five one. We work, eat and sleep with each other every day. One is bound to get on the other's nerves occasionally. When I asked her where was she staying she told me with Ann Hewitt, the trainer, who at the time had recently got married and lived in Cheshire. A couple of times I went to see her there. She also came back and stayed at Moss Side overnight, but went back to Ann's the next day.

Jo had an interview in London for a job in the Isle of Man looking after a stud owned by Noel Souter, and got it! She was giving thought to going, and even thinking of going abroad. Thankfully she didn't. It was like starting courting again, or making up. Ian Clark of the *Manchester News* rang me up as he had heard we had parted. I told him we were having problems and were sorting them out. I would appreciate it if he kept quiet or we had too much going for us and we were trying to sort things out. Next night in his paper he had it in we were going our separate ways and so on.

At the time Jo was also considering renting a yard and doing liveries and breaking horses. She is brilliant at that. She has always been the main person breaking horses in. In all my time I have never seen anyone with more patience and understanding of a young horse than Jo. If a horse was upside down tangled up in it's reins, she wouldn't show the slightest signs of flapping. Quietly unravelling it she would say, "You have got yourself in a bit of a mess haven't you?"

The following month we stayed at Doncaster for the Yearling Sales; we were on the road to recovery then. The reporter Brian Radford rang our hotel asking was it true, he'd heard we had parted? I told him we had a fall out like lots of couples do and we had patched our differences up. I would appreciate it if he would let sleeping dogs lie. Unlike Ian Clark, he did! It's business as usual and I don't have to carry all the car keys in my pocket in case Jo wants another trip out.

21

SOMETIMES IT'S HARD

March has always been an in-and-out sort of a month for our family. On 10th March, I broke my leg; on 17th March, my grandad died. The worst possible thing ever to happen was on 5th March 1985.

Sam, our son, was riding our 'chaser, Solares, in a Conditional Jockeys' 3-mile Novice 'Chase at Sedgefield (he had previously ridden him three winners over hurdles) and been placed on him over fences. I was in the stands watching the race with Jo. Going round the back straight, well clear, on the final circuit, "Sol" was jumping like a buck and looking as if he had the race sewn up. Then, he stood right off, outside the wings, and caught the top of the fence. Sam shot out of the saddle and took a terrible fall. "He'll be bad to live with now, for a while," Jo said, thinking about Sam's pride at being unseated, as he was a good little rider with a bit of polish and style.

When Sam didn't get up, I had a gut feeling that he was hurt badly. I ran from the stands to the fence where he was lying, bleeding from the nose and ears – that's a sure sign of a fractured skull. He lay there, spark out. The doctor came and, with the help of the St. John's Ambulance men, put a collar around his neck, then very gently put him on a stretcher and lifted him into the ambulance. By now, Jo had come down from the paddock, and went in the ambulance with Sam. I got my car out of the car-park and followed it to Darlington Hospital. There, they sent him on to Middlesborough General, where Sam was given a brain-scan. It was very dodgy – his breathing was so shallow and he had several skull fractures, as well as a broken collar-bone. Sam was taken to the Intensive Care Unit at Middlesborough General. He was on the danger list as he was in a deep coma.

For the first two weeks, Sam's condition was critical. We lived in the parents' room at the hospital, so we could go in to see him at any time, day or night. He was so helpless, laid there with tubes up his nose, on his chest and out of his arms; he was on a ventilator to help him to breathe. Every so often, a nurse would suck stuff out of his throat to stop him from choking, or prick him with a needle for reaction. He lay like that for five weeks.

Roy Swindlehurst, the ex-jockey who now has a racing video firm at Blackburn in Lancashire, very kindly came to the yard and made a film of the horses working and the lads chatting. We took the video to the hospital and played it to Sam to try and snap him out of his coma. At the time, Sam was courting Dana Mellor, Stan and Elain's daughter. Dana was magic – she sat and cared for him for hours on end. She was studying law at Lancaster University, but in the first three weeks (or so) she stayed with Jo and myself at the hospital just about all the time.

People were absolutely marvellous – Sam got dozens of get-well cards and lovely, touching letters from people giving us hope and encouragement. One of the first cards came from Willie Carson. From time to time, there was a news bulletin on our local radio. It was gratifying to know that there were so many people pulling for him.

Every morning around 5.00a.m., I would set off in my car to come home to work the horses. At the time, Alan was working as an assistant trainer to Willie Jarvis at Newmarket, so we didn't see much of him. After I had finished working the horses, I would return to Middlesborough.

One black day, on my way back there, I crashed the car. Sam had been taken out of Intensive Care and put in the observation ward (which was a great step forward), but late that night he suffered a set back – he stopped breathing – and he had to be put back on the ventilator in the Intensive Care Unit again. This was as big a shock to us as his first getting hurt had been. Jo and I sat up with him. That night was awful.

We also had the taxman on our backs. Our troubles all began when I came home from a day at the races to find our accountant out in a paddock, playing football with the lads. I was livid. He was playing in goal, but by the number of balls he dropped on our accounts, it wasn't his best position!

We appointed a replacement, and things went from bad to worse! We started on a tax investigation, what's known as a "back duty", which was to go on for over five years and nearly ruin the business. In the end, we had to appoint yet another accountant, thankfully one who understood the racing industry and was willing to work hard on our behalf. He was able to show that we were entirely blameless and satisfy the taxman – but not before it had badly affected our health, our business, and our bank account!

I'm told that all our problems started from one tiny oversight that could not have been more innocent. Many of our owners are kind enough to give the stable staff gifts when a horse does well for them. In order to be fair to all our stable staff, we used to put all the gifts in a deposit account and, every so often, have a fair share out among our workers. Jo and I never took a penny, but the deposit account was in Jo's name. The account had to be in an individual's name and, as staff could leave at any time, Jo's name was put forward by them. We closed the account in 1988 on our accountant's advice when we got straight with the taxman. It seemed obvious that the money was nothing to do with our income, so the deposit account was never shown to the taxman. Apparently, this meant that the interest went unnoticed. When the Inland Revenue spotted it, they were worried there might be other problems.

They asked a whole series of simple questions, but our accountants couldn't seem to answer them. We now realise that horse racing and training do not mix well with the U.K. tax system, which is possibly true of many sports and entertainments which have become industries. There are two obvious recent examples from the world of racing and the stage, and I'm sure there are lots of others that have not made the headlines. Racing is increasingly coming under the magnifying glass of the taxman and the VAT-man, and this is a burden we all need to come to grips with.

I don't pretend to understand the complications which came up in our case, but certain things I will never forget. I used to graze sheep for a local farmer in return for a rent per head. Without discussing it with me, the accountant went out into the field and counted the sheep. This must have made him sleepy, as he included the sheep in stock on our balance sheet and the taxman tried to tax us for the sale of wool and lambs!

Meanwhile, we had been spending tens of thousands of pounds improving the yard and building an all-weather gallop, ploughing the profits of the stable back into the business. Little did I realise that huge amounts of this expenditure were not tax-deductible. I still find it difficult to believe the U.K. taxman can tax profits which have been put straight back into the business, with the result that he needs cash when there isn't any!

When we got the bill for the rates, it was virtually double the amount it had been the previous year. At the time, we had lots of empty boxes, and I didn't think it fair that they should be rated if they were empty. After arranging a meeting at the yard with a man from the rates office, I showed him all the empty boxes. "Take the roofs and doors off the boxes in the back yard," he said. "That'll save you a substantial amount. As they are, you could put horses in them tomorrow or next week." Rather than have the yards looking like a bomb site, I told him I would sooner pull them down completely. This is what we did. That year, 1985, we had very few horses.

These times remind me of the plaque we have hung up in our kitchen: "Out of the gloom, a voice said unto me, smile and be happy, things could be worse. So I smiled and was happy, and behold, things did get worse".

We also ran into problems over numerous silly things which our accountants had missed – items paid out of our private bank account not claimed, private motoring and food bills not declared, and so on. Things got to the stage where never a day passed without a letter, phone call, or tax demand from the Inland Revenue. Our accountants seemed totally unable to make progress, but they kept insisting that there was no tax to pay. Jo and I knew we had been totally straight and open with everyone, we had nothing to hide, so we trusted the accountants and the taxman to sort things out between them.

Sam was in Middlesborough General Hospital for nearly three months (from 5th March to the beginning of June). Coming out of the coma was a gradual thing. One day he would have a bit more body movement, the next he would open his eyes a bit, then recognise us and try to talk. Having come out of his coma, his speech was very poor (in fact, hardly understandable) and one side of his body didn't work very well. He had damaged the part of his brain which controls his co-ordination: thankfully, the rest of his brain is perfect.

At the beginning of June he was moved nearer to home, to Sharoe Green Young Persons Disabled Unit at Preston. He had his twentieth birthday there. We took Sam, Dana, and a group of his friends for a pub lunch at The Battalion. It was within walking distance from the Unit, so the able-bodied pushed the disabled to and from the pub.

We made a cardboard board with the alphabet on it in big letters. When Sam wanted to say something, he would point to the letters and we would write them down on a pad so that we could understand him.

On 13th May 1985, Peter Dunn had a bad fall at Hexham Races, giving him head injuries and putting him in a coma. He was taken to the Intensive Care Unit at Newcastle Hospital. Fortunately, Peter has made a remarkable recovery and is nearly 100% better.

It never rains but it pours; things often happen in threes. On 8th November 1986, Jayne Thompson had a horrible fall at Catterick. She was taken, like Sam, to the Intensive Care Unit at Middlesborough General with severe head injuries and in a coma. Ron and Joan, her parents, stayed at the hospital, just as we had done. Sadly, Jayne didn't pull through – she died on 14th November. At the crematorium, her mother had a song played that Billy Jo Spears sings, 'One Day At A Time'. I always think of Jayne when I hear it – it was her favourite. She was such a lovely, bubbly girl, always full of fun.

By 1987, things had become desperate. Our accountants insisted we owed no tax, but the Inland Revenue disagreed. The bailiffs arrived at the stable and even threatened to impound some horses to cover our tax bills. It's hard to describe how angry, yet helpless, this made me feel. The business suffered, as I made life hell for Jo and everyone around me. Many of our friends will undoubtedly remember how, even for a Yorkshireman, I was hardly ever in a good mood. I probably upset lots of people – friends and owners – without knowing it, and I hope they forgive me.

Our new accountant got precious little help from either the Inland Revenue or the old accountants, but within weeks had prepared us for the worst – the errors and misjudgments of the previous five years had left us with a huge tax bill and the possibility of high penalties and interest. We were devastated.

There was no suggestion that we had ever tried to falsify our finances (in fact, the co-operation we had given all along was stressed by the taxman when the penalties were decided). Through no fault of our own, the business owed so much to Her Majesty's Tax Collectors that we half considered throwing in the towel. With penalties and interest, the final bill was over £100,000. One penalty (£50 per day, for eleven days) was for a paying-in book that couldn't be found among six plastic sacks full of bills, receipts and paying-in books.

It took nearly a year to get all the books and information back from our old accountants, and a further six long months to come to an agreement with the taxman. By then, we had done everything in our power to raise the money we needed. We had sold all our eighty-six cattle. They were nearly beef and we should have put half a dozen per week in the auction then re-stocked with stores. But, we put forty-three in one week and the other half in the next, which flooded the market as there weren't enough butchers, locally, to take that quantity in a week. We didn't get the true value and had it not been for my old pal Robin Winder (a wholesale butcher) buying the majority, we would have got even less money.

We made the remaining owners we had aware of our plight. Bearing in mind we had very little time to raise the capital for the Inland Revenue, I asked them if they wouldn't mind paying up front for their horses' keep which we would then work off. This, the majority did.

Just when we needed a final push, Olly must have known because he showed a clean pair of heels at Chester. Our accountant later told us he'd given the tip to the chaps at the Revenue Office, who were having an office day out at the races, so Olly did us two big favours that day!

We negotiated a payment plan with the tax authorities, and before the 1988 season ended, we had paid every penny – in advance of the promised deadline. I suppose the story has a happy ending, because we came out of those gloomy years determined to beat the system and make Moss Side Racing Stables the flagship of The North. But, it will be a long, long time before Jo and I forget how miserable and frustrated we sometimes were and how the burden of the tax system almost cost us our livelihood.

Now that Sam can walk using elbow-crutches, with the money so kindly given by the Injured Jockeys' Fund, he has bought a ground-floor flat in Tenerife and one at Catterall, about eight miles from us, where he lives entirely on his own. His pad is an absolute credit to him – beautifully kept and spotlessly clean, which he does all by himself from his wheelchair.

Sam is a very strong character. He goes shopping once a week with Lynne Rowe, a pal of his, and gets his milk and *The Sporting Life* delivered every day. There is a small shop near to where he lives which he goes to for everyday things, always on his crutches, never in his wheelchair. He has had a number of falls, getting cuts and bruises (and a few stitches here and there) on account of them, but it doesn't bother him. It gets to me more than him. Our lads and girls in the yard are brilliant with him, as are jockeys and valets at the races. In fact, the jockeys played a very big part in getting him going again. He loves the crack with the lads in the weighing room. The ultimate came for him on 19th September 1987, when Paul Cook, president of The Jockeys' Association, presented Sam with a Jockeys' Association badge at Ayr Racecourse so that he can still go into the weighing room. One day at Catterick Races, before he got the badge, the doorman wasn't for letting Sam into the weighing room. Archie Birch and Dandy Nicholls said, "If he doesn't come in, we're coming out!"

People are good, and never a day goes by without someone asking Jo or me how Sam is.

Sam has never held a grudge or any bad feeling towards Solares. In fact, when he came out of hospital he wanted to buy my half-share in him. At first I didn't sell my share, I leased it to him. With being the majority share-holder, Sol ran in Sam's name, and the following season I sold him my half. Sam enjoyed going to see him run and Sol went on to win six races for him and his partners.

When Sam bought his pad in Tenerife, we sold Sol at Doncaster on 26th March 1990 with an engagement to run in the National. Les Eyre bought him and Sol finished 12th in the great race, ridden by Paul McMahon. Unfortunately, he hurt a stifle in the race. However, I rang Les recently and his daughter told me the horse is now better and in roadwork.

Every Friday, when he's at home, Sam goes to a riding school owned by a girl called Christine Pollet at Wrea Green. One day when I took Sam there for his riding lesson, Jeff Nicholl (Chris's boyfriend) said, "You're a clever beggar. Come and see if you can get this fellow to win a race." He took me to a box and showed me a wallaby inside it. Jeff is a super lad, and always has unusual things for sale – one of these days, he will sell his own mother! I ended up buying the wallaby from Jeff, and named him Walter. We put Walter in a cage, then put him on the back seat of my car to take him back to Cockerham. "How can I break it to your mum that I've bought a wallaby?" I asked Sam on the way home. No solutions came from him – all he could do was laugh!

When we arrived home, Jo was out shopping. Jo loves shopping – that's why we send her to so many race meetings: to keep her out of the shops! I put Walter in a spare stable for the night and fed him. He looked like a giant rat, sat in the corner of the box. That night, while we were having our meal, I thought we'd set Jo up about this wallaby. So, I said, "Today, I saw the biggest rat I've ever seen in my life, in the school yard."

"Don't be daft," Jo said. "We haven't got any rats!"

With this, Alan, Sam, and Neville all cracked up. Jo thought we were all mad! So, I got her to come out and see where this rat was. "Where on Earth did you get that?" asked Jo when she saw Walter. "What the hell are you going to do with it?" After she had got over the shock, she was O.K.

177

Walter had cut his nose while travelling, so I got one of the lads to hold him whilst I bathed and powdered the wound. Walter was not very well handled – the beggar was kicking and ramming about, giving me a really hard time. It's right when you see kangaroos kicking in films! I finished up on the floor, with water all over me. By the time we had done, I was in a far worse state than he was: a long scratch down my cheek and a puffed cheek-bone!

The next day, I put a collar on Walter, with a lunge-line attached, and tied him to an apple tree on our lawn. A couple of hours later he got tangled up in the line around the tree. Jo attempted to free him, but he slipped his collar and started hopping around the yard. When our two Labradors, our five Jack Russells, and Dick (our sheep-dog) saw him, they set chase and followed him until he was out of sight! It was like a day out with the Vale Of Lune Harriers! While all our staff and I joined in the hunt for my recent purchase, we came across a farmer ploughing a field. "Hey, mate, have you seen a wallaby come over this field?" I asked him.

"A wallaby? That's a small kangaroo isn't it?"

"Yes."

"Oh yes, he went that way," he said. "And yesterday, a herd of elephants came over this field, and they went that way, too!" He must have thought that I was either taking the piss, or wasn't a full shilling! Anyway, we never saw or heard of Walter again.

A few years ago at about 5.00p.m. on the eve of an Edinburgh meeting, I got a phone call from Tommy Taylor, who trained at Litchfield, Staffordshire. His horse-box had broken down on the M6 motorway, about forty miles away from our yard, so I sent our 'box to pick him, his lad, and his two horses up, then bring them back to Cockerham. We rang a garage to get Tommy's 'box from the motorway and mend it.

The following day, we took Tommy's horses to Edinburgh Races in our 'box with our two runners. However, Tommy's horses couldn't run as their injections in their passports weren't correct. Tommy was fined something like £300, which was a lot of money to him. He also wasted four days waiting for his 'box to be mended in the bargain. I thought he had been hurt enough without a fine.

When I went to the next Trainers' Federation meeting in London (I was on the Council), I brought this up to see if it was possible for the fine to be reduced or waived. Michael Pope, the chairman of the Federation, wouldn't hear of it. He killed it stone dead and didn't want to know. "He should put his house in order," was all Michael would say.

Injections were very complicated in those days – people hadn't got used to them. Tommy hadn't got secretaries to check up on things like passports. As The Trainers' Federation was meant to help the trainer, and they had done nothing for Tommy, I resigned. This is why, when I am seen at the races, I often have cardboard badges on my binoculars as I don't have the metal badge most other trainers have.

The Trainers' Federation serves its purpose regarding staff wages, etc., but trainers still advertise for staff in *The Sporting Life* and *The Racing Post*. When Richard Whitaker advertised for a "stablelad who was a competent rider", I applied for the job – it went as follows:

31st March 1987

Dear Sir,

Would you please consider me for the job you advertised in The Sporting Life on Friday, 27th March, 1987?

I am 6ft. 9ins. tall and weigh 13st. 12lb. I have riding experience.

One day, a horse got loose on National Day at Liverpool and my pal gave me a leg up. I rode it from the Melling Road to Anchor Bridge. A policeman stopped me from taking it any further. He then made me give the horse back to a small man in very wide trousers.

My last employment was in 1963, when I was a window-cleaner in The Pioneer Corps. I work very hard. My age is fifty-nine. If you consider me for the job, sir, you will not be disappointed with me.

I must also add, could I bring my mother-in-law, a rabbit and two cats with me? Would it be possible to stay in your house with you? I get up very early in the morning – always before 10.00a.m. – and I could bring you a cup of tea before you start work, if you like.

Yours hoping,

J. Berry.

22

ALBERT YOU'RE A STAR

I was introduced to Tommy Doherty, a breeder from Knocklong, Ireland, by Willie Stephenson. Tommy told me that he had a lovely 4-year-old (by Dalsaan) at home that he couldn't sell; So Careful was his name. "I tried to sell him at the sales, but the vet wouldn't pass him because of his wind," Tommy said. "Would you train him for me?"

So Careful duly arrived at Cockerham. After a while, our girls nick-named him "Albert".

We gave Albert a month's roadwork, then started steady cantering him, listening all the time for the whistles that the Irish vet had said this fellow could do better than Ronnie Ronald. Thankfully, they never came: Albert's wind was never a problem with us. Tommy must have fed him on cigarettes!

In Ireland, Albert had run many times and never looked like troubling the judge. The first time he ran for us was on 30th May 1987, in a conditional race at Thirsk, The Dick Peacock Memorial Stakes. Albert finished 3rd behind two good horses, Luna Bid and Atall Atall, beaten a head and 3 lengths. The *Raceform Notebook* read, "A sturdy sort, showed modest form in Ireland last year. He raced upsides the winner until weakening in the last hundred yards."

On 8th July 1987, he went on to win a maiden at Catterick, ridden by Steve Perks. On 24th August 1987, when So Careful ran at Hamilton with John Carroll in the plate, John had "Albert" tucked in, just behind Lindsay Charnock. "I can take this fellow whenever I like," thought John. A furlong out, he pulled Albert from the backside of Wesbree Bay, Lindsay's mount. On the far side of the track, these two both thought they were clear. "Did you win, John?" asked Lindsay.

"Yes," John said.

"Good, then I was 2nd."

John rode So Careful straight into the winner's enclosure and Lindsay went straight into the 2nd slot. The judge called a photo. "First – Miami Bay;

second – Tufuh; third – Shari Louise; fourth – Shy Mistress," was the announcement. Not even in the first four! We were stood in the winner's enclosure like right wallies. Never again have I let J.C. go into the winner's enclosure when we have had a close photo. The other jockeys also gave John and Lindsay some stick!

In our profession we travel thousands of miles in a season. To make good use of the mileage, we try to put our horses in races that they have a chance of winning. This takes us all over Britain to find suitable races. Ron Smyth, the Epsom trainer says when I am down South (which is quite often), "See you tomorrow Jack". John Hills, the son of Barry Hills the Lambourn trainer, tells me that he has a cottage to let to cut out some of my roadwork.

Once, at Newcastle Races, whilst watching our horses running at Hamilton and Nottingham on SIS, Bill Watts, the Richmond trainer, was stood with me when a greyhound race came on the screen. Bill asked, "Have you got one in this Jack?" Of course all of them take the piss.

One day, as John and I were travelling back from a meeting at Hamilton, a fellow in a car cut us up on the M6. John (who will fight anyone when he gets excited or annoyed) got a bit fiery, and a bit of verbal went on, with a show of fists and a V-sign or two. John indicated onto the hard shoulder, keen to sort him out. The man in the car pulled in behind us and got out of his car. It looked as though these two terriers were going to set to and have a do – until John saw the size of him. He must have been six inches taller than Bob Willis and as broad as Big Daddy! John soon bottled-out and drove off. "Did you see the size of him?!" John said.

One very hot day, on my way to Pontefract Races, tanking on in my car (as usual), I spotted a police car parked up on the M62. So, I slowed right down (to keep within the speed limit), looking at the police car as I drove past. The bobby in it was either dead or fast asleep – mouth wide open, head bent right back! I pulled up onto the hard shoulder, got my camera off the back seat, put it on the passenger seat, then reversed very steadily back towards the police car. When I got there, I wound down the passenger window and got hold of my camera. Just then, he woke up! I didn't hang about to bother with a photo; I kicked on towards Pontefract. Luckily, he didn't follow me. I had every intention of putting the shot on our Christmas Cards – it would have been a change. It was that or the print I have at home called the "Handicappers Welcome".

Talking of handicapping – our early 2-year-olds are fit as our facilities here at Moss Side are good so we don't have many hold ups. It is often said that our horses carry more than their fair share of weight in handicaps and nurseries. When I complain to the Handicappers, they can always justify the weight.

We can't all be total idiots and know nothing. If a horse is in a handicap with 9st. 12lbs, 20/1 in the betting and runs out the back trying his heart out, he has too much weight. He should be dropped in the handicap quickly, not just one or two pounds, while if a horse starts winning races from bottom ratings, he shouldn't be allowed to win six or more races before he is collared. All the horses are supposed to be handicapped to have a chance on the day.

I appreciate the Handicappers have a difficult job. I have never told one that he has thrown in a horse of mine and I don't suppose that many other trainers have either. To me, when a horse is picked on for a long time (as some are), it would be fitting if we could go to a referee or ombudsman. As it is now, one man has the say and that's it!

It costs the same money to train a good horse as it does to train a poor one. It also costs the same to train a well-handicapped horse as a badly handicapped one; there is little difference between a horse with no ability and a horse overrated by the Handicapper, as neither can win!

I would rather sell our 2-year-olds at the end of their first season, unless they look good enough to be entered in Listed or Group Races as 3-year-olds. This is especially true of ones which have been over handicapped in nurseries as it becomes a waste of expenses unless one runs them in claiming or selling races. It often makes sense for an owner to sell his horse on, then get involved in another yearling as there are plenty of maiden and condition races to be won before the "man with the pen" handicaps them in nurseries.

On a lighter note, punters will have seen me struggling at the races, taking huge weights from the weighing room to the saddling-up boxes. When Great Chaddington ran at Newmarket, in April 1988, there was talk of me receiving a hernia from carrying the saddle. Thankfully, it was only a suspected one, but I do appreciate people's concern! The next time I run a sprinter in a handicap at Epsom, I am seriously thinking of applying for permission from The Jockey Club to wheel my tack down in a barrow!

Since I was a boy of fifteen years, riding out Mr. Gosden's flying machines at Towton, my burning ambition was to win The Ayr Gold Cup. We ran I Don't Mind in The Cup in 1978, Touch Boy in 1981 and Clantime in 1984. At fifty years old, on a lovely day, Friday 16th September 1988, on the greatest racecourse in Britain, we achieved the ultimate – So Careful won The Ayr Gold Cup, ridden by Nicky Carlisle.

The race, sponsored by Ladbrokes, carried a prize of £32,304. Albert was very fortunate to get in the race. There were twenty-nine runners, and if two more above him in the handicap had declared, he would have been balloted out. At the generous odds of 33/1, carrying 7st. 7lb., he beat by a length that great old horse, Chaplin's Club, ridden by Kevin Darley, trained by David Chapman and owned by Peter Saville, who was nearly as keen as me to win the great race. The *Raceform Notebook* read: "So Careful tracked the leaders going well, and sent on almost 2 furlongs out. He ran on in great style and was never going to be caught."

What a day – I have never been so chuffed in all my life! Everyone in

Northern Racing knew what it meant to me. For years I have told the racing world, or anyone else who would listen, that my ambition was to win The Ayr Gold Cup. David McHarg, the Ayr Clerk of the Course, even had a dream a couple of days before the race that So Careful won. Linda, his lovely wife, backed his dream and won herself a few pounds!

Albert's previous win was the Philip Cornes Sponsored Match at Haydock Park with Klute on 12th August. Klute was owned by Miss Leslie Bruce. She had broken the world record on him at Haydock Park – a trial. Haydock Park asked me if I would challenge Klute with a horse so I sent Albert. The match was very kindly sponsored by Philip Cornes Ltd. They must have got more mileage, by way of advertising, out of that match than they did for the Philip Cornes Final at Newmarket. The build up to it was in most of the papers, radio and on T.V. lots of times.

That Friday, Albert went to Haydock full of confidence to be ridden by John Carroll. With both horses carrying 9st. 4lbs, he made all to win by 25 lengths at the odds of 1/14. The same day we won the seller with a filly called Meine Vonne Lady. This filly used to rub her heels on the wood chippings on our all-weather gallop. We used to put some ointment on her heels, made by Pettifers who have been selling this ointment to the racing stables for 153 years without a problem. After the filly had won, she went in the dope box for a urine test. She was found to have traces of camphor in her. That was the first case of this sort in Britain at the time. So, unfortunately, the filly got disqualified. We worked hard for Meine Vonne Lady's win. Albert's was a piece of cake. It just shows it's six and two threes, swings and roundabouts . . . . . .

. . . You win some, you lose some!

After winning The Ayr Gold Cup, everything else is a bonus. Of course, I would like to win other things – I am still as keen as the first day I rode out for Mr. Hall. In due course, I would like to win some of the prestigious 2-year-old races, like The Gimcrack, The Heinz 57, The Coventry, The Middle Park Stakes, The Richmond, The Queen Mary, The Flying Childers[1], The Norfolk, and so on. It would give me great pleasure to win the Racecall Gold Trophy, a race put on at Redcar with the forward thinking and initiative of their Chairman, Earl of Ronaldshay[2], in conjunction with his son. However, for us to win any of these races now does not seem as far-fetched as winning The Ayr Gold Cup did for me over thirty years ago.

We knocked one race off our list when Almost Blue won The Molecomb at Goodwood in 1988. It would be nice to train the winners of some of the bigger sprints. It would also be marvellous to find a good home

Editor's Notes
[1] Jack won this with Robert Sangster's Distinctly North in 1990 after he had written the book.
[2] Now Lord Zetland.

183

for Albert, where he can cover a few mares and enjoy the rest of his days[1].

Most of the credit is given to me for our successes. In fact, one of our owners, Bernard O'Brien, often says it's lucky for McAlpine I am not a builder. However, without our loyal staff, and the love and dedication that goes into caring for the horses, especially when things are not going right in a yard, much of it can seem an up hill struggle. It was lovely to see Albert's lass Polly Coleman being interviewed on T.V. by Brough Scott when he won. I wished they could have interviewed old Bob our gardener – they are all part of our team. Whatever we do now, I have fulfilled my greatest ambition. Lots of people never get around to doing that, as when they achieve their goal they want something else. But one can only wear one suit at a time, drive one car and live in one house. I am at peace with my little lot. As I have already mentioned, I would still like lots of things, but you can't have everything you want and there's a price for everything you get. To win The Ayr Gold Cup, after waiting for so many years, was the ultimate. Without a shadow of doubt it was the happiest day of my life. All of us at Moss Side Racing Stables are truly grateful to Mr. Doherty for sending us Albert to train. Albert, mate – thank you. You're a star!

WE WON THE CUP!!

Thank you for your time reading my book. I hope you enjoyed it.

Jack.

Editor's Note
[1] *Albert is standing at Mr. Graham Heal's Vauterhill Stud, High Bickington, Umberleigh, N. Devon.*

EDITOR'S NOTE

The Seasons 1989 and 1990

First and foremost, it has been the greatest fun producing this book for Jack Berry. We tried a few little editorial changes early on but soon gave up the unequal struggle.

Jack's story takes us up to the great day in September 1988 when Jack fulfilled what could really be called a life-long ambition – thirty-five years is a long time to wait for a victory – when So Careful won The Ayr Gold Cup.

The 1988 Flat season for Jack and his team at Moss Side, leaving aside So Careful's victory, was a great one with 70 winners compared to his previous best back in 1983 of 43 winners. He was of course leading Flat trainer in the North.

The 1989 season yielded another all-time best for Jack of 92 winners, and once again he was leading Northern trainer.

Jack's achievement in the 1990 Flat season is already racing legend. Jack and Jo have 106 boxes at the Moss Side Racing Stables and they won 127 Flat races, making him the Champion Trainer, by races won, in Britain last year.

Furthermore, last year, Jack had a couple of smashing 2-year-olds; Boozy, who won a Group Three race at Phoenix Park near Dublin; and Distinctly North who won the Group Two Flying Childers Stakes. It can only be a matter of time before the Moss Side Racing Stables houses a Group One winner.

Odd as it may seem, only eight other British trainers have achieved the magical 100 Flat winners in a season this century and like Jack their names will forever be honoured in racing circles. They include names such as Henry Cecil, Michael Stoute and John Dunlop. Some of Jack's fellow members of the '100-Up-Club' have achieved this a number of times and I am certain most readers of Jack's delightful book will wish him every success in becoming another multiple member of this exclusive Club.

At my first meeting back in August 1990 with Jack, after I received the manuscript, I naturally tried to persuade Jack to cover in full the 1988 and

1989 Flat seasons. Further in December, I wanted him to write an extra chapter, or better two, on his stupendous 1990 season. Jack was unyielding and was firm that the book was to end with Albert's win in The Ayr Gold Cup in September 1988.

Someone close to Jack has told me that he would find it hard to write the story of his great successes in these last two years at the moment due to his inherent modesty. However, I join with many members of the racing public in hoping that he will soon write a companion book on the years covering the times when he was far from the bottom.

Rupert Collens

Index

189

192